THE 1954 GENEVA CONFERENCE
INDO-CHINA AND KOREA

combining

*Documents relating to the
discussion of Korea and Indo-China
at the Geneva Conference
April 27-June 15, 1954*

and

*Further documents relating to
the discussion of Indo-China at
the Geneva Conference
June 16-July 21, 1954*

With a new introduction written especially
for the Greenwood reprint by

KENNETH T. YOUNG
President of the Asia Society

**GREENWOOD PRESS, PUBLISHERS
NEW YORK**

Introduction

What were the Geneva Accords? Were they a success or a failure? Why do they still have an application today? These are relevant questions for all Americans who want a workable peace in Southeast Asia. These documents remain an enigma of the past wrapped in the reality of the present. Hardly a day goes by without some mention of them. They have given the present discussions in Paris a common theme. Yet we know too little about the documents, for they have been twisted out of shape by events and misinterpretations. The present Greenwood reprint edition of the Geneva Accords makes the original material easily accessible in book form.

The Geneva Conference of 1954 was convened primarily to provide for Korea's unification. It failed to accomplish this, but it did succeed in ending the war in Indo-China. Several crucial international bargains produced the Geneva Accords on Indo-China. The Russians agreed to them with the understanding that France would not join the European Defense Community. The Chinese Communists joined on the assumption that the Americans would stay out of Southeast Asia. The North Vietnamese agreed to peace and a temporary partition of Vietnam at the 17th Parallel in return for French withdrawal and unification, within two years, of all Vietnam under Hanoi's control. In sum, the Geneva Accords came out of a major exchange: the non-Communists gave up territory to achieve peace, while the Communists made peace to get that territory.

Nine governments participated in 1954: Cambodia, the Democratic Republic of Vietnam (Hanoi), France, Great Britain, Laos, the People's Republic of China, the Soviet Union, the State of Vietnam (Saigon), and the United States. Sessions were both public and secret. However, most of the negotiating, compromising, and drafting was done behind the scenes and is not recorded in the public documents. The British and Soviet heads of delegation served as alternating co-chairmen who mediated the critical disputes to produce the final compromises. Without them the conference would have collapsed.

It was a harsh time and a tense conference. Hanoi was toughly demanding French capitulation and virtual dominance of all Indo-China. The French wanted to pull out of Indo-China at almost any price. Ruthlessly employing its "fight-talk" stratagem, Hanoi refused to stop fighting until talking produced favorable results: what Ho Chi Minh called a "glorious victory" and withdrawal of French forces. Yet Hanoi lost its demand that its Communist representatives from Cambodia and Laos be treated as spokesmen for sovereign nations and be seated independently at the conference. This move foreshadowed later demands, in the 1960's, for treating the National Liberation Front similarly.

Among the real issues, then, were Vietnamese partition, Cambodian and Laotian independence, and effective international supervision. Many compromises and much hard negotiating produced the three agreements on cessation of hostilities in Vietnam, Laos, and Cambodia and the "Final Declaration of the Conference," which together form the Geneva Accords. In addition, and in important relation to them, were nine unilateral statements by individual governments. Each of the three cease-fire agreements was signed by a military officer from each side. They were military documents, not treaties or international compacts. The "Final

Declaration," which was the significant international and political document, was not signed by anyone. It was orally approved in the closing minutes of the conference by only five of the nine participants. The Laotian delegate made no comment, and the North Vietnamese answer is not recorded, notwithstanding Hanoi's implicit acceptance of it. The American delegate dissociated the United States entirely from the Geneva Accords, but pledged not to disturb them by force. At the same time the United States warned the Conference that it would consider renewed agression with "grave concern." The South Vietnamese delegate, in effect, also abstained after protesting most of the Accords. Accordingly, the Declaration is not a treaty, and its binding character is at best dubious.

All the Geneva documents divide into three kinds of provisions: organizational, military, and political. The machinery established the Conference as a body; the two Co-chairmen, who have been active; the three International Commissions, which remain in limbo; and the Joint Commissions, which soon lapsed. This was a lot of machinery without much motive power for peace-keeping.

The main purpose of the Geneva negotiations, and the Accords themselves, was to set up military provisions designed to end the fighting in Indo-China, separate the belligerents, and discourage resumption of hostilities. The three cease-fire agreements and related unilateral statements had detailed stipulations on five categories: 1) a general and simultaneous cease-fire throughout Indo-China; 2) the disengagement and regroupment of military forces in specified assembly areas and, in the case of Vietnam, the important establishment of the Demilitarized Zone on or about the 17th Parallel; 3) prohibitions and restrictions on troop reinforcements, new military materiel, and foreign advisers; 4) neutralizing safeguards to prevent military bases, military alliances, the resumption of hostilities, and any "aggressive policy"; and 5) the rules governing the commissions.

The political articles concerning Laos and Cambodia treated them as united sovereign nations which unilaterally pledged at the Conference to hold general elections under their current constitutions, and to follow a neutral policy without alliances or military bases "unless their security was threatened." Concerning Vietnam, the political provisions were significant but enigmatic. The cease-fire agreement provided for a "provisional demarcation line" and a demilitarized zone of some five kilometers "to act as a buffer zone," thus again partitioning Vietnam temporarily into two political areas, the South and the North. Political and administrative measures were outlined for the "two-regrouping zones." The cease-fire agreement also provided for free movement of civilians from one zone to the other, forbade reprisals or discrimination against any persons or organizations because of their activities during the war, and called for guarantees of their "democratic liberties" as well as protection of individuals and property.

The Final Declaration was the principal political work of the Conference. Paragraphs six and seven, to be applied in conjunction, contained the core of the Geneva Compromise of 1954: the exchange of territory for peace, space for time, and a temporary division of Vietnam before a permanently united Vietnam. The Declaration called for "settlement of political problems" in Vietnam by elections in 1956 to unite the country under one regime, and recognized that "the military demarcation line is provisional and should not in any way be interpreted as constituting a political or territorial boundary." Paragraphs six and seven posited two joint prerequisites for "achievement in the near future of a political settlement in Vietnam," i.e., unification under a single authority: first, by the "execution of the provisions" of the cease-fire agreement and the Declaration; and, second, by the "fundamental freedoms, guaranteed by democratic institutions established as a result of free general elections by secret ballot." The Declaration vaguely called for a two-stage process of Vietnamese unification: consultations between the "competent representative authorities" of the two zones "will be held from July 20, 1955 onwards," and general elections under the supervision of another international commission, also composed of India, Canada, and Poland, "shall be held in July 1956," Nowhere did the Conference or its Accords indicate how either the consultations or the elections were to be undertaken. South Vietnam and the United States at the Conference, moreover, dissociated themselves from these political provisions. They did not ever represent a treaty or compact law as some have claimed or assumed. Just what the legal status or the binding effect of that Declaration was has remained cloudy.

The Geneva Accords, nevertheless, achieved some results, despite their weaknesses. As Lord Avon, British co-chairman and virtual architect of the Accords, observed some ten years later: "The Geneva Conference fell short but not by so wide a margin." It ended hostilities, underwrote the independence and neutrality of Cambodia and Laos, and created a temporary equilibrium in a partitioned Vietnam which facilitated French withdrawal. Nearly one million refugees were able to move south. Its supervisory machinery monitored the whole new "Geneva order" in Indo-China. For several years after the Geneva Conference these arrangements partially worked. In fact the equilibrium between South and North Vietnam soon reached the stage where even the Soviet government proposed *both Vietnams* for membership in the United Nations in 1957. The United States and others opposed North Vietnam's admission, fearing a precedent for a divided Germany and Korea. Had such dual representation succeeded, we all might have been spared the present tragedy and war in Southeast Asia.

Unfortunately, however, the Geneva Accords could not undo the enmity between Communists and non-Communists in Vietnam and Laos. Their actions, rather than the Accords, decided the keeping of peace or the renewal of war. The Geneva Accords had no power of enforcement. Their veto provisions vitiated the Commissions in important cases of violations. From the outset Hanoi prevented the Commission for Vietnam from doing any significant inspection or supervision in most of North Vietnam, where military forces and repressive measures were rapidly expanded in 1954 and 1955. Vietnamese authorities in both zones restricted the operations and effectiveness of the Commission. In Laos, the Communist Pathet Lao turned their assembly areas into forbidden sanctuaries which became springboards for massive North Vietnamese infiltration into South Vietnam. From Hanoi's viewpoint the Americans "intervened" illegally to strengthen South Vietnam as the French withdrew, although the three Western powers had publicly indicated, during the Geneva Conference, their intention to help the "retained half" of Vietnam, as Lord Avon once put it. Although not bound by the Accords, the American government scrupulously tried to follow the stipulations of the cease-fire agreements, as I can personally testify, having been responsible in 1954-1958 for American observation of them.

The political process for settling political problems in Vietnam as outlined in the Declaration never took place in 1955 or 1956 and became a dead letter. The American and South Vietnamese proposal at the Conference to have free elections under United Nations supervision was rejected. The paradox of the Geneva Compromise, was exposed when Hanoi once again reverted to force in the 1960's, seizing the territory of South Vietnam which it had temporarily yielded to make peace, or at least a truce. The textual ambiguity and political unreality of paragraphs six and seven overlooked several factors. The participants at Geneva openly dealt with two different and unreconciled kinds of Vietnams: the two temporary "zones" which were supposed to be united in 1956, on the one hand, and the two sovereign states which followed their own designs on the other. Indeed, South Vietnam had explicitly dissociated itself at Geneva from carrying out that particular process of electoral unification, as did the United States. Neither nation considered itself bound to the agreement, although Washington in 1955 tried to persuade the Saigon regime to proceed with the consultations. In any event, as Lord Avon wrote in looking back on this controversial issue, "The brief two years allowed by the Geneva Agreements before an election in all Vietnam was altogether too short." It was argued, at the time, that nonexecution of the cease-fire agreement—restrictions on the Commission's activity, the military build-up, widespread reprisals, and a repressive police state, all in the North—nullified the spirit and letter of paragraphs six and seven. The members of the Geneva Conference preferred to allow those paragraphs to lapse without provoking a major issue at the time. In view of this background, the recent war in Vietnam was not caused solely by the inadequacy of the Accords or by nonfulfillment of those two key paragraphs.

To restore peace again, the question is whether, and to what extent, the Geneva Accords of 1954 are still relevant. A strong case can be made to prove that their inherent weaknesses and world changes have made them obsolete, unsuitable, and irrelevant. On this side of the argument one can cite Chinese Communist intractability, two divergent societies in South and North Vietnam, American power in Asia, a different war, Asian regionalism, and, accordingly, the need for a whole new set of provisions. On the other hand, the Accords of 1954 and 1962 are all that the warring parties have in common except distrust, death, and destruction. Both sides at the present Paris talks speak of "respect" for the Geneva Accords. The American delegation, in particular, urges a return to their "fundamentals" and "essential elements" as a "framework" or "basis for peace." These elements were a cease-fire, disengagement and regroupment of military forces, separation of the belligerents, reestablishment of the demilitarized zone near the 17th Parallel, renunciation of force, international supervision, and a free expression of the will of the Vietnamese people without intimidation to determine Vietnam's political future with neutrality. To end suffering in Vietnam, these principles derived from the Geneva Accords must be made available. It is thus timely that this book should be published.

—Kenneth Young
Larchmont, New York, 1968

Miscellaneous No. 16 (1954)

Documents relating to the discussion of Korea and Indo-China at the Geneva Conference

April 27—June 15, 1954

Presented by the Secretary of State for Foreign Affairs to Parliament by Command of Her Majesty
June 1954

LONDON
HER MAJESTY'S STATIONERY OFFICE

DOCUMENTS RELATING TO THE DISCUSSION OF KOREA AND INDO-CHINA AT THE GENEVA CONFERENCE

April 27—June 15, 1954

CONTENTS

Part I.—Korea

CONTENTS

Part II.—Indo-China

CORRIGENDA

Part I.—Korea

Document 21 should be read immediately after Document 22.
Document 23 should be read after Document 26.

Part II.—Indo-China

P. 107.—Above " *Document No. 1* " insert—

FIRST PLENARY SESSION ON INDO-CHINA

P. 114.—Delete " Head of the " in heading.

PART I

KOREA

INTRODUCTION

In the communiqué issued by the Foreign Ministers of the United States, France, the United Kingdom and the Soviet Union at the end of their Conference in Berlin between January 25 and February 18, 1954([2]), they proposed that " a Conference of representatives of the United States, France, the United Kingdom, the Union of Soviet Socialist Republics, the Chinese People's Republic, the Republic of Korea, the People's Democratic Republic of Kcrea and the other countries the armed forces of which participated in the hostilities in Korea, and which desire to attend, shall meet in Geneva on April 26 for the purpose of reaching a peaceful settlement of the Korean question."

The Conference opened in Geneva on April 26. Nineteen countries sent Delegations. The Korean question was considered during fourteen plenary sessions of the Conference and one restricted session attended only by representatives of the United States, France, the United Kingdom, the Union of Soviet Socialist Republics, the People's Republic of China, the Republic of Korea and the Democratic People's Republic of Korea. The Korean section of the Conference ended on June 15, having reached no agreement on the settlement of the Korean question.

Part I of this White Paper contains a selection of speeches made and documents tabled in the Korean plenary sessions of the Conference.

Foreign Office,
June, 1954.

([2]) " Miscellaneous No. 5 (1954)," Cmd. 9080.

LIST OF COUNTRIES REPRESENTED AT THE KOREAN PHASE OF THE GENEVA CONFERENCE

Australia.
Belgium.
Canada.
Colombia.
Democratic People's Republic of Korea.
Ethiopia.
France.
Greece.
Luxembourg.
Netherlands.
New Zealand.
People's Republic of China.
Philippines
Republic of Korea.
Thailand.
Turkey.
Union of Soviet Socialist Republics.
United Kingdom of Great Britain and Northern Ireland.
United States of America.

THE FIRST PLENARY SESSION ON KOREA ON APRIL 26 WAS PURELY FORMAL AND NO SPEECHES WERE DELIVERED

SECOND PLENARY SESSION ON KOREA

Document No. 1

Speech by Mr. Pyun, Foreign Minister of the Republic of Korea, April 27, 1954

Mr. Chairman,

I feel deep gratitude for the immense honour of this privilege of speaking first, accorded the delegation of the Republic of Korea, the only recognised legal government in Korea, in this august and important Conference convened for the purpose of unifying Korea by democratic means. At the same time, I find myself smitten with inexpressible emotions, standing among the delegations from these friendly nations that have borne arms steadfastly beside us through bloodshed and sacrifice in this great crusade for human freedom.

I am extremely sad, however, to meet my brethren from North Korea here in this international gathering as if they belonged to some foreign country. For the past forty centuries we, North and South, have been one homogeneous and indivisible people, with the same blood, same culture, same habits, same language, same national consciousness, same interests, same destiny. For forty years under Japanese domination, we stood together like one man in the bloodless revolution of 1919. We resisted together our oppressor's inhuman policy of Japanisation and escaped unhurt together. Now, kin as they are to us, they are going a different way from ours, against their will, intimidated by a ruthless alien régime. This spectacle grieves me indeed. We who are still in the free part of the country cannot help feeling all the more determined to bring deliverance to these groaning and vanishing brethren of ours.

Those millions of North Koreans who have escaped South, stealing through the Iron Curtain, have been far from discriminated against when they came among us. Proportionately speaking, they are now occupying more top positions than are South Koreans. Is this not a proof that the thirty million Koreans, North and South, are one family—of one stock? Even those brethren still cooped up in North Korea, if a chance is offered them, will cleave to us and put heart and soul into overcoming this national tribulation and in rehabilitating our devastated national economy. Even among the North Korean brethren present here, I am inclined to believe that some must feel as we do, though they can hardly dare say so.

Those few changeling Koreans who oppressed their own kin, in league with foreigners they have welcomed in, and who fondly call a foreign country their fatherland, will, of course, stand condemned before the nation for generations. As for those innocent North Koreans who form the great majority, we embrace them in spirit and silently weep with them in sympathy, though we cannot do so physically.

Mr. Chairman, the right solution of the Korean question must come from sound conclusions based on facts. It would not be utterly meaningless, therefore, for me here to recapitulate the events that took place since the liberation of 1945, exactly as they were.

The demarcation along the 38th parallel was originally a temporary military expediency, with the Soviet Union disarming the Japanese above the

1

line—the United States below it. But it has been hardening into a boundary line all these nine years.

The Moscow Decision of December 27, 1945, stipulating a United States–Union of Soviet Socialist Republics Joint Commission for framing proposals for the establishment of a Korean provisional Government, says in paragraph 2 : " In preparing their proposals the Commission shall consult with the Korean democratic parties and social organisations. . . . . "

When the news got abroad that the Moscow Decision was for a five-year four-Power trusteeship, the entire nation, both North and South, was convulsed with a movement against it similar to the 1919 Mansei movement. A Moscow directive, however, compelled the few Communists to fall away from the national movement. In North Korea, suppression was complete, and Mr. Cho Man-sik, a most prominent national leader, was imprisoned as a result and finally was spirited away by the Russians.

On May 20, 1946, the first United States–Union of Soviet Socialist Republics Joint Commission opened at last. The Soviet Union insisted on excluding the majority of the Koreans from consultation on the ground of their anti-trusteeship tendencies. Finally, after nearly two months of fruitless talk, the Commission broke up because of this undemocratic attitude of the Soviet Union. One year afterwards. on May 21, 1947, the Joint Commission was reconvened. But the Soviet Union persisted in the undemocratic demand that all the nationalist elements forming the majority of the people be excluded from consultation, with only Communists and their fellow-travellers being eligible. After dragging on for months, the Joint Commission ceased to meet.

Thus it became apparent that the Soviet Union had not the slightest intention either of living up to the Moscow Decision or of unifying the country. So the United States submitted the question to the United Nations. The November 14, 1947, resolution of the United Nations called for a general election throughout the country for the purpose of establishing an independent, democratic Korean Government. But the plan failed because of the Communist refusal to admit the members of the United Nations Temporary Commission on Korea as observers.

On February 26, 1948, the Interim Committee of the United Nations adopted a resolution authorising the United Nations Temporary Commission on Korea to observe general elections and thereby set up a democratic government in an accessible area, that is, in South Korea. In a speech delivered in the Interim Committee on the previous day, Mr. Lawford, delegate of the United Kingdom, said : " The United Kingdom delegation will vote in favour of the United States draft resolution in the hope that the elections in South Korea will constitute a first step towards Korean unity and independence."

The Korean people have a right to independence and it is the duty of the United Nations to remove, so far as possible, any obstacles in the way of that independence. It would be unfair to refuse to recognise the right of the two-thirds of the Korean population because one-third of the total population is prevented, against their will, from enjoying those rights.

In the opinion of the United Kingdom delegate, which I strongly share, to hold free elections in North Korea, when made accessible, was the remaining task to be fulfilled for the completion of Korean unification.

Fully in step with this original intent of the United Nations resolution, our National Assembly held about 100 seats vacant, always ready to be filled by holding free elections in North Korea under United Nations observation.

It is beyond dispute that to open North Korea to such elections as have been carried out time and again in South Korea in the last six or seven years will be to complete the tasks to which the United Nations set its hand, and

2

that that alone will be compatible with United Nations prestige and former resolutions on Korea. Making an issue of holding free elections in South Korea, as if discrediting the previous ones as devised and observed by the United Nations, cannot but constitute a serious reflection upon the prestige and authority of the International Organisation.

The foundation of the Republic of Korea strengthened as popular confidence in it grew. Despairing of taking it over from within through infiltration, sabotage and guerrilla warfare, the formidable Communist army in North Korea, supported by a great number of Russian-made tanks, cannon and jet fighters, without previous notice on June 25, 1950, launched an all-out attack on the Army of the Republic of Korea, which was hopelessly under-armed and small in numbers. Led by the United States, fifteen other United Nations member States sent fighting units to Korea to give succour to the victim and punish the aggressor, an act of collective security never before known in human history.

On February 1, 1951, the United Nations passed a resolution condemning Communist China as an aggressor. Some are prone to think that it is reasonable for the United Nations forces to withdraw simultaneously with the Chinese Communist troops, but this is against logic and reason. The United Nations forces were in Korea before the aggression by the Chinese Communists, to take a police action in punishing the North Korean aggressors. Only when that police action is regarded as accomplished will they withdraw, and not before. We fail to see why their withdrawal should be tied up with that of the Chinese Communist aggressors. It would be like a burglar agreeing to drop his criminal weapon on condition that the policeman was disarmed at the same time.

Like all real communists, the Chinese Communists, too, regard the Soviet Union as their fatherland. If they were independent of the Soviet Union, they would not have come into the war. The present Communist China is in the same situation as was the Soviet Union in the 1920's. Their primary task is to consolidate their internal situation, not to wage a foreign war of expansion. Yet, abjectly submissive to the directives of Moscow, Communist China is prepared to offer its multi-million nationals as cannon fodder in the Soviet cause of global conquest.

During the recent Sino-Japanese war, whereas the Japanese invaders did not send one single bombing mission to Yenan, the Red capital lying close by, they sent many hundreds to Chungking, which was hundreds of miles away, in a difficult terrain. This is an historical fact. The reason was obvious. The communists never fought the Japanese, though they pretended to. They were so absorbed in their own aggrandisement, to the utter neglect of their national interests. The growth of the communist strength, off-setting that of the Nationalist Government, was thus found advantageous to the Japanese invaders.

For over one thousand years, Korea and China lived side by side, on very friendly terms. China never interfered with the internal affairs of Korea. She went so far as to create a no-man's land on her own territory, contiguous to ours, to prohibit her own people from migrating to Korea and causing friction. Those who transgressed this barrier received capital punishment. When communism came into power, however, China's national character underwent a complete change, suddenly becoming aggressive, quite contrary to her long tradition. This is a matter of regret for world peace as well as for peace in the Orient.

Communist China has placed the whole of North Korea in occupation status. Not only that, it sends in an endless stream of Chinese farmers to supplant the Korean population. How can such a policy ever hope to win

3

Korean friendship? If aggressive acts are stopped and the traditional Chinese policy of peace is resumed—if a real good neighbour policy is put into practice—the numerous neighbour nations surrounding China are more likely than not to prove a protective wall. It would be a blessing to everyone concerned. If, on the other hand, aggression is extended to more neighbours, China will be encircled by hostile nations only.

Since the signing of the Armistice Agreement([1]), the Chinese Communists have in disregard of the Agreement built military airfields throughout North Korea, and amassed immense quantities of munitions, dodging the inspecting eyes of the Supervisory Committee and often forcibly hampering its activities. the Communists have unilaterally repudiated the Armistice terms. Even if we should come to conclude that the Armistice terms so utterly disregarded by the Communists need no longer bind us, they will be held responsible for this state of affairs.

Mr. Chairman, I have frankly recounted the past events as they actually have occurred. Without bravely rectifying past errors, the prospect of peace will not be bettered by the mere wish to have it. It entirely lies with the communists to maintain peace in the Orient, and indeed in the world, by backing their professed wish for peace with real acts of peace.

Some outsiders say that the Republic of Korea alone loves fighting. Nothing is further from the truth. For what reason on earth should my country be bellicose? Never in all our long history have we ever fought any war outside of our own boundaries. We have no intention of carrying on any warfare against any other people, but only to protect what is our own. Surely we have seen enough of war to be weary of it. Has not much of our country been turned to cinders? Has not our economy been shattered beyond remedy? Have we not suffered casualties defying computation? No other nation can have more cogent reasons to hate war than the Republic of Korea. All through our history we have preferred peace in obscurity to celebrity achieved through bloodshed.

Nevertheless, we cannot buy peace at the price of freedom. We cannot seek to survive at the expense of honour. Our determination to die for what is right alone may yet lead us to life. We believe, along with our friends abroad, that right will win out in the end.

In conclusion, Mr. Chairman, the Korean delegation should like to stress most emphatically that there should be co-operation all round to help the discussion that is to take place here finally to achieve the objective of establishing by peaceful means a united, independent and democratic Korea. We have been longing for complete unification and freedom all these years, and prayerfully hope that this cherished wish of ours may be accomplished at this Conference.

Document No. 2

Proposal by the Delegation of the Democratic People's Republic of Korea tabled by Mr. Nam II on April 27, 1954

In order to achieve the speedy restoration and unification of Korea and the establishment of a democratic, independent, unified State :—

1. The Government of the Democratic People's Republic of Korea and the Government of the Republic of Korea are urged—

   (a) to hold general elections for a national assembly for the formation of a unified Korean Government, based on the free expression of the wishes of the inhabitants of the whole of Korea;

[1] Korea No. 2 (1953) Cmd. 8938.

4

(*b*) to organise an all-Korean Commission, with representatives from North and South Korea, to make the necessary preparations for free general elections for a Korean assembly, and to take urgent measures for the economic and cultural rapprochement of North and South Korea, the members of the Commission to be selected by the Supreme People's Committee of the Democratic People's Republic of Korea and the National Assembly of the Republic of Korea respectively, and to include representatives of the largest democratic social organisations in South and North Korea;

(*c*) to bear in mind that one of the primary tasks facing the all-Korean Commission would be to arrange for the drafting of a law on general elections, which would guarantee the true democratic character of the elections and enable them to be carried out in a free atmosphere by the elimination of pressure by foreign interference, by local authorities and by terror groups. The Commission should further take the necessary measures for guaranteeing freedom of assembly and of the press for the Korean people, and freedom for all citizens in the country to propose candidates for the legislative organ irrespective of their political views, sex, religion or race;

(*d*) in order to assist the economic reconstruction of Korea, which is the first important step for the creation of the conditions necessary for realising the national unification of Korea and with a view to promoting the material well-being of the Korean people and to maintaining and developing the culture of the people, the all-Korean Commission should immediately take measures to establish and develop economic and cultural relations between the Democratic People's Republic of Korea and the Republic of Korea, in such matters as commerce, finance, transport, frontier relations, free movement across the frontier, freedom of correspondence, scientific and cultural exchanges and all other relations.

2. The necessity should be recognised of the withdrawal of all foreign forces from Korean territory within six months.

3. The necessity should be recognised for all those countries most interested in the maintenance of peace in the Far East to guarantee the peaceful development of Korea, thus creating the conditions likely to contribute to a swift conclusion of the task of unifying Korea by peaceful means as a united, independent, democratic State.

Document No. 3

Speech by Señor Eduardo Zuleta Angel, Leader of the Colombian Delegation, April 27, 1954

The Colombian Republic has no direct interest in the affairs of Korea, any more than in those of other Asian countries.

It is represented at this Conference because it felt it to be its duty to respond to the appeals made by the Security Council on June 27 and July 7, 1950.

It responded to them because the course it has adopted in international politics has invariably been that of sincerely and honestly fulfilling undertakings entered into under international conventions. Having approved and signed the San Francisco Charter, Colombia felt it must honour its undertakings and to the best of its ability fulfil the obligations laid on it by the decisions and recommendations of the United Nations Security Council and General Assembly. The manner of Colombia's response to the Security Council's appeals of June 27 and July 7, 1950, shows the respect our country has for the United Nations, and our intention to make the Organisation set up at San Francisco in 1945 as effective as possible.

Small countries without sufficient armed forces of their own for their national security look to the rules of international law for protection, and consequently are very glad to support anything that can secure the effective application of legal principles.

International organisations, and more particularly the United Nations, are the effective means in present-day international law of enforcing, so far as possible, the supremacy of law and justice in relations between peoples.

It is to the interest of these States not only to respect, but also to do their utmost to make others respect, the recommendations and resolutions of international organisations for the maintenance of peace and security and the establishment of friendly relations between nations. This is the sole interest Colombia has in the Korean question and the sole interest of the Colombian delegation in this Conference, for we have no direct political interest, no commercial or economic interest whatever in the Asian problem.

The Colombian Republic was invited to take part in this Conference as a result of what was agreed on February 18, 1954, at Berlin, at the Meeting of the Foreign Ministers of the United States, France, the United Kingdom and the Union of Soviet Socialist Republics. This agreement was proclaimed in a communiqué of the same date, which began by declaring the importance of establishing by peaceful means a unified, independent and democratic Korea and went on to state that it would be the task of this Conference to try to secure a peaceful settlement of the Korean question.

The United Nations General Assembly on its side, by its resolutions of November 1, 1947, December 12, 1948, October 14, 1949, and October 7, 1950, laid down as the primary objective in connexion with the Korean question the establishment of a united, independent and democratic Korea.

Even before the United Nations was created, President Roosevelt, Generalissimo Chiang Kai-shek and Mr. Churchill had expressed, in the Cairo Declaration, their intention to secure Korea's independence.

After the United Nations Charter was signed, but before the General Assembly met, the Moscow Agreement emphasised the necessity for re-establishing Korea as an independent State under conditions which would promote democratic principles in that country.

In the light of the foregoing, my delegation wishes to state that in its opinion it is clear that the sole purpose of this Conference, regarding Korea, is to seek a peaceful agreement which will establish the unity and independence of Korea on a democratic basis.

There can be no doubt but that what Article 60 of the Armistice meant by a peaceful settlement of the Korean question was a settlement establishing the unity, independence and democratic life of Korea.

Any doubts on the subject were dispelled by the Berlin communiqué, which declared that the object of this Conference would be to find a peaceful solution for the Korean question, after having stated explicitly that the establishment of the unity and independence of Korea by peaceful means would be an important factor in reducing international tension and establishing peace in other parts of Asia.

For all these reasons, the Colombian Delegation hopes that this first point, which is vital will not even need discussion. The purpose of this Conference is to establish, by peaceful agreement, a unified, independent and democratic Korea.

The problem we have to study, therefore, is what are the proper means to achieve this end.

The Colombian Delegation takes the view that these means have been laid down very clearly by the General Assembly resolutions already referred to.

The General Assembly, from the outset, took the view that the way to achieve the independence and unity of Korea was to hold free elections by secret ballot. Such elections would enable all the inhabitants of Korea to choose representatives, who would then meet as a National Assembly to set up a Government for Korea (paragraph 2 B of the resolution of November 14, 1947).

In 1948, the General Assembly, seeing what had happened in Korea on the occasion of the elections, after stating its views on the legitimacy of the Government of the Republic of Korea, decided to set up a Commission on Korea, with instructions to investigate and advise on the possibility of extending the representative Government based on the freely-expressed wishes of the people.

In 1949, the Assembly urged that the Commission must be prepared to carry out investigations, throughout the whole of Korea, on the possibility of extending the representative Government based on the freely-expressed wishes of the people, adding the phrase " and in particular on the possibility of holding nation-wide elections."

Finally, the Assembly, in its resolution of October 7, 1950, recommended that, under the auspices of the United Nations all the prescribed measures, including the holding of free elections for ascertaining the wishes of the people, be taken to establish a unified, independent and democratic Government throughout the whole of Korea.

We do not think there will be any discussion on this second point either. We believe that there is general agreement regarding the need to hold free elections in Korea and so achieve the unification and independence of this country.

But how can we guarantee genuinely free elections expressing the will of the majority of the people?

There is, in our opinion, only one means of doing so, the means recommended by the General Assembly and dictated by the situation itself: that such elections should be held under the auspices of the United Nations, *i.e.*, under the supervision and with the assistance and advice of the United Nations Commission for the Unification and Rehabilitation of Korea.

From the preceding, it follows: —

(1) that the purpose of this Conference, as far as Korea is concerned, is to establish, by peaceful means, a unified, independent and democratic Korea;

(2) that in order to achieve this result, there must be free elections which will reflect the wishes of the people;

(3) that this last condition can only be met if the elections are held under the auspices of the United Nations.

There thus remains, in the opinion of the Colombian Delegation, only one problem requiring the attention of this Conference, namely, how to reconcile the idea of free and democratic elections with the express declaration, made on several occasions by the Assembly itself, that a legitimate Government has been established in Korea (the Government of the Republic of Korea); that this Government exercises effective authority and jurisdiction over that part of Korea where the temporary Commission was able to carry out investigations, and in which the great majority of the total population of

7

Korea lives; and that this Government was set up on the basis of elections held under the supervision of a United Nations Commission and which represent the true expression of the free wishes of the electorate of this part of Korea.

The first way of reconciling these two ideas is that recommended by the United Nations Assembly in its resolution of 1948: to extend to the whole of Korea the representative Government formed in accordance with the freely expressed wishes of the people. In that case elections would now only be held in that part of Korea where, formerly, elections could not be supervised and controlled by the United Nations Commission. The results of the elections already held under the supervision of that Commission would continue to be respected.

A second method would be for the Government of the Republic of Korea, which is the only Government expressly recognised by the United Nations as legitimate, to agree to fresh elections throughout the whole of Korea.

A third possibility has also been mentioned; for the National Assembly of North Korea and the National Assembly of South Korea to meet in a single body and take all necessary decisions on the holding of elections and the setting up of a new Government.

This third solution would be excellent if the number of members of both Assemblies were proportionate to the number of inhabitants in the parts of Korea represented by those Assemblies; and if, moreover, there were evidence, acceptable to the United Nations, that the elections in North Korea had in fact been conducted by democratic methods.

Lastly, it has just been proposed that a joint Commission should be set up, in which North and South Korea would be equally represented, to control everything to do with the elections.

This, too, would be a very helpful solution if North and South Korea had the same population. Such, however, is not the case, and it is hard to see how a system which starts out by establishing a representation ratio that does not fit the facts can be called democratic.

To be democratic, the system must be representative, and to be really representative, it must be a proportional one.

Since North Korea does not possess the same population as South Korea, there seems no reason why the two countries should be given an equal number of representatives on the Commission.

However that may be, it seems that the primary endeavour of this Conference regarding Korea should be to find a formula that will reconcile the desire to unify Korea and give it its independence through free and democratic elections supervised by the United Nations, with the General Assembly's reiterated declaration that the Government of the Republic of Korea is a legitimate Government founded on elections which truly expressed the free will of the electorate of the part of Korea in which the United Nations Commission was able to observe and advise, and that this Government is the sole such Government in Korea.

Any other formula should be acceptable provided it combined three essential conditions:—

(1) if it established a democratic and representative régime—which means that the number of electors belonging to each political party must be proportionate to the number of their representatives;
(2) if it involved no violation of United Nations resolutions;
(3) if it provided that the elections should be held under United Nations supervision so as to ensure the electors' independence and freedom.

The material strength of the country I represent is not such as to lend great weight to the suggestions I have ventured to make, but a certain weight

8

may be attached to them as the expression of Colombia's steadfast hope that this Conference will yield results that will strengthen, not weaken, the United Nations.

In conclusion, I wish to state that we cannot take part in these discussions if the United Nations is to be regarded as a belligerent or as subject to the rules applying to belligerents.

When it engages its armed forces in any part of the world the United Nations does so in the performance of the sacred duty conferred on it by the most important of all multilateral international treaties, namely, that of protecting peace and security by meeting aggression whenever it may be necessary.

Colombia cannot bring pressure to bear to secure any particular solution of the Korean question. All it can do here is to ask this Conference to respect United Nations decisions and the Powers represented here not to disregard them.

THIRD PLENARY SESSION ON KOREA

Document No. 4

Speech by Mr. Dulles, Secretary of State of the United States of America, on April 28, 1954

Mr. Chairman and fellow delegates,

We are here to establish a united and independent Korea. It may be given us to write a new page in what has been a tragic history. The people of Korea for centuries lived together as one nation, and together they have long endured foreign subjugation and aggression. They have sought to be united in freedom and independence. This is a right which no nation or group of nations can legitimately deny them.

The United States has come here with the Republic of Korea and with the other Governments whose armed forces came to Korea's assistance, in a renewed and determined effort to aid the Korean peope to realise their reasonable and rightful aspirations.

Why does Korea remain divided? The 1943 Declaration of Cairo promised that victory over Japan would be used to make Korea " free and independent." But that has not happened.

The present phase of Korea's martyrdom goes back to August, 1945. Then the United States, which had for four years borne the burden of the Japanese War, agreed that the Soviet Union might move into Manchuria and Korea north of the 38th parallel, in order to accept there the surrender of the Japanese. But the Soviets, having gotten into North Korea for one purpose, stayed on for another purpose. Their goal has been directly or through puppets, to turn North Korea into a satellite state and, if possible, to extend their rule throughout all Korea. In so doing, they have consistently defied agreements with their former allies, and also the collective will represented by the United Nations.

It is important that we should constantly have in mind that what is here at stake is not merely Korea, important as that is; it is the authority of the United Nations. The United Nations assumed primary responsibility for establishing Korea as a free and independent nation. It helped to create the Republic of Korea and nurtured it. When aggressors threatened the

9

Republic of Korea with extinction, it was the United Nations which called on its members to go to Korea's defence.

Korea provides the first example in history of a collective security organisation in actual operation. If this Conference is disloyal to the United Nations and its decisions, then each of us will bear a share of responsibility for destroying what protects us all.

Yesterday, the Delegates of the Republic of Korea and of Colombia told eloquently of the mission which the United Nations had assumed in relation to Korea. It is a story that bears repetition.

The United Nations first took jurisdiction of the Korean problem in the year 1947. It then created a Temporary Commission for Korea to help organise a government of Korea and to observe the initial elections. The Soviet Union refused to permit the United Nations Commission to have access to North Korea. Elsewhere the Commission functioned as the United Nations had intended.

In December 1948 the United Nations General Assembly received the report of its Temporary Commission and it adopted, by a vote of 48 to 6 with one abstention, a resolution which I shall read. The resolution declared:

"That there has been established a lawful Government (the Government of the Republic of Korea) having effective control and jurisdiction over that part of Korea where the Temporary Commission was able to observe and consult and in which the great majority of the people of all Korea, reside; that this Government is based on elections which were a valid expression of the free will of the electorate of that part of Korea and which were observed by the Temporary Commission; and that this is the only such Government of Korea."

The United States, trusting to the moral authority of the United Nations and the Charter undertakings of its members, withdrew its own armed forces from South Korea. That left South Korea with only local forces suitable for maintenance of internal order. In contrast, the Soviet Union rapidly built up the war power of the Communist régime it had installed in North Korea, and on June 25, 1950, these forces launched a full-scale attack, implemented with many Russian-made tanks and planes.

The United Nations Temporary Commission, which was present on the spot, and the membership of which included India, instantly and unanimously found that this was armed aggression, and so reported to the United Nations Security Council. That Council in turn, by a vote of 9 to nil, with one absence and one abstention, certified to the fact of aggression, and called on the members of the United Nations to help to resist the aggression. Sixteen nations responded with military contributions, and over forty responded with either military or material aid.

The small and lightly armed forces of the Republic of Korea were initially overpowered by the assault. The Communist aggressors quickly occupied all of Korea except a small beachhead at Pusan. But the forces of the Republic of Korea quickly rallied and the United Nations members gave increasing support. A brilliant military operation, involving a bold landing at Inchon, caught the aggressors off balance, and enabled the United Nations Command to break out of the Pusan beachhead. The aggressors were routed and destroyed as an effective force.

It seemed that the United Nations could now complete its earlier action to unify Korea. Accordingly, on October 7, 1950, the General Assembly set up a new body, known as the United Nations Commission for the Unification and Rehabilitation of Korea—initials UNCURK and usually used—to complete the task of the previous Commissions. The new Commission proceeded to Korea.

10

But the long-sought unification and freedom of Korea was not yet to be. Another Communist aggression intervened. In November 1950 the Chinese Communist régime sent masses of its armed forces into Northern Korea. The United Nations General Assembly by a vote of 44 to 7, with 9 abstentions, adjudged this intervention to be aggression.

The United Nations Command was forced to withdraw again to the South of Korea. But again they fought their way back to a point where the aggressors held less territory than when they had committed the initial aggression from the 38th parallel.

On July 27, 1953, an Armistice[1] was concluded with the United Nations Command. This was no free-will gift of peace by the Communists. It came only after final fanatical efforts to break the line of the United Nations Command had failed with ghastly losses to the attackers. It came only after the Communists realised that, unless there was a quick armistice, the battle area would be enlarged so as to endanger the sources of aggression in Manchuria. Then and only then did the Communist rulers judge that it would be expedient to sign the Armistice.

The Armistice contemplated that there should be a political Conference with reference to Korea within three months. But the Communists found it inexpedient to live up to that agreed recommendation. They desired first to consolidate their position in North Korea.

Only now does the Korean Political Conference meet, after long haggling over its composition and place of meeting.

The composition and the place of the Conference are precisely those which the United Nations side proposed six months ago.

This fact enables one to judge where lies the responsibility for the delay.

The seven-year story I have summarised is a story of persistent attack against the forces of international law and order represented by the United Nations. Whether this attack will still prevail may be determined by this Conference.

During the seven-year period of 1947 to the present time, which I have briefly reviewed in relation to Korea, the Governments of France, Great Britain and the United States have been working with the Soviet Union to bring about the unification of Germany and liberation of Austria. There have been hundreds of meetings of the Foreign Ministers or their aides on these subjects. Nothing has been accomplished. But something has been learned. This Conference can usefully have that in mind as we judge the proposals which come before us here.

It seems to us that Soviet Communist conduct has been largely influenced by fear of freedom.

It seems that the communist ruling class believe that a society is most peaceful and most productive if its members conform to a pattern which is prescribed by rulers possessed of absolute power. This inherently involves a suppression of freedom, for freedom implies diversity, not conformity, but it is not enough that freedom be suppressed within what is now the Soviet orbit, because freedom is contagious. Accordingly, freedom outside that orbit cannot be acquiesced in and the area of suppression must be constantly expanded in order to preserve the existing area of suppression.

Thus, the Soviet Communist rulers seem to have been driven by their own doctrine, by their own fears, to seek constantly, in one way or another, to extend their control until there is finally achieved the goal which Lenin referred to as " the amalgamation of all nations " and which Stalin referred to as " the amalgamation of the masses into a single State Union."

[1] Korea No. 2 (1953), Cmd. 8938.

11

It may be said that Lenin and Stalin are dead—and so they are. But their doctrine is not dead. It continues to be taught to communists throughout the world, and communists continue to practise it throughout the world.

As the record stands to this date, the communist rulers have at no time, at no place, voluntarily relaxed their grasp on what they had. This is so even though, as in the case of Eastern Germany, Austria and North Korea, they had promised that the grasp was to be only temporary. Also, in every non-communist nation of the world the agents of international communism work to achieve the amalgamation of the nation and its people into the system of communist dictatorship.

The problem which we face here at Geneva is the same problem that has been faced elsewhere. It is the problem of achieving " peace " and " democracy "—in the historic meaning of those words. They are alluring words, rich in their traditional meaning. Communist propaganda has adopted them as lures, to trap the unwary. It must be remembered that when the Communists speak of " peace " they mean a society of conformity under a single directing will. When they speak of " democracy " they mean a " dictatorship of the proletariat."

The sum of the matter is this :—

When we negotiate with the Soviet Communists and their satellites, we are confronted with something far more formidable than individual or national lust for glory. We are confronted with a vast monolithic system which, despite its power, believes that it cannot survive except as it succeeds in progressively destroying human freedom.

I do not present this analysis in a mood of pessimism, but rather in a mood of realism. Communist doctrine authorises accommodation when the opposition is strong. It is our task here to show such strength—strength of honourable and non-aggressive purpose—that the communists will find it acceptable to grant unity and freedom to Korea.

Yesterday, we heard three proposals for the solution of the problem of Korea. The Republic of Korea and the Republic of Colombia advocated a solution giving vitality to the resolutions of the United Nations—those resolutions which refer to the establishment of a united and free Korea.

The proposal of the North Korean Communist régime was, however, something different. It did not so much as mention the United Nations or its resolutions. These, it seems, are to be treated as nullities.

The communist proposal is in essence the same as that made in June 1950, as a prelude to the armed attack upon the Republic of Korea. Also, it is strikingly similar to the scheme which the Soviet Union presented at Berlin last February for the unification of Germany.[2] Conformity, you see, is the communist rule.

The present communist proposal on Korea provides that the freely-elected Government of the Republic of Korea, representing at least three-quarters of the Korean people, would be forced into combination, on a basis of equality, with the communist régime ruling a small minority of the people in the North.

General elections are proposed by the communists under a law, the terms of which would be subject to veto by the communist régime. The proposal stipulates that the election conditions should exclude all " foreign interference." Presumably, this is intended to exclude United Nations supervision.

The scheme is designed to destroy the authority of the existing Government and to replace it by a communist puppet régime.

[2] "Miscellaneous" No 5 (1954), Cmd. 9080.

The North Korean Communist proposal likewise requires that all foreign forces should be withdrawn from Korean territory within six months. The United Nations forces would have a long way to go. The Chinese Communist forces would have only a few miles to go—and they could quickly return.

The United States does not desire its troops to remain indefinitely in Korea. But we remember that once before we had our troops in Korea and withdrew them prematurely as it turned out. We do not want that history to repeat itself.

This, then, is the North Korean proposal. The United States must reject that proposal because it does not meet the requirements of a free, unified and independent Korea, for which so much blood has been expended and suffering endured.

Peace is always easy to achieve—by surrender. Unity is also easy to achieve—by surrender. The hard task, the task that .confronts us, is to combine peace and unity with freedom.

The people of the Republic of Korea know freedom, and they have fought and suffered as have few others to preserve their freedom.

I have myself seen the freedom of the Republic of Korea.

I have been to the University of Seoul and seen the young men and women of Korea eagerly acquiring knowledge in a free, liberal educational institution.

I have attended sessions of the Korean Assembly and seen the functioning of this body, whose members had been chosen by freely contested elections observed by a United Nations Commission.

I have met in a vast auditorium with thousands of Christian refugees who had recently fled from North Korea into the Republic of Korea to escape the religious persecution of the Communist North and to gain the freedom of religion which prevailed in the Republic of Korea.

The Republic of Korea, which fought so valiantly for freedom, will never accept unity at the price of thinly-disguised annexation by the Soviet-Chinese Communist *bloc*. The United States sent over one million of their youth to fight in Korea to save Korea from violent annexation by aggressors. Of them, over 140,000 became casualties. Certainly we are not disposed, here at the Council table, to give away what our sons battled so bravely to preserve.

It is basic that whatever programme is adopted here for the unification of Korea must in fact also be a programme which will assure the freedom of Korea.

A workable programme for unifying Korea does not have to be invented by us. It is already at hand. It was laid down by the United Nations General Assembly resolution of October 7, 1950. That is the resolution to which I have already referred, the resolution which established a Commission to complete the unification of Korea by observing elections in that part of Korea where observed elections had not yet been held.

That United Nations Commission (UNCURK) is at this very moment waiting in Korea ready to fulfil its clear and precise mandate from the United Nations.

Accomplishment of that mandate would complete the unification and freedom of Korea which was interrupted first by Soviet obstruction in 1948, then by North Korean Communist aggression in June 1950, and then by the Chinese Communist aggression of November 1950. Now that aggression has been thwarted, the interrupted work of the Commission should proceed. That is our proposal.

It would require the Chinese Communist régime to withdraw their forces of aggression and occupation from North Korea so that the United Nations can complete its task in an atmosphere free of menace.

13

It is important to think of freedom not only in terms of the freedom of individuals but also in terms of national freedom. Korea is a peninsula of such strategic value that it has for many years been the subject of big-power politics. Russia, Japan and China have successively sought to use Korea to serve their own policies of aggrandisement. For a long time the Koreans have not been the masters of their own destiny. That state of affairs should be ended.

The United States seeks no advantages in Korea. We are in the process of concluding a Mutual Security Treaty with the Republic of Korea. But that treaty implies no aggressive purpose and the United States does not seek thereby to gain a forward position which could menace anyone.

Japan is no longer an aggressive force and has loyally undertaken to refrain from the threat or use of force against the territorial integrity or the political independence of any other country.

The Republic of Korea has itself no ambitions which extend beyond its natural borders.

Are Soviet Russia and Communist China willing to renounce ambitions which would be served by control of Korea. If so, it will be possible to give Korea that national independence which the United Nations has been seeking for Korea, and which the Koreans want for themselves.

Such a Korea should of course be a member of the United Nations and enjoy the added dignity and protection which membership may give. It may be recalled that the Republic of Korea applied for membership in the United Nations in 1949. It was prevented only by a Soviet Union veto in the Security Council. That is another of the wrongs which we should agree here to remedy.

There are those who feel that past experience and cold reason combine to show the futility of the task which we here undertake. I do not under-estimate the difficulty of that task. But I still feel that we need not be' discouraged, and that it is not a waste of our time to seek resourcefully to achieve our allotted goal.

We properly recall the failures of the past, so that we may profit by experience. But we can also remember that the future is never a mere repetition of the past.

We need not let cold logic chill our hopes. We know that those who live by faith prevail in the end over those who live by calculation.

It is right that Korea should be united and should be a free and independent nation able to realise a destiny which conforms to the peaceful aspirations of its people.

It is right that the United Nations should be sustained as an authority to which all peoples, for all time, may turn to save them from the scourge of war and to assure the dignity and worth and equal rights of nations large and small.

Our duty is to pursue these goals with dedication, and with a purity of purpose which admits of no self-aggrandisement. Then we shall have done our part in serving principles of moral order, which imposes themselves on men and nations.

Document No. 5

Speech by Mr. Chou En-lai, Head of the Delegation of the People's Republic of China, April 28, 1954([3])

The Geneva Conference to which the people of the whole world have been looking forward with enthusiasm has already begun its session. This Conference should have for its aim the lessening of international tension and the consolidation of world peace. That is a task of tremendous significance.

([3]) This text is the unofficial English translation provided by the Chinese delegation.

This is the first time that the Foreign Ministers of the Union of Soviet Socialist Republics, the United States of America, the United Kingdom, the Republic of France, the People's Republic of China and other countries concerned have met together at the same table, to examine and solve the most pressing problems of Asia. Our task is intricate. However, the convening of this Conference signifies in itself the growing possibility of settling international disputes by the peaceful means of negotiations. The Delegation of the People's Republic of China hopes that all the delegates to this Conference will make due efforts to fulfil this task.

The peoples of Asia, like the peoples of the rest of the world, love peace and freedom. They were oppressed and enslaved for a long time. Their struggle for liberation from the foreign imperialist enslavement for national independence and freedom is a just struggle. There is not a force which can stop this historical development. The influential circles of the United States of America, however, for the purpose of setting up their colonial rule in Asia intensify their interference so that they can obstruct the movement of the Asian peoples for national liberation; they develop plans to create an aggressive *bloc* in Asia and spread the war over Asia. Such a policy of the United States of America is in conflict with the aspirations of the people of Asia. It is the source of tension and trouble in Asia.

After a long and resolute struggle, the Chinese people put an end to the rule of the imperialists and of the Kuomintang, which was a scourge to them, and in accordance with their independent will, chose their own State system of people's democracy and founded the People's Republic of China. The Central People's Government of the People's Republic of China represents the will of all the Chinese people, and the policy it has pursued enjoys the unanimous support of the entire nation.

In less than five years, the People's Republic of China has recorded great achievements in the political, economic and cultural fields without any parallel in Chinese history. The Central People's Government of the People's Republic of China has achieved the unification of the nation and has carried out social reforms. It has succeeded in stabilising the financial and monetary conditions of the nation, and in rehabilitating the national economy which had long been ravaged by war, and is steadily improving the material and cultural life of the people. At present, China is carrying through the plan of large-scale industrialisation of the country. And on a national scale democratic elections are being held for organs of all levels wielding political power.

This is the first time in China's history that the Chinese people have become the real masters of their country. All nationalities throughout the country have united into a big family of nationalities with freedom and equality for all. The Government enthusiastically loved and supported by the people of all nationalities of the entire country is as solid as a rock. No force in the world can prevent the Chinese people from marching along the road of making China strong and prosperous.

The victory of the Chinese people has radically changed the state of affairs in Asia. It inspires the peoples of Asia to struggle for their national independence, and for their ultimate liberation from the imperialist yoke.

The Government of the People's Republic of China and the Chinese people consistently work for peace and against war. We have never committed and will never commit aggression against other countries; but we most emphatically shall not tolerate aggression against us by any country. We respect the right of all the nations to choose and preserve their own way of life and their own State system without interference from outside. At the same time we insist that other nations treat us in the same way. We believe if all the nations of the world observe these principles and are motivated by

15

the mutual desire for co-operation, the peaceful co-existence of the countries with different social systems will be secured.

It is generally known that after the People's Republic of China had been founded, the Government of the Union of Soviet Socialist Republics was the first to establish friendly diplomatic relations with the new China. The Treaty of Friendship, Alliance and Mutual Assistance between the People's Republic of China and the Union of the Soviet Socialist Republics was concluded, which is an important factor in the maintenance of peace in the Far East. Traditional firm friendship has long existed between the great peoples of China and the Soviet Union. From the very beginning the Soviet people have expressed enthusiastic sympathy with the glorious struggle of the Chinese people for national liberation. For nearly five years, the Soviet Union and China have established and have been successfully developing economic co-operation and cultural interchange between the two countries in accordance with the principles of equality and mutual assistance. The ever-increasing consolidation of Sino-Soviet friendship has played and is playing a mighty role in safeguarding peace not only in the Far East but throughout the world as well.

The People's Republic of China has already been recognised by more than twenty countries with an aggregate population of over one thousand million. However, certain States—the United States of America, first and foremost—still refuse to recognise the People's Republic of China and endeavour to ignore the right of the Chinese people to choose their own State system. Refusing to reconcile themselves to the defeat suffered by them in China, they continue to scheme to impose by force upon the Chinese people the Kuomintang remnant clique, a clique long ago thrown out by the five hundred million Chinese people. Up to now at various international conferences they are still planting the henchmen of the Kuomintang clique to pose as representatives of the Chinese people. The People's Republic of China has been subjected to improper discrimination with respect to its international status and rights. The peaceful development and security of China are being constantly threatened. The utter unreasonableness and the extreme unfairness of that are obvious. The existence of this state of affairs and its further continuation hinder the peaceful settlement of the urgent international questions, especially those of Asia, and aggravate uneasiness and tension in international relations. It is clear that this state of affairs should not prevail any longer. Our Conference should mark the beginning of change in this situation.

Although the hostilities in Korea have now terminated, peace in that country has not yet been consolidated, the unification of Korea has not yet been realised, other problems relating to the Korean question still remain to be solved and, moreover, war is still going on in Indo-China. The people of the whole world are displaying a profound concern and anxiety in regard to this state of affairs and they hope that through this Conference it will be possible to change the situation, namely, to bring about a peaceful settlement of the Korean question and to restore peace in Indo-China.

The present Conference has already proceeded to discuss the peaceful settlement of the Korean problem.

The People's Republic of China attaches great importance to the settlement of this problem in the interests of consolidating peace in the Far East and in conformity with the national interests of the Korean people.

Korea is a close neighbour of China. She is separated from China only by a river. Long since Korea has maintained with China the most intimate and friendly relations and shared her weal and woe in common with China. The Chinese people could not but be concerned with Korea's peace and security. In June 1950, the United States launched her war of intervention against Korea. Simultaneously the United States occupied China's territory —Taiwan—and then incessantly bombed North-East China and bombarded China's merchant shipping, thereby encroaching upon China's territorial air space and waters.

Moreover, in defiance of the warnings of the Chinese people and world public opinion, the United States Government ordered its troops to cross the 38th Parallel. These troops approached the Yalu and Tumen Rivers, thus endangering seriously the security of China. Quite obviously, the United States was playing the old game of the Japanese militarists of invading Korea to establish a base for invasion on the mainland of China. In view of painful historical lessons and in consideration of their vital interests, the Chinese people had no choice but to volunteer assistance to Korea, fighting aggression shoulder to shoulder with the Korean people in defence of the security of their motherland.

The Chinese people could not permit such a situation in which Korea could be used once again as a springboard of aggression against China.

After the Korean People's Army and the Chinese People's volunteers had driven back the interventionist troops and reached the vicinity of the 38th Parallel, the Korean and Chinese peoples, in conformity with their consistent policy of the peaceful settlement of the Korean question, quickly responded to the proposal of the Union of Soviet Socialist Republics made on June 23, 1951, at the United Nations regarding negotiations on the cessation of hostilities in Korea. Under the pretext of the so-called question of war prisoners, the United States Government dragged out the subsequent negotiations, thus preventing over a long period of time any agreement being reached in the Korean armistice negotiations. Nevertheless, the Korean-Chinese side made great efforts in this respect. As a result, an Armistice(¹) was concluded in Korea to the immense relief of all peace-loving peoples. In spite of this, the authorities of the United States and South Korea continued as before to create complications so as to put up obstacles in the way of the settlement of outstanding questions between the two sides. This has found its expression particularly in the fact that before and after the Armistice the authorities of the United States and South Korea forcibly retained more than forty-eight thousand Korean and Chinese war prisoners who thus were prevented from returning home. The Government of the People's Republic of China in no way considers this question closed. The Delegation of the People's Republic of China holds that this Conference should not by-pass this question.

These are the facts. However, not all the participants in this Conference reckon with these facts. For instance, the delegate of the Republic of Korea, without regard to the facts, merely trots out a version of the events in Korea which started in 1950 that has long since been refuted. Turning black into white, trying to foist the blame on to the People's Republic of China and at the same time on the great neighbour of the Chinese and Korean peoples —the Soviet Union—he has sought to defend the real culprits of the Korean war. Such methods cannot alter the righteousness of the voluntary help given by the Chinese people to Korea, of the Chinese people's resistance against aggression and of their safeguarding the security of their own fatherland. Neither can such methods obliterate the consistent efforts of the Chinese people and their Government to settle the Korean question peacefully.

Since the Armistice, the flagrant violations of certain important Articles of the Korean Armistice Agreement by the United States and the Republic of Korea offer additional evidence in this regard. Paragraph 60 of the Armistice Agreement explicitly provides that one of the questions to be considered by

(¹) Korea No. 2 (1953), Cmd. 8938.

17

the Political Conference convened after the Armistice is that of withdrawal of all foreign troops from Korea. The United States Government, after the Armistice Agreement had been signed, concluded, however, the so-called " Mutual Defence Treaty " with the Government of the Republic of Korea which grants the United States of America the right to station its armed forces in South Korea. Moreover, until recently the Government of the Republic of Korea made much noise about " march to the North to unite Korea " and openly declares that on expiration of 90 days after the present Conference is convened it will, together with the United States of America, withdraw from the Conference and will again appeal to military force to unite Korea. All this not only proves who unleashed the war in the past and started the aggression but also testifies as to who is continuing at present to prevent the peaceful settlement of the Korean question in an attempt to break once again the peace in Korea. But the war in Korea has taught a significant lesson, namely, any foreign interference in a country whose people have awakened will invariably suffer defeat; any attempt to suppress by the means of foreign arms the liberation struggle of one's own people is also doomed to failure.

The Delegation of the People's Republic of China fully supports the three-point proposals put forward by Foreign Minister Nam Il of the Democratic People's Republic of Korea in respect to the restoration of national unity of Korea and the holding of free all-Korean elections.

The Korean people, after their liberation from the enslavement under Japanese imperialism, have consistently aspired for the realisation of Korea's independence and unity. The unification of Korea should be achieved through the holding of the all-Korean general elections under conditions precluding any foreign intervention and pressure from any terroristic group thus enabling all the Korean people to freely express their will under peaceful conditions.

Some people do not like this, the only correct solution, that is, the holding of general elections in Korea to form an all-Korean Government and reunite Korea in a united, independent and democratic state. The Syngman Rhee Government does not like it, according to yesterday's speech made by the delegate of the Republic of Korea.

He obviously ignores the national interests of the Korean people, trying to make it appear that without foreign interference in the internal affairs of Korea, the Korean people could not solve their domestic problems, the holding of free all-Korean democratic elections included.

This view was most vividly expressed by the delegate of the Republic of Korea when he spoke of the problem of the foreign troops in Korea. He openly called for the staying of American troops in Korea. This fact alone shows how much such claims that the South Korean régime expresses the interests of the people of Korea are worth. But the Chinese people are interested not only in this aspect of the problem, but more so in the direct effect of the presence of the American troops in Korea on the preservation of peace in Korea and the security of the People's Republic of China.

The peaceful unification of Korea is a matter for the Korean people themselves. Therefore, for the purpose of holding nation-wide free elections in Korea without foreign interference, all foreign troops must first of all be withdrawn from Korea.

From the first day of the negotiations on the cessation of hostilities in Korea, we have formally put forward the proposal for the withdrawal of all foreign troops from Korea. Now as the Armistice in Korea has already been achieved, there is even less excuse for any foreign troops to remain in Korea. Our proposal is obviously in full accord with the interests of the peoples of both North and South Korea and with the interests of the peoples of all the countries which took part in the Korean War. Since the Armistice the peoples of all nations whose sons are stationed in Korea demand their early return to lead a peaceful life. All Korean people aspire for a free life without foreign interference. They naturally ask: Since there is no more fighting, why should foreign troops remain in Korea? We believe that this question is wholly justified and the demand of the people for the withdrawal of all foreign troops is quite legitimate.

The peaceful unification of Korea has a great bearing on the maintenance of peace and security in the Far East. The successful carrying out of the peaceful unification of Korea depends on the will of the respective States concerned with the maintenance of peace in the Far East to take measures for ensuring the free and peaceful development of Korea without allowing foreign interference in the internal affairs of Korea.

To summarise, we consider that the proposals made by Foreign Minister Nam Il, Head of the Delegation of the Democratic People's Republic of Korea, are entirely fair and reasonable. We hope that all the participants in this Conference will seriously consider those proposals which could form a basis for achieving an agreement on the peaceful settlement of the Korean problem.

Since the outbreak of the war in Korea a territory belonging to China—Taiwan—has been occupied by the United States of America. This question is not yet settled. As is generally known, Taiwan is part of China's territory, and its occupation by anybody can in no case be tolerated. The United States occupation of Taiwan is an act seriously violating the territorial integrity and sovereignty of China. At the present time Taiwan is turned into a base of the United States of America for conducting subversive activities and further aggression against the People's Republic of China. Japanese militarism which had committed aggression against nations in Asia for a long time is now being revived at an accelerated pace. This state of affairs is menacing with daily increasing seriousness the peace and security of the Far East and Asia.

The Government of the United States of America, as far back as during the period of the war in Korea, sought to create the so-called " Pacific Mutual Security System." Now it is further intervening in the Indo-China war and using it as a pretext to scheme for the organisation of the so-called defence communities in the West Pacific and South-East Asia. These *blocs* have actually agressive purposes and are directed at the establishment of a new colonial rule in Asia and preparation of a new world war.

We consider that the aggressive acts on the part of the United States should be stopped, that peace in Asia should be ensured, that the independence and sovereignty of the Asian nations should be respected, that the national rights and freedom of the Asian peoples should be safeguarded. We also hold that interference in the internal affairs of the Asian nations should be stopped, all foreign military bases in Asia be removed, foreign armed forces stationed in Asian countries be withdrawn, the revival of militarism in Japan be prevented and all economic blockades and restrictions be abolished. The statement just made by Mr. John F. Dulles is contrary to these demands. His proposals are completely contrary to the interests of the Asian peoples. We absolutely cannot agree to his views.

The Government of the People's Republic of China considers that the countries of Asia should consult among themselves with a view to seeking common measures to safeguard peace and security in Asia, by assuming obligations mutually and respectively.

The people of China, as all the peoples of Asia, are concerned not only about peace in Asia but also about peace in Europe and other parts of the world. The policy of reviving German militarism and splitting Europe into mutually hostile military *blocs* now menaces the peace and security in

19

Europe and at the same time affects the situation outside Europe, aggravating tension and uneasiness in Asia. That is why we consider that in order to safeguard world peace it is necessary, through negotiation, first and foremost between the great Powers, to put an end to the rearmament of Western Germany and to ensure security in Europe on the basis of joint efforts of all the European States, as proposed by the Soviet Union.

We also consider that the interests of peace demand the termination of the armaments race, the reduction of armaments and armed forces, the prohibition of atomic, hydrogen and other weapons of mass extermination.

The peoples of the whole world, especially the peoples of Asia, are following the progress of our Conference with great concern. They all expect the Conference to achieve positive results. Unfortunately, some Asian States which express concern about peace in Asia, such as India, Indonesia, Burma, &c., are unable to participate in our Conference; this certainly cannot be considered good.

Allow me to express the hope that the delegates to this Conference, guided by the interests of consolidating peace and security in Asia and in the whole world, will make joint efforts to find ways and means for solving the present urgent problems listed on the agenda of the Conference.

FOURTH PLENARY SESSION ON KOREA

Document No. 6

Speech by Mr. Casey, Minister of External Affairs of Australia, April 29, 1954

Following the Conference at Berlin earlier this year between the Governments of the United Kingdom, the United States, France and the Soviet Union, we are meeting here in Geneva for the purpose of reaching a peaceful settlement of the Korean question—an objective of great importance to the peace of the world and the well-being of mankind.

Let me say, to begin with, that we of Australia approach this Conference in the spirit of restrained optimism—restrained since our hopes of peace have received too many disappointments in the past for us to feel that there is any easy solution to problems of this sort in these days of international rivalry and suspicion, but optimistic in that we do not admit they are insoluble, however complicated they may be.

Speaking on behalf of Australia, I may say that we shall, for our part, do our best to contribute to the success of this Conference. This is not a time for recrimination about the past—but for an attempt to make a fresh start.

As my friend from Colombia has pointed out, we have very clear directions in approaching our problem. These are contained in a number of international agreements and more particularly in the United Nations Charter and in the resolutions of the United Nations General Assembly on Korea. I have personally visited South Korea and I know very well the intense desire of the people to achieve a unified, independent and a democratic country which would allow them to live in peace and freedom without oppression from outside or interference in their internal affairs.

Throughout the course of United Nations intervention in Korea, Australia has played a direct and responsible part. From the beginning, we have been represented in the various United Nations Commissions, where we have tried to play an active and constructive role. We have supplied sea, land and air forces to resist aggression in the interests of collective security.

We have contributed to the great cause of Korean relief and reconstruction. Our concern is a natural one. As a country situated close to Asia, the affairs of our neighbours—and Korea is one of our neighbours—are of great interest and concern to us. Then again, as a member of the United Nations, we accept the responsibility of furthering its policy in Korea. In this Conference we will strive to continue to play a constructive part designed to support United Nations principles and objectives and to develop the armistice in Korea into something more permanent and satisfactory.

It is against this background that I should like to discuss the problems we are facing here. In doing so, I believe our task can be clarified by keeping in mind the existing United Nations decisions to which I have referred.

In the first place, in accordance with United Nations principles and objectives, we believe the settlement in Korea must be found by peaceful means. That was the basis on which we supported the Armistice in Korea, which, a little more than nine months ago, successfully concluded the first endeavours to enforce the principle of collective security through a world-wide international organisation. That armistice was not a peace settlement, but it provided the opportunity of seeking by peaceful means the ultimate goals of the United Nations and the Korean people, through a conference such as the one we have at last succeeded in arranging here. In the interests of peace, we must collectively endeavour to make this Conference succeed.

Secondly, in accordance with the principle of self-determination, emphasised in so many of the previous United Nations Assembly decisions on Korea, we believe that the Korean problem must be settled through the free expression of the will of the Korean people.

This means, of course, that the unification and independence of Korea must be based on free elections. There is undoubtedly a strong case for arguing that these elections should be held only in North Korea, since elections have already been held in the South under the supervision of the United Nations and have led to the recognition by the United Nations of the Republic of Korea as the only sovereign Government of Korea. We hope, however, that, if it were necessary in the interests of a final settlement, the Republic of Korea Government would agree to elections throughout Korea. This would be a gesture which would not only be in keeping with the Republic of Korea Government's support of democratic principles but which should, if the other side is sincere in its approach, lead to a peaceful solution of the Korean problem.

We believe, of course, that the elections should be based upon fair, proportionate representation as between the North and the South—that a free atmosphere both before and during the elections must be assured by specific guarantees—and that the elections should be held under United Nations supervision to ensure fair play.

As Mr. Dulles has pointed out, United Nations supervision of elections is not only the existing policy of the United Nations, but there is at present in Korea a body established by the Assembly—the United Nations Commission for the Unification and Rehabilitation of Korea—U.N.C.U.R.K.—which has the express task of supervising, assisting with and advising on elections.

Thirdly, in our approach to the Korean problem, we must pay special attention to the welfare of the Korean people. Their grievous suffering and the need to alleviate their hardships must remain a prominent objective in any discussions on Korea. Not only have the Korean people suffered heavy casualties, but the country has been devastated by the fighting and to-day the rehabilitation requirements are very great. Substantial contributions in the way of international assistance have been made and will continue to be made, but only a settlement which will provide security and stability for

21

Korea will enable the people to concentrate on building up a viable and durable economy and society. This Conference must therefore take heed of the pressing need for effective reconstruction and rehabilitation measures in Korea and of the need for ensuring, as far as possible, the future security and stability of the country.

I should now like to turn to the North Korean proposals. As compared with what I have said, the plan of the North Korean Delegation appears to be inadequate on a number of important points. Nevertheless, these North Korean proposals require careful consideration and, in pointing out what I believe are their basic weaknesses, I should like to take the opportunity of seeking further clarifications. It will be remembered that the North Korean plan advocates a joint commission made up of representatives of Northern and Southern Korea elected by the Supreme People's Assembly and the National Assembly respectively, for the purpose of preparing for and holding Korean elections.

In the first place, I should like to ask whether the number of members of both Assemblies on the Commission would be proportionate to the number of inhabitants in the parts of Korea represented by those Assemblies or, if not, on what basis they would be represented. As Mr. Dulles has pointed out, the Supreme People's Assembly of North Korea, although a far larger body than the Republic of Korea National Assembly of South Korea, represents far fewer people. It would seem to be quite unreasonable to have a joint body which was not based upon the relative size of the populations in the North and in the South.

Secondly, I should like to point out that, whereas the elections to the Republic of Korea National Assembly have been carried out under United Nations observation, no evidence is available to show that the elections in North Korea were freely and democratically conducted, in the generally accepted meaning of the words.

This lack of independent observation of the elections in the North brings me to the third point—how, in the present circumstances, can free elections in Korea be assured without international supervision? To argue that the Korean people can decide this among themselves seems unrealistic in view of the major issues involved and the bitter feelings that have been aroused in recent years. Moreover, the United Nations has its own responsibilities and an important stake in seeing that there is an eventual settlement in accordance with United Nations principles. The United Nations Assembly would certainly want to be assured through independent observers about the conditions of such decisive elections.

Fourthly, I would see little prospect of the proposed joint Commission reaching satisfactory agreements and would expect that inevitably there would be long delays which would be most damaging to the interests of the Korean people. I should like to enquire how the North Korean Delegation envisages the breaking of deadlocks and what time-limit would be placed upon completing arrangements for the elections.

In addition to the establishment of a joint Commission, the North Korean plan places much emphasis on the withdrawal of foreign troops within six months. If I may say so, this is a deceptively simply proposal. It overlooks the fact that withdrawal of United Nations forces from the south would, as Mr. Dulles pointed out, be quite a different matter from the withdrawal of Chinese forces from the north. Withdrawal of Chinese forces means a withdrawal of maybe only five miles, whereas the withdrawal of the United Nations forces from the south could mean a withdrawal of 5,000 miles. Chinese forces could be brought back into Korea in a matter of hours, whereas it would take at least many weeks for United Nations forces to return.

I am sure we all agree that the sooner our troops can be safely withdrawn from Korea the better pleased we shall all be. But the dangers of an over-hasty withdrawal have been all too bitterly demonstrated and the heavy sacrifices that this has involved must surely preclude the United Nations from agreeing to withdrawals before United Nations interests and objectives are properly safeguarded. It may be that some United Nations forces will be needed in Korea until a unified and independent Government has been democratically established. Nevertheless, I would hope that, on the basis of satisfactory agreements and firm commitments, it might be possible to begin withdrawals at some early date. Moreover, irrespective of the stage of the withdrawals, I would expect that an agreement would be possible to ensure that such of our troops as remained in Korea would in no way interfere or influence the conduct of the elections.

And now let me say something on another matter.

Mr. Chou En-lai, in the course of his speech yesterday, said that " in June 1950 the United States launched its war of intervention against Korea." References of this sort have been made on many occasions since June 1950 in a desperate effort to obscure the facts of the case. I say "facts" because it is facts and not opinion or wishful thinking with which we must deal.

Since the beginning of 1948 the United Nations has been in Korea. The United Nations has attempted to bring about the unification of the country by peaceful means and, until 1950, to prevent hostilities. In pursuance of these objectives, a United Nations Commission and its military observers used to make regular inspections of the situation. They wanted to observe military dispositions on both sides of the boundary between North and South Korea, but, though they were given every facility by the South Korean Government, they were not allowed north of the 38th parallel by the Communists.

Though the United Nations Commission was unable to report on this because it was denied access to North Korea, it was able to report on the situation in South Korea. And, actually, on June 24, 1950—the day before the invasion—a report was submitted to the United Nations Commission by United Nations field observers who had just returned from a field trip along the 38th parallel beginning on June 9. The field observers included two Australians—Major F. S. B. Peach and Squadron-Leader R. J. Rankin, R.A.A.F. The Report of this United Nations Commission was made public, and conclusively demonstrated that the South Korean Army was not in a position to launch an attack. The observers reported, for example, that there was no concentration of troops and that there was no dumping of supplies. ammunition or petrol in forward areas in order to prepare for a large-scale attack. " So far as equipment of the South Korean forces is concerned, in the absence of armour, air support and heavy artillery, any action with the object of invasion would, by any military standards, be impossible."

This report, I repeat, was submitted *before* the invasion. Subsequently, the United Nations forces captured various documents whuch further estab-lished the fact that preparations had been made by the Communists to launch an attack. There is no doubt where responsibility lay, or who was the aggressor.

I think it is clear to all of us that, in the present international atmosphere, it is not going to be easy to reach a practical and durable solution of the Korean problem. However, a solution has to be found. Already in Korea the United Nations has made history by successfully establishing for the first time the principle of collective security. But beginnings are not as important as the carrying through of programmes to a final successful conclusion. "Korea" has become a symbol in the minds of many anxious peoples throughout the world. We must finish what we have begun. The Korean problem has become much more than a local problem.

And now let me finish by saying this. We are here in Geneva to deal with two problems which I believe have some relationship to each other— the problem of Korea and the problem of Indo-China. In Korea there has been war in which countless thousands have lost their lives and vast destruction has taken place. But, after all the suffering and destruction, Korea is back where it started four years ago. Because of United Nations intervention, the people of South Korea are still able to maintain the way of life they want. The Communist world has gained nothing, at a great cost to themselves. The Communist world has been faced by the might and purpose of the free world in defending one of our number from being overwhelmed and absorbed. Maybe the Communist world will recognise that Korea presents a lesson and a warning to those who set out to overwhelm and absorb other countries by force of arms.

But even before this bloody drama began in Korea, a Communist enterprise, on rather different lines but with the same objective, was in train in Indo-China. The end of the war in Korea—and the lesson of Korea—came when the attempt to communise Indo-China by force of arms was well advanced. But, it is to be expected that the recent reactions of a significant part of the free world to the Communist war—and Communist-supported war—in Indo-China will not have been lost on the communist world.

It is no empty form of words on our part when we say we want no more than for the free countries to be left alone to pursue the way of life that they want. We are not out to force our democratic way of life on others— nor will we abide efforts to force the communist way of life on any of our number—whatever may be the slogan under which this is done.

Wars do not stand still. They expand or they contract. If all of us here—all—sincerely want a diminution of international tension, there is no more suitable or appropriate gathering of nations than this present Conference in which to achieve it.

Document No. 7

Speech by M. Molotov, Soviet Foreign Minister, April 29, 1954

Mr. Chairman and Delegates,

It has been decided, at this Conference in Geneva, to examine two questions: first, the peaceful settlement of the Korean problem; and second, the restoration of peace in Indo-China.

It may thus be said that the Geneva Conference is devoted to Asian matters. Both the Korean and Indo-Chinese questions are amongst the most urgent problems of Asia.

In this connexion, we cannot help noticing that only a few Asian countries are present at this Conference. We are bound to find a disadvantage in the fact that a whole number of Asian Powers such as India, Indonesia, Burma, Pakistan and others are not taking part in our Conference, although their presence here would be very valuable for our work.

On the other hand, we must not under-estimate the importance of the fact that this is the first Conference of recent years to be attended by all the great Powers: France, Great Britain, the United States of America, the People's Republic of China, and the Soviet Union. In this connexion, we must stress in particular that one great Asian Power—the People's Republic of China— will be able to make its contribution to the discussions at this Conference on the aforementioned urgent problems of the situation in Asia.

The Conference as at present composed is dealing first with questions affecting Korea.

The problem before us is as follows: how to establish by peaceful means, a unified and independent Korea. A settlement of this problem, besides being of paramount importance to the Korean people, would also constitute an important factor in the easing of international tension.

The settlement of the Korean question is of course first and foremost the business of the Koreans, of the Korean people themselves. No solution imposed upon the Korean people by other countries can satisfy the Korean people or lead to a lasting settlement of the Korean problem.

It is essential to take into consideration Korean history, and in particular the history of the Korean people's struggle for independence.

At the beginning of the present century, as we know, Japanese imperialism, with the support of a number of other Powers, first turned Korea into a Japanese protectorate, and subsequently occupied it and assumed full control of the Korean Peninsula. This aggressive imperialistic policy inevitably aroused the resistance of the Korean people. The Korean people's struggle for its independence and freedom was a hard one, calling for heavy sacrifices. It dragged on for many years. In our day, however, such an aggressive policy is bound to meet with the determined opposition of peoples defending their independence and freedom.

As we know, the Japanese imperialists, after occupying Korea, turned the Korean Peninsula into the main springboard for an all-out attack on China and the Chinese people. They sought to extend their domination throughout the whole of China and South-East Asia. For this purpose, they formed an alliance with Hitlerite Germany, concluded the so-called " anti-Comintern Pact " and, on the pretext of waging a " struggle against communism " made plans for partitioning the world in collusion with German imperialism.

We all remember how this ended. The Japanese militarists suffered defeat in the autumn of 1945, and were driven back to their own home. Korea was able to free itself from the clutches of the Japanese militarists and begin a new, free and independent life.

Since, owing to circumstances of a military nature, Korea was divided into two parts—North and South—immediately after its liberation from the Japanese Occupation, the Korean people were faced with the task of establishing a unified Korea and setting up a unified and independent democratic Korean State. This task was not completed during the early years following the end of the Second World War. The Democratic People's Republic of Korea, established on the territory of North Korea, succeeded during that period in carrying out a series of major democratic reforms, including the transfer to the peasants of land belonging to the landowners and former servants of Japanese imperialism.

This constructive work on behalf of the Korean people was cut short by a war forced upon the country from abroad and the brutal military intervention of the United States of America, which lasted three years and was carried out under the United Nations flag. After the conclusion of the armistice in Korea in the summer of 1953, there once again arose the question of restoring Korea's unity and creating a single Korean State on democratic lines.

The chief task of the Geneva Conference is to help the Korean people to restore Korea's unity. We must make every effort to enable the Korean people to find, by peaceful means, the path to the creation of a unified, independent, democratic state. All States desirous of decreasing tension in international relations and strengthening universal peace have an interest in achieving a peaceful settlement of the Korean problem. We cannot ignore the fact, however, that the United Nations, as a result of pressure brought to bear upon it by certain States, has taken a one-sided attitude and shown itself incapable of settling the Korean problem. Suffice it to say that not once in the whole of the last four years have representatives of, for example, North

25

Korea been given a hearing in the United Nations. As to the fallacious account of events in Korea that the United States representative has once again repeated here, it has been repeatedly refuted and denounced by the Soviet Union representatives in the United Nations.

In considering the Korean question, we cannot leave out of account the fundamental changes that have taken place in the political development of the Asian countries in recent years, particularly since the end of the Second World War.

It is common knowledge that for many years, in some cases for several centuries, other non-Asian States have held sway in the countries of Asia and the people of those countries have been deprived of the opportunity of self-determination. This was due to certain States' acquisitive, imperialist policy. However, that policy has already discredited itself. Attempts to pursue the old colonial policy at the present time are ending in more and more obvious failure. This is to be borne in mind at the Geneva Conference in dealing with both the Korean and the Indo-Chinese questions.

The peoples of the Asian countries have met with considerable success in their struggle to achieve independence and free themselves from foreign domination. That is a fact which cannot now be ignored.

The world population is in the region of 2,400 million. More than half this population inhabits Asia. Yet even at the beginning of the twentieth century the great majority of the population of Asia had the status either of colonies or of semi-colonies and dependent countries.

Since then, fundamental changes have taken place in Asia.

The decisive change in this connexion occurred when the Socialist Revolution took place in Russia in 1917 and the Union of Soviet Socialist Republics was established, which put an end to the imperialistic policy of Tzarism and based its relations with other countries on the recognition of their national freedom and independence. This new situation inevitably helped to lift up the hearts of peoples who had been struggling for centuries for their national freedom and independence.

These events are sometimes completely misinterpreted by people of old-fashioned views who are incapable of understanding the historic changes that have taken place, for example, in the countries of Asia. They are prepared to find " communist intrigues ", " agents of the Kremlin ", &c., everywhere. These persons ascribe every movement for freedom and national independence on the part of the oppressed peoples to communism. Contrary to their own intentions, they are raising the communists' prestige even in cases in which the communists are not involved, not realising that the real causes of the unselfish struggle for national freedom and independence among people of diverse political views and convictions, are the aspirations long cherished by nations to achieve freedom from dependence on the foreigner and from colonial servitude. As far as the views and convictions of the Soviet people are concerned, however, we cannot conceal our warm sympathy with the movement of the peoples, including the peoples of Asia, for national freedom.

The fundamental political changes in Asia have found their supreme expression in China, which has a population of over 500 million. Since the creation of the Chinese People's Republic, and the establishment of the firm foundations of a popular democratic régime there, it would be absurd to ignore that fact. The social and economic and the political reforms in China are taking place before the eyes of all, and to ignore this is to ignore major events of historic significance.

Who, furthermore, can deny that a country like India, with a population of over 300 million souls, has also entered the historical arena—India which was until quite recently in the position of a colony? Yet nobody can now deny that India is taking an increasingly prominent place among countries that are asserting their national independence and striving to play the important part in international affairs which is their due. The importance of such States as Indonesia, Burma, and a number of other countries is steadily increasing. That does not mean that the efforts being made to establish real independence in those countries are everywhere proceeding smoothly, without strife and without complications in their relations with certain countries. Nevertheless, what has been said bears witness to the fact that in Asia highly important historical changes have actually taken place. And this fact cannot be ignored when any problem relating to the countries of Asia is being considered.

Reference must be made to the question of China, which now occupies a special position in international affairs.

I do not reveal any secret when I say that between the Soviet Union and the People's Republic of China lasting friendly relations have been established. Many other countries also have already established political and economic relations with the People's Republic of China. It is a well-known fact that a country like Great Britain attaches great importance to the development of its relations with the People's Republic of China. It is also common knowledge that quite a number of other countries have not established normal relations with the People's Republic of China, only because they have been prevented in every way from doing so by outside pressure.

As for the United States of America, the Government of that country is pursuing an openly aggressive policy towards the People's Republic of China. This aggressive attitude of the United States of America is reflected, moreover, in the whole state of affairs in modern Asia.

Everyone knows that on the part of the People's Republic of China there have been no acts of aggression against the United States of America. But the case is quite different when one considers the policy of the United States of America towards the People's Republic of China.

Ever since the Chinese people drove from Chinese territory the discredited Chang Kai-shek clique, which took no account of the needs of the Chinese people but was simply a servant of foreign capitalism—and set up the People's Republic of China, act after act of aggression has been committed against that people. The main responsibility for this lies with the ruling circles of the United States of America.

They seized the island of Taiwan and established the die-hards of the Chang Kai-shek clique as lords of that island. They took all sorts of inadmissible measures to prevent the People's Republic of China from taking its rightful place in the United Nations. In addition, they introduced, through the United Nations, a decision to place an embargo on trade with China. They are preparing the re-establishment of the armed forces of Japan, thus threatening China. They have accused China of aggression in Korea, although the participation of Chinese volunteers on the side of the People's Democratic Republic of Korea was due not only to a completely natural feeling of friendship towards the Korean people, who were fighting for their national freedom, but also to the security requirements of China itself, to whose frontiers aggressive foreign troops had advanced. While openly preparing aggression against the People's Republic of China, constantly threatening its frontiers with attacks from Taiwan and the Korean Peninsula, and establishing new military bases near Chinese territory on the Pacific Islands and in Pakistan, the ruling circles of the United States of America depict all this as if China, and not the United States of America, were the aggressor.

Recently, under the pretext of defending the puppet régimes in Indo-China, plans are being made to create a military alliance in South-East Asia, although

27

not a single self-respecting country of Asia proposes to take part in this alliance. These plans once again provide evidence of the intentions of the colonial Powers to play one group of Asiatic peoples against another.

At a time when events of the greatest importance have been occurring, denoting the beginning of the national and social rebirth of the countries of Asia, and above all China, on new democratic foundations appropriate to the present epoch of democratic progress and development, certain circles in the United States of America are clinging to the past and struggling to preserve the colonial and semi-colonial systems. An unwillingness to reckon with the historic changes in the development of the peoples of Asia cannot, however, justify the policy of those States which still regard it as their task to preserve reactionary cliques and colonial systems in that continent. The United States of America's hostile policy to the People's Republic of China is reflected in its highly negative effect on the solution of current Asian problems. This aggressive policy has no prospects of any kind, for it is contrary to the whole march of historic development in Asia—and not only in Asia—and is, in present circumstances, the main obstacle to the settlement of current Asian problems in accordance with the principles of freedom and the national rights of peoples.

The United States Secretary of State's most recent pronouncements on the situation in Asia bear witness to the fact that certain quarters are still powerfully attracted by the outworn past and that in places the old out-dated colonial policies of Imperialism still exert a strong pull.

On April 16, American newspapers published a statement by the United States Secretary of State in which the establishment of the People's Republic of China, which, as is well known, was set up in accordance with the wishes of the Chinese people, is described as " a great catastrophe," signifying " the loss of mainland China." In this statement Mr. Dulles also said that " this catastrophe will be multiplied, if to it is added the loss of the millions of inhabitants, the extensive economic resources and the strategic positions in South-East Asia and the islands of the Pacific Ocean."

In this statement by the American statesman, there is not a single word about the national interests and rights of the peoples of China and South-East Asia and the islands of the Pacific Ocean. Moreover, it clearly expresses a desire to use all means to oppose the advance of the great Chinese people and the other peoples of Asia from the old colonial and semi-colonial way of life to a new, free, way of life and a new democratic system. The profound transformation which has occurred in China is here described as " a loss," although China never belonged to anyone and had no intention of belonging to any foreign State. The reference to " the loss of mainland China " clearly reveals an attraction to the Imperialist, colonial policy which has outlived its time, and shows no recognition of the principles of freedom and the national rights of peoples. Yet the United States representative has found it possible to deliver here his trivial moralisations on communism and the principles of freedom.

The Geneva Conference presents an opportunity for all sides to improve their knowledge of those problems of Asia which are at present recognised as being most urgent. Here we can listen to different points of view and, as a result of the exchange of views, find a solution to the questions before us which will be in accordance with the aspirations of the peoples concerned and also with the interests of progress and the strengthening of peace. Such an approach, for example, to the Korean question can greatly facilitate a peaceful solution of the problem of creating a unified and independent democratic Korea; it can help us to arrive in fact at a peaceful settlement of the Korean question.

Such will be the outcome of the Geneva Conference if it proceeds on the basis of the principle that the peoples of Asia are fully entitled to decide their own affairs themselves and, above all, that this is their own business.

Other States, including also the participants in the Geneva Conference, are called upon to assist the peoples of Asia with their friendly endeavours in this matter.

Such an understanding of the tasks of this Conference would accord in the highest degree with the interests of the freedom and national advancement of the peoples of Asia and, at the same time, with the interests of the strengthening of peace in Asia and with the interests of peace in general. The achievement of positive results at the Geneva Conference would also contribute towards the settling of other problems, and not only in Asia.

The Head of the Delegation of the People's Republic of China, Mr. Chou En-lai, has expressed here the view that it is desirable that the Asian countries should be united in their endeavours to safeguard peace in Asia. The Soviet delegation entirely shares that view. As the European peoples in Europe, so also the peoples in Asia must take such measures as would accord with the interests of the strengthening of peace in Europe, in Asia and throughout the world.

The Conference has heard the representative of South Korea, but in that jejune statement no positive concrete proposals whatever were made.

The point of view of the Government of the Democratic People's Republic of Korea on the subject of the peaceful settlement of the Korean problem has also been expounded here.

The Soviet Delegation considers that the proposals put forward by the Minister for Foreign Affairs of the Democratic People's Republic of Korea, Mr. Nam Il, can serve as a basis for the adoption of an appropriate decision on the Korean question. These proposals are designed to meet the national aspirations of the Korean people for the restoration of the unity of their fatherland and to accord with the interests of the strengthening of peace among the nations.

SIXTH PLENARY SESSION ON KOREA

Document No. 8

Extract from Speech and Proposal by Mr. Chou En-lai, Head of the Delegation of the People's Delegation of China, May 3, 1954

I have already pointed out at our meeting on April 28, that this Conference cannot possibly by-pass the question of war prisoners, which still remains an unsettled issue of the Korean Armistice. If the United States Government had faithfully abided by the international conventions to which the United States is a party. the question of war prisoners would never have arisen, since the Geneva Convention[4] explicitly stipulates that war prisoners shall be released and repatriated without delay after the cessation of hostilities. But in the Korean war the United States Government conducted the war by savage and inhuman methods and, in violation of the various provisions of the Geneva Convention for humanitarian treatment of war prisoners, maltreated and persecuted Korean and Chinese captured personnel and persisted in its erroneous view which is contrary to the Geneva Convention as regards the release and repatriation of war prisoners. thus delaying the Korean Armistice. The Korean and Chinese side made repeated efforts for the conclusion of an armistice in Korea, and finally reached agreement with the other side on the question of war prisoners. Both sides agreed to ensure for every prisoner-of-war the opportunity of

[4] " Miscellaneous No. 4 (1950)," Cmd. 8033.

exercising his right to be repatriated. But only ten days after the agreement on war prisoners was signed, the United States induced the authorities of the Republic of Korea, starting on June 18 and for several days thereafter, forcibly to retain more than 27,000 Korean and Chinese captured personnel and impressed them into the army, thereby depriving them entirely of the opportunity of exercising their right to be repatriated. This action of the authorities of the United States and of the Republic of Korea in violation of the agreement on war prisoners almost endangered the Korean Armistice and met with widespread criticism and condemnation. General Mark Clark, Commander-in-Chief of the United Nations Command, stated on June 29, 1953, that " the United Nations Command is continuing its efforts to recover the prisoners-of-war who have escaped." But up to the present not a single man of the more than 27,000 prisoners-of-war who were forcibly retained and impressed into the army has been recovered.

After the Korean Armistice, the authorities of the United States and the Republic of Korea used every means to obstruct the work of the Neutral Nations Repatriation Commission([5]), which was presided over by an Indian representative. As a result, the overwhelming majority of the Korean and Chinese captured personnel in the custody of the said Commission did not have any opportunity to exercise their right to be repatriated. Consequently, the said Commission did not fulfil the functions and responsibilities entrusted to it by its terms of reference under the Korean Armistice Agreement. On January 20 and 21, 1954, the Neutral Nations Repatriation Commission handed over to the United States side the more than 21,000 Korean and Chinese captured personnel in its custody; the said Commission also pointed out in its Final Report of February 18, 1954, that " unless the two Commands agree on alternative procedures or courses of action in regard to status and disposition of prisoners of war, any unilateral action by any party concerned will not be in conformity with the said terms of reference." However, the United States side used force and threats of force and handed over these more than 21,000 Korean and Chinese captured personnel to the South Korean Government and the Chiang Kai-shek remnant clique, which impressed these captured personnel into their respective armies.

The action of the authorities of the United States and of the Republic of Korea in forcibly retaining on two occasions over 48,000 Korean and Chinese captured personnel is a serious breach of the Geneva Convention([4]) and the Korean Armistice Agreement. In order to solve this problem in a reasonable manner, the Delegation of the People's Republic of China, after obtaining the consent of the Delegation of the Democratic People's Republic of Korea, hereby proposes:

(1) That measures be taken to ensure the return to their motherlands of those Korean and Chinese captured personnel who were forcibly retained in June 1953, and January 1954, and impressed into the army;

(2) That a Commission, composed of representatives of the United States, the United Kingdom, France, the People's Republic of China, the Soviet Union, the Democratic People's Republic of Korea and the Republic of Korea, be set up to assist in carrying out the measures for the repatriation of Korean and Chinese captured personnel as provided in the foregoing paragraph;

(3) That, pending the handling of the prisoner-of-war question by the afore-mentioned Commission, joint teams composed of representatives of the Red Cross Societies of the States concerned on each side in the Korean Armistice Agreement be formed and sent to the present locations of the war prisoners for purposes of inspection.

([4]) " Miscellaneous No. 4 (1950)," Cmd. 8033.
([5]) " Korea No. 1 (1953)," Cmd. 8793.

SEVENTH PLENARY SESSION ON KOREA

Document No. 9

Speech by Mr. Lester B. Pearson, Secretary of State for External Affairs of Canada, May 4, 1954

If I venture to take part in this debate, it is because I do not wish my silence to be interpreted as indicating any weakening or slackening of the strong support that my country has steadily given to United Nations policy on Korea; or as indicating, even by omission, approval of the distortions in some previous speeches on Korean and Asian developments; or indifference to the false charges that have been levelled, particularly at the United States of America, in respect of these developments.

Canada is represented at this Korean Peace Conference because she is a member of the United Nations and, as such, has participated, on land, water and in the air, in United Nations operations against aggression in Korea. Similarly, our responsibilities here derive solely from the decisions taken by the United Nations on the Korean question.

These decisions were concerned with, first, the determination of the fact of aggression in Korea; second, the repulse of this aggression, something that has been accomplished by the United Nations forces under the resolute and unselfish leadership of the United States, and by the heavy and gallant sacrifices of the Korean people themselves; and, third, with the establishment, under the auspices of the United Nations, of a free, united and democratic Korea, rising from the tragedy and devastation of that unhappy land.

Every one of these United Nations decisions was accepted by the vast majority of the members of that organisation, including—we should not forget this—many who have often declared their intention of remaining outside what has been called the "cold war," and whose foreign policies could not be remotely considered as aimed against the communist Powers.

The Canadian Government has supported and remains bound by these United Nations decisions. Therefore, we cannot support any proposal which denies their validity, or which would equate at this Conference the moral and political status of the United Nations in respect of the Korean question, with those Governments which have broken the United Nations Charter by taking aggressive military action against the Republic of Korea.

The leader of the Soviet delegation in his one-sided and unconvincing analysis of recent Asian history stated that the Western countries, and the United States in particular, were "incapable of understanding the historic changes that have taken place in the countries of Asia." He added that, instead of trying to understand these changes, we were prepared to find "communist intrigues" and "agents of the Kremlin" everywhere.

Leaving aside the fact that fear of "communist intrigues" and of "agents of the Kremlin" is, for many free States, something that has grown out of hard and unhappy experience, M. Molotov is completely wrong in his charge that we do not recognise the significance of what has taken place in Asia in recent years, in the march of the peoples of that great continent to national freedom and greater human welfare. On the contrary, we do understand and fully accept the significance of these developments, and the fact that this march cannot and should not be reversed.

M. Molotov also said in his speech, "We cannot conceal our warm sympathy with the movements of the peoples, including the peoples of Asia, for national freedom." We can all echo that expression of sympathy while insisting, at the same time, that this freedom should be more real than that to mention a few examples, of Lithuania or Bulgaria or the Mongolian People's Republic; or, indeed, of those members of the United Nations who belong to a *bloc* so tightly controlled that no member in all the years of its existence has ever publicly disagreed with or voted against a proposal of the leader of that *bloc*.

We, therefore, hope that *all* the Asian peoples in their forward march will secure for themselves, as India, Pakistan and Ceylon, for instance, have already done, a better kind of national freedom than that which is a mere façade to conceal imperialist and aggressive domination by any power, whether Asian *or* European.

The right to be free does not include the obligation to be communist; and "Asia for the Asians" is not the same as—indeed is the opposite of— "Asia for the Cominform." It would be no contribution either to Asian peace or prosperity, independence or dignity, if the Japanese East-Asian co-prosperity sphere were exchanged for the Chinese East-Asian co-Communist empire.

In their speeches to this Conference the leaders of the delegations of the Soviet Union and the People's Republic of China have attacked the United States for a policy of aggressive imperialism in Asia, which, they allege, stands in the way of freedom for the Asian peoples. As the leader of the delegation of a country which is a neighbour of the most powerful State in the world, I can say with a conviction based on our national experience that the people of the United States are neither aggressive nor imperialist; and it is the people of the United States that freely elect their Governments.

If, indeed, the United States did not respect the rights and interests of others, Canada would not to-day be an independent Power, but merely a satellite of her great neighbour. Her representatives would not be able, as they certainly *are* able, to speak their own minds and stand up for their own views in conferences of the nations, even if this means, as it has more than once meant, disagreeing with some aspects of the policy of the United States of America.

I hope that the fact that we have on occasion so disagreed (indeed, we differed on the composition of the United Nations Korean Political Conference) will be taken as convincing evidence, not only of our own independence, but also of the respect which the United States has for smaller countries, and of the value which it attaches to co-operation and support based on free will, and not imposed from above. Our own experience of free partnership and co-operation shows the rest of the world how little it has to fear from this so-called "aggressive imperialism" of the United States.

What kind of "aggressive imperialism" was it that brought about, after World War Two, the quick and virtually complete dismantling by the United States, and the other Western allies, of the greatest military machine in history in the hope that arms would now no longer be necessary for security?

What kind of "aggressive imperialism" was it that caused the United States, at a time when it alone possessed atomic weapons, to agree that those weapons and the materials from which they were manufactured should be put under the exclusive jurisdiction and control of an international authority?

It is also strange to the point of phantasy that, if the United States was following in Korea "colonial policies of imperialism," as Mr. Chou En-lai described them, she should, in 1949, have withdrawn all her armed forces from that country. And when United States troops returned to Korea, they did so under United Nations auspices to repel the aggression launched on the Republic of Korea from across the 38th parallel.

Ignoring all this, and in support of his charges of imperialist aggression, the head of the Chinese Communist delegation brought up once again the old accusation that "in June 1950 the United States launched its war of intervention against Korea."

This false charge has long since been disproved; not merely on the evidence produced by one Government, but by the unanimous verdict of a United Nations Commission which, as has already been pointed out by the Delegate of Australia, was on the spot in Korea, and which included among its seven members the representative of India.

These unfounded accusations and arguments about American aggression against Korea are strikingly similar to those which came out of Moscow and Berlin in September 1939, to prove that peace-loving Nazi Germany had been the innocent victim of aggression by Poland.

No amount of distorted or false or manufactured evidence, however, can alter the truth. This is as true of June 1950, in Korea, as it was of September 1939, in Berlin. Facts are facts, and they can be left to history to record and confirm.

There was another observation of the leader of the Chinese Communist delegation which invites comment. He stated that all foreign military bases in Asia should be removed and foreign armed forces stationed in Asian countries withdrawn. It would be interesting to know whether he includes in this sweeping generalisation the Russians in Port Arthur.

In his second statement, made yesterday, Mr. Chou En-lai brought up the question of prisoners of war. It is difficult to understand why, if he is sincere in his desire to press forward with a peaceful solution of the Korean problems.

We all know of the efforts made last winter at Panmunjom, under the skilful and impartial administration of Indian representatives, and the direction of the Neutral Nations Repatriation Commission, to give all prisoners the opportunity of making up their own minds whether to return to communism or not. We know also that this question has now been settled—and to re-open it at this Conference would serve no useful purpose.

If the Geneva Convention([4]) is cited by the leader of the Chinese delegation, I would remind him of the thousands of South Korean prisoners who disappeared without a trace shortly after capture; of the failure to account for many United Nations prisoners, of the refusal to allow the Red Cross to visit them, or to give information concerning them, of the cruel treatment and torturing interrogations to which many of them were subjected.

Certainly, if this question were raised for discussion at this Conference, there would be much to talk about. But the net result would be merely to delay, and possibly to prevent the work we have come here to accomplish, namely to bring peace and freedom to a united Korea. Any delegation which introduces proposals for such a purpose, or which would have such a result, would bear a heavy responsibility indeed.

While, Mr. Chairman, the questions I have been raising are all important, our primary concern at this Conference is a peace settlement for Korea. On that subject the leader of the North Korean delegation has presented a number of proposals which have been endorsed by the delegations of the People's Republic of China and the Union of Soviet Socialist Republics. Those proposals have not, however, been adequately defined or explained. My delegation is not alone in its suspicion that they include words and phrases designed to camouflage a scheme which would bring to Korea the reverse of freedom and independence.

The first point concerns the method of selection and operation of the proposed all-Korean Commission. The question on this point which I had intended to ask was answered yesterday by the leader of the delegation from North Korea. He said that his proposed all-Korean Commission must be

([4]) "Miscellaneous No. 4 (1950)," Cmd. 8033.

simple in its organisation and function in all matters, procedural and otherwise, by agreement on "both sides." This resolves any ambiguity arising out of the scope of representation of North and South Korea, and over how decisions should be reached. It is now clear that even if North Korea had only ten representatives in a Commission of 100, they would have a veto over the activities and decisions of that Commission which is to be given such far-reaching responsibilities. We know from long and bitter experience what this means. It means that the all-Korean Commission would operate as the Communist members wished, or not at all. This device of "agreement on both sides," irrespective of the number of members or the number of people represented, would make, if nothing else made, the all-Korean Commission completely unworkable, unfair and unacceptable; and that Commission seems to be a central and vital part of the North Korean proposals.

There are one or two other questions about these proposals that occur to one.

What is meant by "the largest democratic social organisations in South and North Korea"? Does the word "democratic" exclude anti-communist or non-communist organisations?

How would the representatives of these "democratic social organisations" be chosen for the all-Korean Commission, and would there be an equal number from North and South Korea?

Does the phrase "terror groups" mean anti-communist political parties?

Furthermore, if no United Nations or other impartial international supervision of Korean elections to ensure that they will be free is permissible, as Mr. Nam Il states, how can this freedom be guaranteed in districts where bitter animosities and fears and local tyrannies would make impartial Korean supervision quite impossible?

If the Government of the Republic of Korea is really guilty, as charged yesterday by the Foreign Minister of the Democratic People's Republic of Korea, of tyrannical and savage repression of freedom in elections, how can he expect us to take seriously his proposal for elections which he says will be free because they will be conducted under arrangements which must be agreed to by the representatives of this Government which he so viciously attacks? Does Mr. Nam Il really wish us to believe that representatives of North Korea feel that they can work amicably and constructively on the all-Korean Commission with the representatives of what he contemptuously calls the " Syngman Rhee clique "?

It is clear, Mr. Chairman, that the most superficial examination of the North Korean proposals, with its veto provisions for the all-Korean Commission, with its rejection of free elections, guaranteed by impartial and effective outside international supervision, with the voters in North Korea, for instance, left to the tender mercies of the communist governmental machinery in expressing their views, it is clear that such an examination of these proposals shows that they provide no hope for bringing about a free, united and democratic Korea.

Such hope lies in the acceptance by this Conference of the principles laid down by United Nations resolutions for the solution of this problem; principles accepted by the vast majority of the nations of the world. These provide for a union of all the Korean people, under a Government chosen by those people.

This united Korea will need some international guarantee against aggression. It will also require, and be entitled to, economic assistance from other countries to repair the cruel devastation and destruction of war.

Along these lines, a solution can be found for the problem with which we are faced.

The other day M. Molotov said, "Here we can listen to different points of view." We must do more than listen to them. We must try to reconcile them, so that the Armistice which now exists in Korea can be converted into an enduring and honourable peace.

My delegation pledges its best endeavours to that high purpose.

Before concluding, Mr. Chairman, I would like to refer briefly to the interesting and significant communication which we have received from the conference of Asian Prime Ministers which has just met in Colombo. This represents an important and constructive effort by a group of free Asian States to assist in, and I hope take some responsibility for, the peaceful settlement of Asian problems in their part of the world.

As the communication deals primarily with the question of Indo-China, I do not wish to make any detailed appraisal of the recommendations it contains. I would, however, like to call attention to the importance attached by these Asian leaders to the rôle of the United Nations in furthering the peaceful purposes of this Conference, particularly in respect of Indo-China.

If these peaceful purposes are not achieved by a just, honourable and negotiated settlement, the consequences will be bad, and probably far-reaching. Failure here may well necessitate further collective consideration—by those who, as a result of such failure, will feel increasingly threatened, —of further ways and means to meet that threat. This, in its turn, may harden and make more dangerous the great and tragic division in the world which now exists.

The reward for success at Geneva will be great in terms of peaceful progress; but the penalty of failure may be even greater in terms of increasing tensions and the risk of a war which would engulf and destroy us all.

EIGHTH PLENARY SESSION ON KOREA

Document No. 10

Speech by Mr. Clifton Webb, Minister for External Affairs of New Zealand, May 7, 1954

The events which have led up to this Conference have already been recounted by a number of speakers and there is no need for me to repeat them here to-day. There is no point in dwelling further on the past: what we need to do is to concentrate our thoughts on the present and the future and hope to bring about an honourable and lasting settlement in this unfortunate country of Korea. Such a settlement is important and urgent, not only for the people of Korea but also for the tranquillity of the whole of East Asia and indeed for the peace of the world. To succeed in this aim we must approach our task in a spirit of conciliation and moderation. If we adopt a rigid uncompromising attitude not prepared to yield an inch for fear of losing face, this Conference is foredoomed to failure and it were better almost that we had not met at all. My delegation trusts that other delegations—like our own—have come here in a spirit of give and take. That does not mean that we should make any sacrifice of principle—but it does mean that we should not maintain a rigid unbending attitude on what might be called the mechanics of any proposal—in other words, the methods by which our aims would be carried into effect. I believe that nothing less than this will fulfil our duty to mankind. Conciliation, however, demands the right mental approach, and from the outset it has been apparent that the attitude of the Chinese and North Korean delegates has been based on a fundamental fallacy.

In particular, there is the constantly repeated accusation that the United States is a militaristic nation bent on territorial aggrandisement. These accusations will not stand a moment's impartial investigation. Indeed, they have already been the subject of impartial investigation and proved to be groundless. The United States is one of the bulwarks of the United Nations, the best instrument man has yet devised for ridding the world of the scourge of war. That it has not fulfilled the highest hopes expected of it cannot be denied, but it has shown that some of its members—and I am proud to think that my country was one of them—were prepared to go to war for the sake of a principle—the principle of collective security. And, as has already been pointed out on more than one occasion, it is the first time that international military action to repel aggression has been taken—the first time we have seen an international police force in action. From this action small nations like our own have derived great comfort.

Let it be clearly understood that nothing will shake our belief—our conviction—that action by the United Nations was necessary because the North Koreans took the law into their own hands and embarked upon a policy of aggression contrary to the principles of the United Nations Charter. Nothing has disturbed us more than the assertion so often repeated that the United Nations is a belligerent in this matter—an aggressor. It will indeed be a serious situation if the Communist countries persist in their assertion that because the United Nations have undertaken collective security action it is no longer neutral, no longer impartial. The grave implications of this assertion must be pondered very seriously. If these attempts to discredit the United Nations and the principle of collective security were successful it would be a sorry day for small and weak States. On this principle we must stand together for it is on our unity and only on our unity that we can rely for our defence.

To blame the United States for the action taken in Korea is to distort the facts of history. So far as the United States is concerned, therefore, the accusation needs no answer. It is an obvious attempt to discredit the nation, which is one of the main pillars of collective security, and thereby to undermine the system of collective security itself.

The United States can afford to ignore such baseless accusations, but what I find disquieting is that the Chinese and North Koreans should profess to believe them. I would ask them seriously to consider whether it is likely that small countries like Colombia, Netherlands, Belgium, Luxembourg, Greece, Turkey, Ethiopia, the Philippines and my own—not to mention the larger ones—would allow themselves to be dragged into a war merely to gratify any territorial ambitions of the United States. This Korean episode has cost my country men, materials and money, all of which we can ill spare. Is it likely, I repeat, that we would incur this cost just to assist a mighty nation bent on conquest? If the Chinese and North Korean delegates really do want this Conference to succeed they must get this false notion out of their heads. We are not likely to grow an olive tree in that climate.

Mr. Chou En-lai has laid claim to a seat in the United Nations. I confess I am unable to understand why he should wish to join an organisation he has so roundly condemned. In my country, and not only in my country, that is called approbating and reprobating and we find, by experience, that it never pays.

We consult the Charter of the United Nations and read that its first purpose is " to maintain international peace and security, and to that end to take effective collective measures for the prevention and removal of threats to the peace, and for the suppression of acts of aggression . . . ." It is more than a little surprising therefore that people who have attacked and sought to undermine the basic principles upon which the United Nations is founded should profess to be offended at being excluded from membership of an international organisation so sinister in their eyes. In view of this attitude, is it any wonder that we should seriously doubt whether the representatives of the People's Republic of China are sincere in the claim they make for admission into membership of the United Nations?

The first qualification for admission to membership of any society is willingness to uphold its principles and abide by its rules. I am bound to say that neither by its words nor its actions has the Government of the People's Republic of China yet given any evidence that it could be relied upon to fulfil this elementary qualification. Moreover, the chilly reception it has accorded those nations which have granted it diplomatic recognition has not been such as to encourage other nations to make the same gesture of trust.

Passing now to the practical side of the business, it is clear that our basic aims are, or at any rate seem to be, the same. We of the United Nations have proclaimed that our objective is a united, free and independent Korea. Mr. Nam II has defined their aim as " the speedy restoration and unification of Korea and the establishment of a democratic independent unified State ". But a profession of common aim is one thing, the real aims and the methods of achieving them are another.

Clearly free elections are a basic necessity for any Korean settlement, and on this key question the North Korean proposal is not at all clear. When it was first put forward by Mr. Nam II I felt that though it bore a striking resemblance to that which was put forward for Germany by the Soviet Union at Berlin recently,([2]) nevertheless, it should not be rejected out of hand. We ought, I felt, to give it serious study. One point on which clarification was obviously needed was the basis of representation of North Korea on the all-Korean Commission proposed by Mr. Nam II. In his second speech he has left no room for doubt on this point. It is clear now that under his proposal North Korea, despite its infinitely smaller population, would have the same number of members on the Commission as South Korea. We are unable to discover the logical basis for equality of representation, but apart from this, what provision is to be made for overcoming a deadlock? Mr. Nam II offers the simple expedient of letting the two sides agree amongst themselves, but the possibility of disagreement cannot be wished away. It is quite unrealistic to act as if mutual suspicion between people who have been locked in bitter war could disappear overnight.

For this reason, the demand by the Government of the People's Republic of China that all foreign troops be withdrawn immediately—presumably this means within six months—is quite unacceptable. Is it intended that United Nations troops are to be withdrawn before proper provision for impartial and effective supervision both of the elections and of Korea's frontiers has been made? And seeing that Mr. Nam II has complained that the last elections in South Korea were improperly conducted by what he was pleased to call the " Syngman Rhee clique," I should have thought that he would welcome any proposals for impartially supervised elections.

Let us be quite clear—we will not agree to rigged elections. If North Korea regards supervision of elections as " interference " then prospects of reaching settlement are, I fear, hopeless. Supervision or observation of elections by an impartial international body—and the United Nations is the clear choice—is so obviously necessary that further argument against this proposition could serve only to raise doubts as to the motives of the North Koreans in rejecting it. I am sure that the nations here represented look forward to the day when their troops will be withdrawn from Korea, but

([2]) "Miscellaneous No. 5 (1954)", Cmd. 9080.

some provision must first be made for effective supervision to ensure that the troops really are withdrawn and will not come back. In view of the impediments which the communists, in violation of the Armistice, have already placed in the way of the functioning of the observer teams in North Korea, all prudent people will insist that any teams, set up to observe the implementation of any settlement that may be reached, must have free access to all parts of Korea. North and South Korea, the United Nations and the Communist aggressors have been locked in bitter war; as I have already said, it would be unrealistic to act as if mutual suspicion had disappeared overnight. Impartial supervision is the answer, and those whose intentions are honest surely have nothing to fear from it.

The speeches so far made at this Conference reveal a wide divergence of method between North and South Koreans but we do not suggest that all the concession should be made by the North Koreans. As I have said earlier, we should be prepared to negotiate in a spirit of conciliation where not all the " give " is on the one side and all the " take " on the other. It seems to me that if our objective of a united, free and independent Korea is to be achieved one truly representative Government for the whole of Korea will be an indispensable condition. One can well understand, however, the reluctance of the people of South Korea to agree that the Government of the Republic of Korea should give way to another government in which they may not feel able to repose confidence. After all, theirs is the government of a sovereign independent state and it is not their fault that the North Koreans are not represented in it. It was created by resolution of the United Nations and its elections were faithfully conducted along lines approved by the United Nations. It is the only recognised legal government in Korea and I think it is fair to say that in the minds of all unbiased people throughout the world the methods by which it was elected entitle it to a greater measure of confidence than do the methods by which the administration of North Korea came into power. Naturally, therefore, the South Koreans, who feel that their lives and existence are at stake are suspicious of any change they are asked to accept. It would be expecting a very great deal of them to agree to merge the identity of their Government in some wide legislative body that might not prove to be a success; nevertheless, I feel sure that some way of overcoming their understandable fears in this regard could be found if other points of difference were satisfactorily resolved.

Finally, let me say that all of us recognise China's need, and the Soviet Union's need, for security. Korea has been an explosive area. Korea's neighbours, like Korea itself, need reassurances and guarantees. We have, I hope, all come here as reasonable people, determined to strive for a settlement that will meet the legitimate requirements of all the countries concerned and particularly all the people of Korea, both North and South.

NINTH PLENARY SESSION ON KOREA

Document No. 11

Extract from Speech by M. Molotov, Minister for Foreign Affairs of the Union of Soviet Socialist Republics, May 11, 1954

The discussion of the Korean problem at this Conference shows that there are considerable differences of opinion in regard to its solution.

Proposals have been put forward here by the Democratic People's Republic of Korea on the question of re-establishing a united Korea as an independent and democratic State. These proposals had the support of the Chinese People's Republic and the Soviet Union. The basis of these proposals is the view that the re-establishment of a united Korea is, above all, a matter for the Koreans themselves, a matter for the Korean people. Accordingly, any attempts to impose upon the Korean people unacceptable decisions relating to the political and social structure of the Korean State are rejected. Whatever may be said in this respect, the Soviet Government is fully justified in stating that the attitude of the Korean Democratic People's Republic is in accordance with the principles of democracy, and, furthermore, with the fundamental interests and national rights of the Korean people.

Another proposal on the Korean question has also been put forward at this Conference. It is nothing more than an attempt to impose on the Korean people an illegal resolution adopted by the United Nations General Assembly on October 7, 1950, when the Korean war was at its height. In that General Assembly resolution, adopted in spite of protests by the Soviet Union and a number of other States, members of the United Nations, an attempt was made to support aggressive plans to place not only South Korea but North Korea also under the factual control of the armed forces of the United States of America. In accordance with that resolution of the General Assembly, a "United Nations Commission for the Unification and Rehabilitation of Korea" was set up. At the same time, steps were to be taken to ensure "conditions of stability" not only in South Korea, but "throughout Korea," or in other words an attempt was made to bring about the military occupation of the whole of Korea and justify the extension of American aggression in the Far East. The Government of the Korean People's Democratic Republic resolutely protested against that illegal resolution which pursued rapacious aims in regard to North Korea. Now, when that policy is advocated here anew, by insisting on the implementation of that illegal resolution, it is merely an attempt to cover with the United Nations flag the rapacious plans of the aggressive Powers in regard to North Korea. By insisting on the implementation of this illegal General Assembly resolution they wish to achieve during the present talks what they did not succeed in doing by force during the three-years' war in Korea.

All this obliges us to dwell on the part played by the United Nations in Korean affairs. And it is all the more necessary to do so in view of the fact that even at this Conference a false light is often being thrown on all known facts relating to events in Korea.

Indeed, the United Nations has, perhaps, never been placed in such a humiliating position as it was during the events in Korea. The facts show that on that occasion the United States of America, in pursuit of its aims in Korea, made use of the United Nations flag for purposes which had nothing to do with the interests, rights and purposes of that international organisation. When considering the Korean question at the Geneva Conference, we must remember how events developed in Korea after the conclusion of the Second World War.

In the summer of 1945, in accordance with an agreement between the Allies in the war against militaristic Japan, Soviet forces entered Korean territory situated North of the 38th parallel, while United States forces entered territory lying South of that parallel. Among the duties entrusted to those forces was that of receiving the capitulation of the Japanese forces, routed earlier on Manchurian territory by the Soviet Army, and thus to help the Korean people to get rid of the Japanese occupation which had lasted for approximately forty years. As a result of this situation, it was natural that the question of the conditions for reuniting North and South Korea in a single democratic State should assume particular importance.

The question of the unification of Korea cropped up already at the Moscow Conference of Foreign Ministers of the United States of America, the United Kingdom and the Soviet Union in December 1945. The plan for Korea then proposed by the Government of the United States of America showed at once that for that Government there was at that time no question of the re-establishment of an independent Korean State. From the American side came a proposal to place Korea for a period of 5–10 years under the trusteeship of four Powers (United States of America, the United Kingdom, China and the Union of Soviet Socialist Republics), which were asked to create a special body of their own for the administration of Korea as a whole. That plan was rejected by the Soviet Union.

On the insistence of the Union of Soviet Socialist Republics at the Moscow Conference of December 27, 1945, the following basic resolution was adopted : —

" With a view to the re-establishment of Korea as an independent State, the creation of conditions for developing the country on democratic principles and the earliest possible liquidation of the disastrous results of the protracted Japanese domination in Korea, there shall be set up a provisional Korean democratic Government which shall take all necessary steps for developing the industry, transport and agriculture of Korea and the national culture of the Korean people."

For the practical implementation of the Moscow Conference resolution, with which the Chinese Government associated itself, a joint Soviet-American Commission was set up, which comprised representatives of the Soviet and American military commands in Korea.

After signing the agreement for the establishment of a provisional Korean democratic Government, the Government of the United States of America, however, did not follow a policy calculated to ensure the implementation of that resolution. During 1946 and 1947 the joint Soviet-American Commission met several times in Seoul to consider that question. No agreement was, however, reached. In fact, the American representatives endeavoured to reduce to nothing the rôle played by the democratic organisations of North and South Korea in their consultations with the Joint Commission. In the territory of South Korea they relied on small reactionary groups remote from the people and concerned to suppress their democratic tendencies. These groups were used to prevent the adoption of any sort of decision relating to the creation of a provisional Korean democratic Government. As a result of the attitude adopted by the American representatives, the joint Soviet-American Commission was unable to take any decision on the question of forming a provisional Korean democratic Government.

From that time the Government of the United States of America began its attempts to use the United Nations flag so as to ensure that the state of affairs in Korea took the direction it desired. At the same time, the United States of America ceased to take into consideration the resolution of the Moscow Conference, although that resolution bore the signature of the United States Foreign Minister. It also ceased to take into consideration the fact that the Korean question, as such, is closely bound up with the after-effects of the war, and that it does not come within the competence of the United Nations, as Article 107 of the United Nations Charter clearly implies.

Throughout the years 1947–1949, the American representatives in the United Nations did all in their power to use that international organisation for their own purposes. In spite of protests by the Soviet Union and a number of other countries, calling attention to the illegality of discussing the Korean problem in the United Nations, they forced the General Assembly to examine that question. Thus began the first stage in the use of the United

Nations flag by the United States of America for the purpose of illegal interference in Korean affairs.

Moreover, the outcome was two sorts of measures, the inadmissibility of which is obvious.

The Commission on Korea set up by the General Assembly resolution was in fact compelled to note that in South Korea there existed the anti-democratic, corrupt, terroristic régime of the Syngman Rhee clique. However, the Commission played the part of protector of that anti-popular régime. Things went so far that the United Nations Commission on Korea even accepted the role of observer at the staging in South Korea of " parliamentary elections " although these elections were purely a police farce at the expense of the Korean people, their rights and elementary standards of democracy. On the other hand, the Commission made attempts to extend its activities even into Northern Korea. Efforts were made to extend the anti-popular Southern Korean régime throughout the whole of Korea. However, all such endeavours met with a definite rebuff from the Northern Korean people and from the Government of the Korean People's Democratic Republic.

Simultaneously with these attempts by the United Nations to intervene in the internal affairs of North Korea, Syngman Rhee began to threaten openly to start a war against North Korea. Thus, in September 1949, he stated in a letter to the American Professor Oliver that " Now is the psychologically most suitable moment for taking aggressive measures and joining up with the part of the Communist army of North Korea which is loyal to us, in order to liquidate the rest of it." On December 30, 1949, Syngman Rhee openly declared that in the new year (i.e., 1950) his aim was to seize North Korea. On that occasion he stated that " In the new year in view of changes in the international situation we must use our forces to unite South and North Korea." In this way, the Syngman Rhee clique prepared war in Korea with the connivance of the United States of America.

The war forced on Korea from outside broke out in June 1950. It turned into a three-year military intervention on the part of the United States of America. At the same time, everything was done to carry on the war under cover of the United Nations flag.

Then began the second stage in the use of the United Nations flag for illegal, nay, openly aggressive interference by the United States in Korean matters, or, to put it more precisely, in the Korean war.

The real state of affairs is shown by the following facts.

On June 27, 1950, President Truman announced that he had ordered the United States armed forces to enter the war against North Korea. Furthermore, the American Fleet in the Far East was ordered to prevent an attack on Formosa (Taiwan), which in reality meant the occupation of the Chinese island of Taiwan. This meant that the United States Government had passed, from a policy of preparing aggression, to direct acts of aggression and had embarked on a course of undisguised interference in the affairs of Korea and China.

It was only after this order of President Truman unleashing American aggression in Korea, that the Security Council met on June 27 and adopted its recommendation on the participation of members of the United Nations in this war, which was represented as furnishing assistance to the South Korean régime. Both the Security Council Resolution of June 27 and its previous resolution of June 25, as well as the resolutions it adopted in July 1950, were gross violations of the United Nations Charter and consequently illegal. They could not have legal force because they had been adopted in the absence of the representatives of two of the permanent members of the Security Council: the Soviet Union and the Chinese People's Republic. According to the United Nations Charter, decisions of the Security Council

41

on matters of war and peace can only have legal force provided the majority of the Security Council's members vote in favour of them and provided this majority includes all the five permanent members. In the case in question, the absence from the Security Council of the representative of China, whose interests are so directly involved in the war in Korea, is particularly important. The participation of the Kuomintang representative in the adoption of those resolutions merely emphasises their illegality.

These Security Council resolutions have been invoked here as justification for a number of States taking part in the Korean war. These illegal Security Council resolutions cannot, however, be regarded as resolutions of the United Nations. Consequently, the participation of a number of States in the Korean war was merely under the cloak of the United Nations flag. This was brought about by the Security Council in violation of the United Nations Charter because aggressive American circles needed such a cloak.

Subsequently many statements were made by official persons in the United States that showed the real reasons for the United States participation in the Korean War. Thus the well-known American General Van Fleet frankly declared in January 1952 that " there had got to be a Korea of some kind either in Korea or in another part of the world." He justified the United States participation in the war by the fact that the war in Korea had created a situation in which " our factories are once more producing armaments in steadily increasing numbers." It is obvious that the war in Korea facilitated the pursuance of an armaments race policy, and that this was just what the aggressive circles in the United States wanted.

From 1950 to 1953, right up to the moment the armistice in Korea was signed, the United Nations adopted a series of resolutions on the Korean question. When the Soviet Union began to attend the meetings of the Security Council again in August 1950, it became impossible to disguise American aggression in Korea under the cloak of the flag of the Security Council. Thenceforward, the cloak was provided by the United Nations General Assembly, whose international authority was thereby greatly undermined.

It also needs to be recalled here that all these Security Council and General Assembly resolutions were adopted regardless of the interests of Korean people and without the representatives of the Korean people taking part in the discussion of such resolutions. Suffice it to say that the representatives of the Democratic People's Republic of Korea were at no time given a hearing in the United Nations during consideration of the Korean problem.

In addition to South Korea, the following sixteen States were participants in the war against North Korea: the United States, Great Britain, France, Belgium, Netherlands, Canada, Australia, New Zealand, the Union of South Africa, Turkey, Colombia, Greece, Luxembourg, Thailand, Finland and Ethiopia. The list shows that most of these are States which have colonies or are interested in maintaining the colonial régime. It is no accident that hardly any Asian countries have taken part in the war. Not one of the Asian States in the British Commonwealth, for example, has desired to take part in it. It is easy to see that such individual Asian countries as did participate in the war are ones that in reality still do not enjoy a minimum of independence and of independent action or are in servile dependence on the big aggressive States.

The facts show that the forces which invaded the territory of North Korea represented the United Nations in name only. In fact at least nine-tenths of the foreign forces which took part in the war against North Korea consisted of United States forces. The remaining fifteen States between them contributed no more than one-tenth of the foreign armed forces which fought in the Korean War. Their participation served only to camouflage the

American aggression in Korea. From that it is also clear who bears the main responsibility for the exceptionally cruel, barbarous and inhuman conduct of the war, concerning which so many facts were reported at the time. That does not, however, lessen the responsibility of the other States which took part in the Korean adventure.

I must also refer to those facts which relate to the period subsequent to the conclusion of an armistice in Korea. As is well known, immediately after the conclusion of an armistice the United States of America and South Korea began negotiating with a view to the conclusion of a military treaty. This treaty was signed on October 1, 1953, and was entitled "Treaty of Mutual Defence between the United States of America and the Republic of Korea." It is plain to everybody, however, that the purpose of this military agreement is not to ensure the "mutual defence" of South Korea and the United States of America, but something quite different. By this agreement aggressive circles in the United States of America are seeking to ensure for themselves another military base for further threatening both North Korea and the People's Republic of China. This treaty is now one of the main obstacles to the unification of South and North Korea.

In concluding the treaty "of mutual defence" with South Korea, the United States of America have not again attempted to shelter behind the flag of the United Nations. On this occasion they have acted in such a way as to have as free a hand as possible in the event of its being considered expedient to start further aggression on the Korean peninsula.

What conclusions may be drawn regarding the United Nations from the facts relating to the war in Korea?

These conclusions are plain.

As the result of a number of illegal steps by the Security Council and the General Assembly, the United Nations has tumbled into the position of one of the belligerents in Korea. In point of fact the United Nations flag was here used only as camouflage for American aggression. In the eyes of the peoples of the whole world the transformation of the United Nations into one of the belligerents has greatly impaired the authority of this international organisation. In the situation which has arisen the United Nations has deprived itself of the possibility of acting as an impartial international organ, and it can no longer play an objective part in the settlement of the Korean question.

Document No. 12

Speech by M. Spaak, Minister for Foreign Affairs of Belgium, May 11, 1954

Like so many of my colleagues I came to Geneva hoping to be able to co-operate in restoring peace in Korea, in the belief that if that great task could be fulfilled, it would not only put an end to a terrible war and the protracted sufferings of a heroic people, but would give the whole world an assurance that an international situation which has for several years caused it such profound anxiety would now begin to improve.

A task of this kind requires that we forgo lengthy discussions on questions of procedure, profitless speeches about the value of our respective ideals, and recapitulations of historical events on which we are in fundamental disagreement. It also requires that we remember that diplomacy is not propaganda and that the only prestige worth while is that acquired by contributing, through understanding and goodwill, to the success of our common enterprise.

Although I was unable to attend all the earlier meetings of this Conference, I have read all the statements made so far and can thus form a fairly clear idea of the stage our work has reached.

The principles I have just mentioned have not all been observed to the same extent. Although we have got very successfully through the first—which are always difficult—stages of the Conference, we have not managed to avoid—or at any rate not all delegates have managed or tried to avoid—carrying our discussions on to ground where unfortunately no kind of agreement is possible.

And yet we have no hope of success unless we confine ourselves strictly to the subject of our agenda. It is not our business to choose between different political, economic and social systems—that in any case has been done long since—or to settle all the problems of the world, or even of Asia. What we have to do is to focus our attention and concentrate our efforts simply on the problems of Korea. Those are quite important and complicated enough.

I nevertheless feel obliged to reply very briefly to certain delegates. They must not misunderstand our fundamental positions. They must realise that certain efforts are absolutely bound to fail and that, consequently, if our work is to be successful, it is better not to repeat them.

They must not try to divide those who, since 1947, have pursued a common policy in Korea, those who since June 25, 1950, have been applying those principles of collective security which they promised to respect and defend when they became members of the United Nations, and which they still believe to-day to be the only ones capable of safeguarding peace.

Nor must they try to isolate the United States of America from this group. The Canadian Minister for External Affairs has already expressed very clearly what we think of the accusation of imperialism which is regularly made in certain quarters against the United States.

For many of us, the United States is first and foremost a great country whose sons twice have sailed across the seas to help us recover our independence and regain our freedom and who, as soon as their job was finished, went back home again without asking or requiring anything of us; a great country which, when peace returned, contributed generously to the reconstruction of Europe; and, perhaps above all, a great country whose power, when South Korea was attacked, enabled the first effective demonstration to be given of the value of collective security.

And that is a sentence which takes on even greater weight and significance when spoken in this city of Geneva and in this Palais des Nations where we now are.

It was here, at the time of a conflict in which the problems of Asia were already involved, that I witnessed the death of collective security. I shall never forget it; the death of collective security was the prelude to the Second World War.

There are certain mistakes that the world has fortunately refused to make twice.

In Korea since 1947 there has been no such thing as American policy, only United Nations policy. I deplore the aggressive and unjust remarks directed against the United Nations. There is undoubtedly something arrogant about a Power, however great, that claims that it alone or almost alone is right, against the vast majority of peoples, and perhaps also something contradictory in such impatience to be admitted to an organisation whose rights it strenuously denies and whose prestige it decries.

I am obliged to dwell on this point at some length because, unless it is properly understood, the ignorance of which it is evidence may compromise the success of our work. It was by 9 votes to none, with 1 abstention, that the Security Council, on June 25, 1950, took note of the act of aggression of which South Korea was the victim, and it was by the same majority that it formally called for assistance from all members of the United Nations in helping South Korea to resist that aggression.

Let us suppose for a moment that this appeal had gone unheeded. A failure such as that would have meant the final bankruptcy of the United Nations, the end of a great experiment, the return of the world to the most odious power politics, with the little states left to the mercy of the ambitions of their powerful neighbours, annexations permitted and encouraged and great wars inevitable.

And let it not be said that this vote was taken under the stress of surprise or emotion. Regularly for several years and by immense majorities, the United Nations Assembly after free debates where every shade of opinion has been expressed and every kind of argument has been put forward, had ratified this decision and renewed this appeal. That is the reason, and the only reason, why countries like mine are present at this Conference to-day.

In a war like that in Korea we have nothing to defend except principles, but they are vital principles on which depend not only our future security but the fate of peace and of the world itself.

We would willingly refrain, in the interests of conciliation, from engaging in further polemics on this subject, but we cannot allow the justifiable intervention of the United Nations in Korea to be depicted as an act of aggression, and the disinterested sacrifice of thousands upon thousands of men for the defence of what is right to be so grossly misrepresented as to be caricatured as a manifestation of imperialism or colonialism.

I am anxious now to leave the subject of the past and to examine our chances of finding a solution for the problems before us.

It is clear from a brief glance at the speeches made so far—and this is, I think, a hopeful sign—that we are unanimous as regards our objective, which is the establishment by peaceful means of a unified, free and democratic Korea. I hope and trust that we are all using the same words to express the same meaning. If that is the case, then it should be possible to reach agreement on the means to be employed.

I note also that we are all agreed that a unified, free and democratic Korea is only possible if elections are held to allow the Korean people to make their own choice between the different parties canvassing their votes.

And I note, finally, that everyone declares that these elections must be free.

Where, then, is the difficulty? It is easily defined.

Some maintain that free elections should be organised by the Koreans themselves, North and South, without any kind of international supervision, and after the withdrawal of all foreign troops. Others insist that, after the disaster which has steeped the country in blood and divided the Koreans into hostile camps, wisdom demands that the reconciliation should be internationally supervised, and that the foreign troops should not be withdrawn until calm has finally been restored, and new institutions are functioning normally.

I am convinced that wisdom lies in the second course alone, indeed that is the only feasible course.

It is amply clear, from the speeches made at this Conference by the representatives of North and South Korea that, if the two sides were suddenly left face to face, filled as they are with passions, anger and fresh memories of the miseries they have suffered, the result would inevitably be chaos, and probably worse.

It is no shame for even the most acutely nationalist people to request the good offices of friendly countries at certain junctures. To ask for arbitration by a trustworthy third party is far from being a sign of weakness; on the contrary, it is evidence of maturity and wisdom.

45

Therefore, before discussing the scope of the elections and the methods of organising them, I think that one absolutely essential question must be settled first: are these elections to be carried out under international supervision, and under the auspices of the United Nations, or are they not? To my mind there is only one possible answer: international supervision is indispensable.

As regards the form to be taken by this international supervision, that can be discussed, once the principle is accepted. The United Nations does not comprise only those nations which fought side by side with the South Koreans. The United Nations is the whole group of all the nations that have joined it. In this connexion, no situation should be regarded as absolutely final and it is obvious that an international organisation for good offices and supervision must inspire equal confidence in all the parties concerned.

It is time we finished with generalities, polemics, and pin-pricking discussions. I must apologise if I myself have not always managed to avoid the pitfalls I warned against. However, I am sure I have spoken with moderation; that I have made no insulting accusations against anyone, and that I have only defended a great friendly country, a great international institution, and the cause of peace with justice.

Let us try to trust each other a little, and try to be practical.

Since our declared aim is the same, it is inconceivable that between us we should not manage to find some way of achieving it.

TENTH PLENARY SESSION ON KOREA

Document No. 13

Speech by Mr. Eden, Secretary of State for Foreign Affairs, May 13, 1954

Our purpose at this Conference is to achieve a peaceful settlement of the Korean problem. The speeches which we have heard show that there is a deep divergence of view between the two sides. This extends to past history and to present facts in Korea.

We shall not achieve our aim by raking over the embers of the past. I have only two comments to make. In our judgment the action of the United Nations in Korea has been no more or less than its duty. If it had failed to take up the challenge of the aggressors its authority would have been destroyed. Secondly, it is true that the United States has borne the major share in the Korean war, both in life and treasure. But the fact that they have done so is a measure not of their imperialism, but of their loyalty to the United Nations. We should all pay tribute to it.

By the same token, I regret that the representative of the Chinese People's Republic found it necessary in his speech of May 3 to revive once again the controversy about prisoners of war. This is a question which Her Majesty's Government regard as settled. The Armistice Agreement(¹) laid down a certain fixed time-table, at the end of which any prisoners who had still not asked to be repatriated were to be released as civilians. The date arrived, and the prisoners were released. This was more than three months ago. The action of the United Nations Command was throughout in accord with the provisions of the Geneva Convention(⁴) and of the Armistice Agreement. It is not true that any of the former prisoners are being retained against their will. I notice that M. Molotov on May 11, in a comprehensive speech, made

(¹) "Korea No. 2, (1953)," Cmd. 8938.
(⁴) "Miscellaneous No. 4, (1953)," Cmd. 8033.

46

no more than a passing allusion to this question. This encourages me to hope that he at least realises that there is no more to be said. We have enough problems to solve here without spending time over those which have long since solved themselves.

I must, however, say a few words about my country's attitude towards Asian problems, since it has been misrepresented in a number of the speeches we have heard. The Soviet and Chinese Foreign Ministers suggest that the countries of the West have no interest in the peoples of Asia except as objects of imperialist or colonial policies. They both set themselves up as the champions of national aspirations in Asia, and claim a monopoly in these sentiments. What are the facts?

In the past few years an immense transformation has taken place in Asia. We have not striven to halt or to impede that change. On the contrary, we have made a contribution to its advance of which we are rightly proud.

Let it not be forgotten that when, in 1947, India, Pakistan and Burma achieved complete independence, the first two of their own free will decided to remain within the Commonwealth. Our relations with Burma, who chose a different path, have continued by the sincere desire of both countries to be especially close and cordial. Ceylon has still more recently become a full member of the Commonwealth and her Prime Minister has in these last weeks presided over a Conference of Asian Prime Ministers, where wide expression was given to independent Asian opinion.

Therefore, Mr. President, I resent and reject the suggestion that we ignore or oppose the tide of national feeling in Asia and I ask, where is there real national freedom to-day—in Colombo or in Ulan Pator, in Delhi or in Pyongyang?

It may well be that representatives of communist states find it difficult to realise that an association of countries like the Commonwealth can come into being on a voluntary basis and flourish upon a footing of equality.

In the Commonwealth there is no one central Power intent upon manipulating the political, economic and military systems of the other countries for its own purposes. The Commonwealth is founded not upon compulsion but upon co-operation. And then we are told that we exploit, indeed " pauperise " was, I think, the word, Asian countries. Have our critics never heard of the Colombo Plan?([6]) That imaginative experiment in co-operation combines the energies of East and West in a humane endeavour to raise the standard of living of the countries of all South and South-East Asia.

It was evolved at a meeting of the Commonwealth Foreign Ministers. It was always the intention that its membership should be open to the other countries of that part of the world. And so it has proved. In addition to Commonwealth countries, Burma, Vietnam, Cambodia, Laos, Indonesia and Nepal have all become full members. This work goes on hand in hand with the Technical Assistance programme of the United Nations and with the Point 4 programme of the United States.

But it is not only a question of technical and material progress. We rejoice that the faith in personal and political freedom thrives in Asian no less than in other soils. We do not see the world in rigid terms of continents, and nations and races. We believe that the principles of freedom are as true for the people of Korea as they are for our own people. That is why we ask that the Koreans should be free to make their own choice of their future. But the choice must be free and the methods employed for ascertaining that choice must be fair and practical.

My criticism of the North Korean delegate's proposals, which he put forward in his speech on April 27, is that they could never, in practice, lead

([6]) Cmd. 8080.

47

to the result which we all desire, namely, the establishment of a single, independent and democratic Government of all Korea. The establishment of such a Government, in his view, would have to await the formation of an all-Korean Commission.

The two parts of Korea are, it seems, to be equally represented on this Commission. This plan ignores the great numerical disparity between the two populations. But more serious still, it overlooks the wide and bitter differences which divide them. Does anyone who has listened to this debate in this room sincerely believe that there is likely to be agreement between the two sides? And if they differ, what happens? There is no provision for outside help of any kind—not even for a neutral chairman or for a tribunal to arbitrate between them and resolve their conflicts. One can foresee only too clearly the complete deadlock which must result. Meanwhile, under this plan, the foreign forces would have been withdrawn, including those of the United Nations, leaving behind them a country still divided, still without a single Government and with no early hope of obtaining one. Where could this lead but to chaos or fresh hostilities?

As the delegate of the United States pointed out on April 28, the proposals of the North Korean representative are in fact a significant echo of those tabled for Germany by the representative of the Soviet Union on February 4 in Berlin.[2] Nor is the similarity only to be found in the wording, though in some places this is identical. There is also a deeper note of resemblance. Each proposal purports to be concerned with free elections. I say " purports " because it is clear that under these proposals the elections either would never happen at all or would not be free. As in the Soviet proposals for Germany, so in the North Korean proposals for Korea, the holding of elections is not the first step, though it is put first on the paper. These proposals impose conditions which would enable the elections to be held only after a long and complicated series of delays. They make no provision for international supervision; they contemplate a packed and nominated commission, not a genuinely elected and representative assembly. In other words, elections come first on paper, but last in practice. They would be free in name but rigged in fact. But the knowledge that the North Korean proposals are not acceptable should not mean that the last word has been said. There are many points on which we are agreed. We have all affirmed that our purpose is to reach a peaceful settlement. We all agree, too, that Korea should be unified. We all desire that, after the independence and unity of Korea has been achieved, the Korean people should be free to carry on their affairs without foreign interference. But at the same time we recognise that their independence will have to be protected by appropriate guarantees from other countries. Finally, we have a common desire to withdraw our forces from Korea as soon as we can do so without again endangering the peace. Where there is so much common ground, we should surely not despair of reaching a settlement. But we should stand a better chance of doing this if we could agree on the basic principles which any solution must contain. I suggest that these should be defined as follows:—

First, elections should be held for the formation of an all-Korean Government. Second, these elections should truly reflect the people's will, that is they should take account of the distribution of the population between North and South. Third, they should be based on universal adult suffrage and the secret ballot. They should be held as soon as possible in conditions of genuine freedom. Fourth, they must be internationally supervised, and in our view this supervision should be conducted under the auspices of the United Nations. The countries selected need not necessarily be those who have taken part in the Korean war: there could be a panel of countries

[2] " Miscellaneous No. 5 (1954)," Cmd. 9080.

acceptable to this Conference. Fifth, any plan for a settlement of the Korean question must provide the conditions in which foreign troops can be withdrawn. The mission of the United Nations forces is to establish peace and security in the area, and as soon as this has been achieved they will be withdrawn. This is clearly stated in the General Assembly's Resolution of October 7, 1950.[7]

If we are agreed about these five principles I have propounded, this Conference can get down to the practical business of working out the terms and stages. This could if necessary be done in restricted session, which would of course report back to the Conference as a whole when it has completed its task. I am convinced that progress by this method is the way, and I believe the only way, to make this Conference a reality. The Korean problem is so hopelessly entangled that it cannot be left to solve itself in a vacuum. After forty years of foreign rule, nine years of division along an arbitrary line and, worst of all, three years of war and devastation, we all have a duty to help the Korean people to attain unity and freedom. The responsibilities which we have assumed towards Korea cannot be simply dropped. We must carry through to its completion the work begun by the United Nations. Shall we not try to do so now?

Document No. 14

Speech by M. Georges Bidault, Minister for Foreign Affairs of France, May 13, 1954

At the first plenary meetings of this Conference, we heard the representatives of several countries recount the principal stages of the political evolution which culminated in the partition of Korea along the 38th Parallel. They mentioned the aggression of which the Republic of Korea was the victim in June 1950, and the conditions in which the Panmunjom Armistice[1] was signed after three years of war. I do not propose to go back over facts which have now passed into history. To deny them serves no purpose; to travesty them, even less.

The impartial and convincing account of the most outstanding events of the last ten years of the tragic history of the Korean nation, given to this Assembly by Mr. Foster Dulles, constitutes for me, as for the great majority of the delegates who have spoken after him, an objective and truthful picture of this period.

The version of these events given by the North Korean delegate, on the other hand, is contrary to the facts.

The attack of June 25, 1950, based on a remarkably thorough and detailed plan, worked out long beforehand yet kept absolutely secret right up to the last moment, came as a complete surprise which in itself is sufficient to prove the Republic of Korea's good faith. But for the immediate intervention of the free world, acting under the auspices of the United Nations, the whole of Korea would have been swallowed up.

That is why France, fully conscious of her obligations as a member of the United Nations, and convinced that any surrender in the face of aggression would have been fatal to peace, took its share in the Korean war.

It has been alleged that peace had its chance, on the eve of the war. In support of this assertion is quoted the offer of peaceful unification broadcast by the Pyongyang authorities over the radio on June 19, 1950. The

[7] " United Nations No. 3 (1951)," Cmd. 8264.
[1] " Korea No. 2 (1953)," Cmd. 8938.

49

very date of this offer, and the fact that one of the conditions was the arrest of the President and the principal members of the Government of the Republic of Korea, show clearly enough that it was merely a device to conceal the aggressive intentions of North Korea just as the final touches were being put to the preparations for attack.

While the proposals contained in General Nam Il's first speech, the one he delivered on April 27, do not, unlike the 1950 offer, call for the arrest of the statesmen who refuse to accept the enslavement of their country, the procedure for unification they propose still falls far short of offering the minimum guarantees without which, in the view of all freedom-loving States, no genuinely free, genuinely democratic Government, can be formed.

I do not intend to embark on a detailed criticism of the proposals put forward by the North Korean representative. I would like, however, to state two principles which, in the view of the French delegation, are fundamental : —

(1) no plan for the reunification of Korea is conceivable which does not include a genuine and effective guarantee that representation of the Korean people in any joint organs which may be set up will be proportional to the number of citizens voting in each of the two parts of the country;

(2) in order for these elections to be regarded as valid, it is absolutely essential that voting should take place in free conditions, checked and vouched for by neutral observers endowed with adequate supervisory powers.

Unfortunately, this is a point on which we seem always to encounter invincible hostility. This idea of international supervision by agents equitably selected in the manner best calculated to ensure that their observations, recommendations and decisions will be objective, impartial and disinterested appears invariably to provoke the other side to suspicion and refusal. We hope and trust that they will reconsider their attitude, and admit that no reasonable and lasting agreement is possible unless we decide together to entrust control of these operations—the holding of elections, concerted movements or withdrawals of troops—to international supervision.

In this connexion it is the opinion of the French delegation that there can be no body better qualified to appoint these observers than the United Nations, in view of its almost universally representative character, and of the weight thereby attaching to its recommendations. I am well aware that the view has been put forward that the United Nations should be regarded as disqualified from taking a hand in the settlement, on the grounds that it has itself been a party to its disputes.

In fact it has even been maintained that the United Nations, by coming to the assistance of the Republic of Korea in June 1950, thereby became an accomplice in aggression, and so was guilty of aggression. Such an assertion is as improbable as it is untenable and cannot be treated as seriously intended.

To accept it would be equivalent to denying the very principles of the international organisation in which we have placed our hopes and at whose service we have put our forces.

Is it not obvious that the aggressor is the side whose armed forces suddenly burst into the territory of its neighbour, without previous recourse to any conciliation or arbitral procedure and without warning, brushing aside any hasty attempt at resistance, as did the North Korean divisions in the territory of the Republic of Korea. Is it admissible that the United Nations, by springing to the rescue and saving this country from total invasion and final subjection, should have forfeited a right whose exercise is the main

50

justification for its existence and its essential attribute, the right to play the part assigned to it by the Charter for the restoration of peace.

The supporters of the opposite view would have it that North American imperialism was the mainspring of this coalition of sixteen nations, united, they contend, in a campaign of conquest and domination, with the steady backing of the majority of the other members of the United Nations.

A very peculiar kind of imperialism it would be that waited until the country it wished to conquer had been almost completely overrun by the enemy before taking action; that right from the very first day proposed to the invader—alas, in vain—a withdrawal to baselines so that peace might be restored; and that, to bring hostilities to an end, made one concession after another, of so sweeping a character as to endanger the forces for which it was responsible. The history of the great conquerors, of the imperialisms of our times shows us a very different picture. It shows that they never withdraw, but always press forward, stifling all opposition and stamping out freedom. Is there any need to carry this argument further?

I cannot but be struck by the attempt that is being made by certain of the delegations here to represent the United Nations as a North American satellite—with the result that this Geneva Conference, which ought to be—and we devoutly hope will really become—a peace conference, seems at times, when the Korean problem is being discussed, to be turning into an arena with the communist world lined up on one side, and on the other the United States surrounded by sixteen states, members of a vassal organisation, known as the United Nations.

The delegate of the Soviet Union considers—I quote his own words—that " . . . . the United Nations has, perhaps, never been placed in such a humiliating position as it was during the events in Korea." According to him, " the facts show that on that occasion the United States of America, in pursuit of her aims in Korea, made use of the United Nations flag for purposes which had nothing to do with the interests, rights and purposes of that international organisation."

Such an interpretation of the situation seems to us highly insulting to the United States, to every Member State of the United Nations and to the United Nations itself. Moreover, it is an interpretation which, by constant repetition, might in the long run endanger the institution's authority and stability, and the very principle of collective security.

France, for its part, will uphold the right of the United Nations, standing above the conflict, to be recognised as the permanent guardian of the concepts of right and freedom by which the world should be guided.

A positive attitude on the part of the North Korean Delegation to the points I have mentioned would be proof that it has come to Geneva with a sincere desire to create a united, democratic and independent Korea, which is one of the essential aims of this Conference.

Contrary to what was asserted here in this building a few days ago, we do not consider that defence of Asian peoples' independence against the new communist imperialism is an obsolete conception. And while we join the Soviet Union representative in his " warm sympathy with the movements of the peoples of Asia for national liberation " we must make it clear that our conception of that liberation is not the same as his.

We are none the less resolved to spare no pains to try to put an end to the unhappy plight of the Korean nation. If we were not inspired with a firm desire to disperse the uncertainty that clouds its future, we would be false to the very purpose of the task we have undertaken; we would be betraying those who, on the field of battle, have made the supreme sacrifice.

It is already a considerable achievement that an armistice has been signed and we who want to see peace spreading like a rash over the whole of Asia,

51

are the first to admit it. But that is only the beginning of our task. We should be failing in our duty if we did not place all our conciliatory power and all our constructive imagination at the service of the Korean nation, which by the trials and tribulations it has endured amply deserves at last to recover its unity in justice and freedom.

ELEVENTH PLENARY SESSION ON KOREA

Document No. 15

Extract from Speech by Mr. Nam Il, Minister for Foreign Affairs of the Democratic People's Republic of Korea, May 22, 1954

During the discussion on the Korean problem nearly all the participants in this Conference have made statements and expressed their points of view regarding a peaceful settlement in Korea. It cannot escape notice that the representatives of the United States of America and of some other states that follow in its wake have been doing their utmost to justify the United States' armed intervention against the Korean people and to impose on North Korea the anti-popular South Korean régime, although it should be obvious to them that such attempts are doomed to failure.

Many of these representatives, while objecting to the proposals of the Democratic People's Republic of Korea, are anxious to get us to recognise the United Nations resolutions on the Korean question. It is, however, common knowledge that these resolutions and actions of the United Nations with regard to Korea were taken under United States pressure in violation of the Charter and principles of that international organisation and in the absence of the representatives of the Democratic People's Republic of Korea.

We fail to understand the statements of some delegates who have called upon the Korean people to respect the United Nations' actions and resolutions on the Korean question. How can the Korean people respect such actions by the United Nations as the placing of its flag at the disposal of the American interventionists who for three years have ravaged our country and caused our people tremendous sufferings and hardships? The Korean people have never recognised and do not recognise the legality of these unjust United Nations resolutions which disregard their national interests and are designed to establish the domination of the Syngman Rhee clique in our country, and with it that of the United States.

By adopting a one-sided attitude from the very outset, under pressure from the United States, the United Nations proved itself completely incapable of settling the Korean question. Moreover, mere words cannot disguise the fact that the United Nations is a belligerent party in the Korean war. It spoke as a belligerent party at the Armistice negotiations in Korea and signed the Armistice Agreement([1]) as one of the belligerents. On the Korean question the United Nations cannot, therefore, occupy an impartial position and claim our recognition of the legality of its resolutions in this regard.

It is quite obvious that in order to settle the Korean question, other ways and means must be sought, which will take into account first and foremost the national interests of the Korean people and the situation actually existing at the present time both in North and South Korea.

As M. Molotov, the Soviet Union Minister for Foreign Affairs rightly emphasised in his statement of May 11, the national unification of Korea can only be achieved on a democratic basis by working out at this Conference

([1]) "Korea No. 2 (1953)," Cmd. 8938.

terms of agreement which will make it possible to preserve the democratic achievements of the Democratic People's Republic of Korea, and will at the same time take into account the peculiarities of the situation that has arisen in South Korea.

In the proposals it submitted on April 27, the delegation of the Democratic People's Republic of Korea indicated the way to re-establish Korea as a single, independent, democratic state and to bring about the peaceful settlement of the Korean question as a whole. Our delegation's proposals received the unanimous support of the Korean people, which found expression in the statement of the Central Committee of the United Democratic Patriotic Front of Korea of May 4.

Document No. 16

Proposal by Mr. Pyun, Foreign Minister of the Republic of Korea, on May 22, 1954

1. With a view to establishing a united, independent and democratic Korea, free elections shall be held under United Nations supervision in accordance with the previous United Nations resolutions relating thereto.

2. The free elections shall be held in North Korea, where such elections have not hitherto been possible, and in South Korea in accordance with the constitutional processes of the Republic of Korea.

3. The elections shall be held within six months from the adoption of this proposal.

4. Before, during and after the elections, the United Nations personnel connected with the supervision of the elections shall enjoy full freedom of movement, speech, &c., to observe conditions and help to create a free atmosphere throughout the entire election area. Local administrative authorities shall give them all possible facilities.

5. Before, during and after the elections, candidates, their campaign helpers and their families shall enjoy full freedom of movement, speech, &c., and other human rights which are recognised and protected in democratic countries.

6. The elections shall be conducted on the basis of the secret ballot and universal adult suffrage.

7. Representation in the all-Korea legislature shall be proportionate to the population of the whole of Korea.

8. With a view to apportioning the numbers of representatives in exact proportion to population in the election areas, a census shall be taken under United Nations supervision.

9. The all-Korea legislature shall be convened in Seoul immediately after the elections.

10. The following questions, particularly, shall be left to the all-Korea legislature: —

   (a) Whether the President of unified Korea should be newly elected or not.
   (b) Amendment of the existing constitution of the Republic of Korea.
   (c) Disbandment of military units.

11. The existing constitution of the Republic of Korea shall remain in force except in so far as it may be amended by the all-Korea legislature.

12. The Chinese Communist troops shall complete their withdrawal one month in advance of the election date.

13. Withdrawal of the United Nations forces from Korea may start before the elections, but must not be completed until complete control over the whole of Korea has been achieved by the unified Government of Korea and certified by the United Nations.

14. The territorial integrity and independence of the unified, independent and democratic Korea shall be guaranteed by the United Nations.

Document No. 17

Speech by Mr. Chou En-lai, Foreign Minister of the People's Republic of China, May 22, 1954

Mr. Chairman and Fellow Delegates,

The Geneva Conference has already held ten meetings to discuss the Korean question. The delegates of many countries have stated their views, touching more or less upon problems involving the whole of Asia. The delegates of the People's Republic of China, the Union of Soviet Socialist Republics and the Democratic People's Republic of Korea have repeatedly pointed out that the root cause of the Asian problems lies in the colonialist aggression in Asia of the imperialist countries and the resistance of the Asian peoples to that aggression. It is only natural that the Chinese people, who have defeated colonialist aggression, should have expressed profound sympathy with the movements of the Asian peoples for national independence. It has been said that we claim a monopoly in the sentiments as champions of the national aspirations in Asia. No, gentlemen, we do not claim any monopoly. What we are voicing is nothing but the aspirations of the Asian peoples for peace, independence, democracy and freedom. However, as one of the major powers in Asia we naturally hold that these aspirations of the Asian peoples are absolutely not to be ignored when pressing problems facing Asia are being discussed and solved.

We have heard at this Conference no small amount of defence and praise of the United States policy of colonialist aggression in Asia. It is easily understandable that the delegates of some Western countries should have defended the United States. The delegates of some Asian States also sang the praise of United States aggression. That is not surprising, either. The reason is that in Asia there really does exist a handful of such people who support foreign domination and favour American aggression. In this connexion suffice it to mention the reactionary clique of Chiang Kai-shek who has already been driven out of the mainland by the Chinese people, and the Syngman Rhee clique which relies on foreign force to maintain its domination. Such persons constitute but a tiny fraction of the minority among the Asian peoples. They have no support from the people and precisely because of this they cannot survive a single day without United States aid and protection. Is it any wonder that this handful of Asians should have considered the United States not to be an aggressor, should have considered that the United States had ended colonialism in Asia, or should have gone so far as to complain about not enough American interference in their country? It is they who serve the American aggressors regardless of the fact that their action conflicts with the national interests of their own countries. Such persons absolutely cannot represent the Asian peoples.

As for the overwhelming majority of the Asians, they are consistently opposed to colonialist foreign rule. They have waged or are waging a determined struggle for their own national independence and liberty. They have never agreed, and they will certainly not agree now, to the colonialist policy which the United States aggressors are carrying out in Asia. Still less will they agree to the war policy of forming opposing military *blocs* and provoking Asians to fight Asians—a policy which the American aggressors are now actively pursuing in Asia.

Mr. Chairman, in order to achieve the unification of Korea on the basis of independence, peace and democracy, Foreign Minister Nam Il of the Korean Democratic People's Republic on April 27 proposed the holding of all-Korean free elections, the withdrawal of all foreign armed forces from Korea within a specified period of time before the holding of the all-Korean elections, and the guaranteeing of Korea's peaceful development by those states that are most interested in peace in the Far East. That these proposals are reasonable is beyond dispute. In the course of discussion, no one has yet been able to advance any valid argument against these proposals. It is quite clear that these proposals, which have obtained the support of the delegations of the People's Republic of China and of the Soviet Union, should serve as the basis for reaching agreement at this Conference. However, the delegates of some countries still persist in their attempt to impose upon this Conference the illegal resolution of the United Nations of October 7, 1950, advocating as they do that the United Nations' forces, which are mainly United States troops, should continue to remain in Korea and that the United Nations should supervise the all-Korean elections, thus obstructing a solution for the Korean problem by this Conference.

We have already pointed out that owing to United States manipulation, the United Nations has been placed in the position of a belligerent in the Korean war and has lost its competence and moral authority to deal impartially with the Korean question. In his statement of May 11, Foreign Minister Molotov of the Soviet Union proved with indisputable facts that the United Nations had never been placed in such a humiliating position as at the time of the events in Korea. The illegal resolutions of the United Nations on the Korean question are fundamentally contrary to the purposes and principles of the Charter of the United Nations. The Charter of the United Nations has for its purpose the maintenance of international peace and security. However, the United Nations gave its approval to United States aggression in Korea, ignored the United States invasion and its occupation of China's Taiwan and then shamefully slandered China as an aggressor, and gave encouragement to the action of the United States in extending the Korean war, thus directly threatening the security of China and of Asia. The principles of the Charter of the United Nations specifically preclude interference in the domestic affairs of any country. But the illegal resolutions of the United Nations were aimed at interfering in Korea's domestic affairs and preventing the Korean people from solving their own problems themselves. Those illegal resolutions were passed in the circumstances that the People's Republic of China was deprived of its right to join the United Nations and that the Korean Democratic People's Republic was unable to be present. These illegal resolutions were, moreover, adopted in the face of determined opposition from the Soviet Union and other countries and in spite of disagreement by many Asian countries. These unilateral, illegal resolutions have long proved to be incapable of leading to a peaceful settlement of the Korean question. It is quite obvious that continued insistence at this Conference on these illegal resolutions of the United Nations will not help to settle anything.

It has been asked: Is it not self-contradictory for the People's Republic of China on the one hand to denounce as illegal the United Nations resolutions on the Korean question and, on the other, to ask to join the United Nations? We must point out that it is not a question of the People's Republic of China asking to join the United Nations, but that the People's Republic of China has been deprived of the right of participation in the United Nations and because of this the lawful place of the People's Republic of China in the United Nations should be restored to it.

China is one of the founders of the United Nations. The Chinese people have consistently supported the purposes and principles of the Charter of the United Nations and have striven incessantly for their realisation. Under the United Nations Charter, the Soviet Union, the United States of America, the United Kingdom, the Republic of France and China assume special responsibility for the maintenance of international peace and security. The fact that the majority of United Nations members have followed the United States in depriving the People's Republic of China of its rightful place and legitimate rights in the United Nations has fundamentally violated the United Nations Charter and seriously damaged the prestige of the United Nations. This act of the United Nations has met with continuous opposition from the Soviet Union and some other countries, especially Asian countries. The Conference of Prime Ministers of five nations, India, Indonesia, Pakistan, Burma and Ceylon, recently held at Colombo also expressed the hope that a change would be made in this state of affairs which constitutes a breach of the United Nations Charter. In fact, the illegal resolutions of the United Nations on the Korean question and the inability of the United Nations to deal with the Korean question impartially are inseparable from the fact that the People's Republic of China has been deprived of its right to join the United Nations. The delegates of several countries have stated at this Conference that the noble purposes and principles of the United Nations Charter should be upheld. Facts have demonstrated that it is we who have consistently upheld the purposes and principles of the United Nations Charter.

It is very clear that the illegal resolutions of the United Nations cannot serve as the basis for a peaceful settlement of the Korean question. The illegal resolutions of the United Nations have long been utilised to obstruct a peaceful settlement of the Korean question. Our Conference has been convened for the purpose of finding other ways to achieve a reasonable solution of the Korean problem. We should not let the Conference remain deadlocked as it is for any length of time. As some delegates have already pointed out, it is not impossible to find common ground for a peaceful settlement of the Korean question. So far, we have not yet heard anybody openly expressing himself at this Conference against the principle that the question of the unification of Korea should be settled by the Koreans themselves. It is therefore apparent that nobody can deny the correctness of this principle.

Since the unification of Korea is a question for the Korean people themselves to settle, it should be our aim at this Conference to create conditions to enable the Korean people to achieve the unification of their own country on the basis of independence, peace and democracy.

In conformity with the above-mentioned principle, we hold that, in order to enable the Korean people to unify their country through nation-wide elections without interference by any foreign State, all foreign armed forces must withdraw from Korea before the holding of such elections.

The all-Korean elections are Korea's domestic affair. The continued presence of American troops in Korea not only threatens peace in Korea and the security of China, but will inevitably create interference in Korean domestic affairs, and make it impossible for the Korean people freely to express their will in the nation-wide elections. The withdrawal of all foreign armed forces from Korea is the prerequisite for the Korean people freely to express their will in the all-Korean elections. With respect to the time-limit for the withdrawal of foreign forces, Foreign Minister Nam Il of the Korean Democratic People's Republic has already pointed out that this question is open to discussion. It is our view that this Conference should reach an appropriate agreement on the question of the withdrawal within a specified period of time of all foreign armed forces from Korea.

The peaceful unification of Korea can only be achieved on the basis of mutual agreement between the Korean Democratic People's Republic and the Republic of Korea. Consequently, Foreign Minister Nam Il very properly proposed that the all-Korean Commission, which will prepare and hold free elections throughout Korea and attend to other matters pertaining to the unification of Korea, should carry on its work on a basis of mutual agreement. If it is considered that there is no need for the Korean Democratic People's Republic and the Republic of Korea to reach mutual agreement on the methods and steps to be adopted in achieving the unification of Korea, how, I ask, will it be possible to bring about peacefully Korea's unification? But some delegates, under the pretext that there is a difference in population between North and South Korea, have utilised the principle of proportional representation to oppose the principle of mutual agreement between the two sides. They overlook the fact that opposition to the principle of mutual agreement between the two sides is nothing but an attempt to impose forcibly the will of one side on the other—an attempt which has long since been proved abortive even when supported by foreign armed forces. Premier Jawaharlal Nehru of India also stated on May 18 in the Council of States that Korea must be united in order to avoid a renewal of the conflict, but unity, he added, could not be forcibly imposed by one side on the other.

As regards proportional representation, it is a problem for the all-Korean electoral law. Since the all-Korean Commission, according to the proposal of Foreign Minister Nam Il, will be an organ through which the Korean Democratic People's Republic and the Republic of Korea jointly prepare and hold the all-Korean elections, its composition fundamentally does not give rise to the question of proportional representation.

In order to enable the all-Korean elections to be held on a genuinely democratic basis, Foreign Minister Nam Il has proposed that the all-Korean Commission should prepare a draft of an all-Korean electoral law to ensure the democratic nature of the all-Korean elections and to provide the necessary measures for guaranteeing the democratic liberties of the Korean people, including the right to nominate candidates in the elections. This proposal is undoubtedly reasonable. It has been said that, as North and South Korea are now in a state of opposition, any Korean organ would encounter many difficulties in examining and verifying the freedom of the all-Korean elections. Of course, we cannot but take into consideration the actual situation arising out of the fact that Korea has remained divided for many years and the strained relations between North and South Korea due to the war. All this has left deep scars upon the relations between North and South Korea and makes it difficult for them to approach each other. Consequently, it is necessary that a neutral organ should be established to assist the Korean organ which is to be entrusted with the holding of the all-Korean elections. Some delegates have suggested that an organ of the United Nations should supervise the all-Korean elections. To that we cannot agree, because the United Nations, as I pointed out earlier, is a belligerent in the Korean war and has long since lost its competence to deal with the Korean question impartially. The delegation of the People's Republic of China is of the opinion that this neutral organ should be composed of representatives of neutral nations, to be agreed upon by this Conference, that did not participate in the Korean war. The task of this organ of neutral nations would be to assist the all-Korean Commission in holding all-Korean elections in accordance with the all-Korean electoral law under conditions which preclude foreign intervention and pressure on the electors by the local administrative authorities or terrorist groups. For this purpose, the delegation of the People's Republic of China proposes that the following addition be made to Article 1 of the proposals of Foreign Minister Nam Il on April 27: —

"In order to assist the all-Korean Commission to hold the all-Korean elections in accordance with the all-Korean electoral law and under free conditions precluding foreign intervention, a neutral nations supervisory commission should be established to supervise the all-Korean elections."

As to the question of war prisoners, it cannot, of course, be considered closed. I have already pointed out in my statement of May 3 that the Commander-in-Chief of the United Nations Command had promised to continue his efforts to recover those Korean and Chinese war prisoners who were forcibly retained in June, 1953. As regards those Korean and Chinese war prisoners who were forcibly retained in January, 1954, the Neutral Nations' Repatriation Commission also has repeatedly pointed out that they should not be the subject of unilateral disposal. We consider that the concrete proposals put forward by the delegation of the People's Republic of China, in agreement with the delegation of the Korean Democratic People's Republic, concerning the disposal of the question of war prisoners should receive serious consideration by this Conference.

Document No. 18

Speech by Mr. Bedell Smith, Head of the Delegation of the United States of America, May 28, 1954

During all these sessions on Korea the United States Delegation has listened, at times with sincere admiration and at other times with profound misgivings, while on the one hand representatives of the free nations of Asia, Africa, Europe and America have called for a constructive effort to unite this unhappy country, and on the other hand our Communist colleagues have denounced and distorted every ideal to which we subscribe and every democratic principle which we cherish.

The date of May 11, 1954, may stand out in the history of our times as an occasion of grave revelation. On that day, in this room, the Soviet Union through its delegate denounced the United Nations and characterised it as a belligerent institution, unworthy of confidence. That the representatives of the Chinese and North Korean Communist régimes reiterated this denunciation is regrettable but is not surprising. Both have been declared aggressors by the United Nations.

Many words, good and bad, have been spoken here since this Conference met, but none have been clearer in intent or more serious in implication than the words of the delegate of the Soviet Union on the eleventh of this month at the ninth plenary session on Korea. All of us who heard them remember, but I repeat them so we may focus on their meaning. He spoke as follows: —

"What conclusions can be drawn with regard to the United Nations Organisation from the facts pertaining to the war in Korea? The conclusions are clear. As a result of a number of illegitimate actions on the part of the Security Council and the General Assembly, the United Nations Organisation became a belligerent in Korea. In fact, the United Nations flag was used there only to cover up American aggression.

In the eyes of the peoples of the whole world, this turning of the United Nations Organisation into a belligerent greatly diminished the prestige of this international organisation. Under the circumstances, the United Nations Organisation has deprived itself of the capacity to act as an impartial international body and can no longer carry out objective functions in the settlement of the Korean problem."

Thus spoke the Soviet delegate.

By the word " American " the Soviet delegate intended to designate the United States. It gives me great satisfaction that there are two other nations from the Americas represented here—Canada and Colombia. They also sent their sons to Korea to defend the ideal that the United Nations flag is not a scrap of cloth. What the sixteen nations here represented did in Korea, acting together under that flag, in accordance with resolutions of the United Nations, was done because of their common belief in deep-rooted moral principles for which men are willing to die. The United States is proud of its role in Korea and of its associates there. It believes that all people who long for a free and peaceful world take pride in the rôle of the United Nations in Korea. The blood of the young men of sixteen nations was shed in Korea for the most noble of causes—to protect the weak from the strong and the predatory. Only if free men continue to be willing to band together for this high purpose can the peace of the free world be assured.

What the Soviet Union, through its delegate, is telling the world from Geneva is that it rejects the principle of collective security, that it intends to do as it pleases without regard to truth or justice or peace—even without regard to the fundamental rights of humanity. It is as simple as that, and it should cause the majority of us to think and to draw closer together.

It is a strange phenomenon that we, who came here to unite a divided and war-torn nation, find ourselves defending the international system of security to which every one of the Governments of the world, if it were truly representative of the wishes of its people, would be eager to contribute all possible moral and material support.

This system was established in 1945 at San Francisco. It is embodied in the United Nations Charter, to which the representative of the Soviet Union at this Conference affixed his own signature. That Charter was, and still is, regarded by the vast majority of us as the world's best hope for peace.

One of the basic pledges in the United Nations Charter is the pledge to resist aggression. A specific case arose in June 1950, when armies from North Korea invaded the territory of the Republic of Korea, which had been formally recognised by the United Nations as the only legal Government in Korea. The Security Council of the United Nations was promptly called into session. It called upon its members to act at once to repel this aggression.

The representative of the Soviet Union in the Security Council absented himself on the occasions of these historic decisions. The Soviet delegate has sought here, and not for the first time, to establish the theory that one absent member is more potent under law than ten who are present and who vote to take a united action.

If one absent member, through the mere circumstance of his absence, can render the operation of the principle of collective security null and void, or " illegal and shameful," to use the words of our communist colleagues, the aggressor in Korea would have swept the entire country unimpeded—and all because the representative of the Soviet Union in the Security Council of the United Nations had gone for a walk. I am not attempting to be sarcastic. I am simply stating a fact.

We are presented here with the paradox that the Soviet Union, while denouncing the acts of the United Nations, insists, nevertheless, on exercising all the rights and privileges of a member and, indeed, goes further by continuously using its veto to keep sovereign and independent and law-abiding nations from being admitted to membership in the United Nations. More than that, the Soviet Union has been insisting that the Government in Peking, so far lawless, shall be seated in the United Nations.

This brings to mind the circumstances that surround the presence here of the Chinese Communist representative. We cannot forget that in the autumn of 1950 when the armed forces of the United Nations had successfully repelled the aggressor armies of the North Korean faction, there came another aggression. At first it was insisted at Peking that the well-organised and well-equipped armies from the mainland of China were merely " Chinese volunteers," and had no connexion with the Peking Government.

Then the world was told after a few months that the Government at Peking acknowledged responsibility for the orders to the armies of Chinese soldiers in Korea. To-day at this Conference in Geneva that same Government, through its representative here, tells us that the United Nations has no right to see to it that the Chinese armies now occupying North Korea will not break the peace again. We are told also by the Soviet Government that the United Nations must not be permitted to supervise the elections proposed for all Korea. Why does the Soviet Government object so vigorously to the conduct of free elections under United Nations observation, and why did it object in May 1948 to the supervision by a United Nations commission of the elections in North Korea? Is the Soviet Government afraid of the votes of the people of Korea in a free, uncoerced election?

Let us now look at the record of the members of the United Nations, who, faithful to the Charter, sent their armed forces to Korea to repel aggression. They sent their troops thousands of miles away from home and they made sacrifices of almost two hundred thousand killed and wounded in order to support the principle of collective security as against aggression—the great objective of the United Nations Charter. They did this only in the interest of achieving peace against aggression. No more dramatic demonstration has ever been given to the world of the collective action of sovereign States in repelling aggression.

Yet after all this, we have been exposed to an effort to distort the facts, a devious, if all too obvious, attempt to pervert an inspiring moral principle. I will not dwell further on this point. The United States did not come to Geneva to lend itself to the destruction of the United Nations.

Here at Geneva we have been confronted by a new challenge to our wisdom, our vision, and our generosity. We have the opportunity to put aside suspicions and antagonisms in a united effort to allow the Korean people at long last to work out their national destiny. We have the opportunity to inspire the whole world with a new respect for the opinions of mankind and a renewed confidence in our only existing institution of international order and justice—the United Nations.

The majority of us came here in the hope that the question of Korean independence and unification would receive the careful sympathetic attention at Geneva that it deserves. Sixteen of our delegations believe sincerely that if the people of Korea, from the Yalu to the Southern shores, are entitled to our most earnest efforts to give them their independence and unity, they must have them. They deserve better than to be made the subject of a propaganda campaign. Yet I grieve to say that this is what we have been witnessing.

If we did not understand the insidious strategy of communism, we would be surprised to find three peoples with such long and infinitely varied histories and cultures as North Korea, Russia and Communist China suddenly appearing so identical on one side of this Conference. Their words and their actions are interchangeable.

And what have they put forward on Korea? After months of delay, this is what they tell us:—

They deny that the United Nations has any authority or moral force to deal with the problem of unification of Korea. They repudiate as "shameful and illegal" the United Nations resolutions on Korea. They reject any United Nations supervision in Korea. They reject overwhelming world opinion which looks to the United Nations as the one fundamental institution for maintaining peace and security.

And thus they erect another iron curtain at Geneva designed to shut out any constructive effort by this Conference toward the attainment of its goals.

Then our communist colleagues ask us to accept proposals for Korea's unification which would provide for elections "first on paper, last in practice, free in name but rigged in facts," as Mr. Eden put it so well. More than this, they have concocted an elaborate device which, when analysed, is nothing more than the Soviet veto system, the paralytic effect of which the world has witnessed on so many previous occasions.

This formula would permit the imposed dictatorship of a minority of the Korean people still living in North Korea to obstruct forever the freely-elected representatives of the great majority of the people in Korea. By this formula a régime which is shrouded in darkness could shackle a Government whose legitimacy and representative character have been repeatedly recognised by the United Nations: and it would not even give the captive minority of Koreans a chance to speak for themselves in genuinely free elections open to the world to see.

As if that were not sufficient, the Communists would have us agree in advance to tie our hands and close our eyes while a divided Korea, quarantined from the rest of the world and isolated from the United Nations, is absorbed into the communist orbit. A few days ago Secretary Dulles made this statement to the people of the United States—"More than 140,000 Americans were killed and wounded under the United Nations command to keep Korea from being over-run by armed invasion. I promise you that we will not surrender at Geneva the principle for which so many fought and died."

I must repeat, as the Netherlands Foreign Minister already has so convincingly pointed out, that ten members of the Security Council, in November 1950, affirmed the policy of the United Nations to hold the Chinese frontier with Korea inviolate, and fully to protect the legitimate Chinese and Korean interests in the frontier zone. This would have produced a genuinely peaceful and united Korea if the Soviet Union had not vetoed the joint resolution, and if shortly thereafter the Chinese Communists had not invaded Korea in force across that frontier.

Despite all this, there remains a basis on which we can still build a new life for all the people of Korea. It is not too late to fulfill our objectives of establishing, by peaceful means, a united and independent Korea. All we need is the courage and the will to accept with honesty the reality of the principles that have been repeatedly expressed and affirmed in our meetings.

There must be a sincere effort toward moderation and a search for an accord, as so many representatives have urged.

There must be clearly reaffirmed our respect for the authority and the moral force of the United Nations. The United States associates itself unreservedly with the support which the large majority of my colleagues here have expressed for the United Nations. It is the only instrument left to us for

61

ridding the world of the scourge of war. It is a moral force for peace. It is the one remaining instrumentality for maintaining collective security. It will be a tragic day for all the people of the world if, as has been threatened here, the United Nations is discredited and condemned, if its resolutions are spurned as scraps of paper, and if the people of the world are cast adrift without this anchor in which they have placed their trust.

There must be recognition of the need to rely on the co-operation of the United Nations in helping the Korean people themselves to bridge the wide gulf which years of separation and war have created. This co-operation will not impair in any way the inherent right of the Korean people to make the decisions that affect their own destiny.

No lasting peace or security can come to the people of Korea unless their right to unity and independence is exercised in an atmosphere of genuine freedom. They must not be coerced as they move through the processes of establishing a united and independent nation.

In the light of these sincere beliefs, Mr. Chairman, the United States delegation has studied the proposals which the delegate of the Republic of Korea presented to us last Saturday. We find them clear, moderate and reasonable. They are within the framework of the basic principles which the vast majority of us here have publicly and repeatedly endorsed. It seems to the United States delegation that these proposals represent on the part of the Korean people an important and significant act of faith in the United Nations and in genuinely free elections. These are the proposals of a nation which conducts its elections under the observation of a United Nations commission, a nation which has fought with enormous sacrifice and great bravery against aggression, and which has demonstrated its dedication to the principles of liberty and freedom.

The United States delegation supports the proposals of the Republic of Korea and recommends their acceptance.

Document No. 19

Speech by Mr. Alan Watt, Head of the Australian Delegation, May 28, 1954

The Australian Delegation has listened carefully to the course of the debate on the subject of Korea and, more particularly, to the speeches which were delivered at our previous meeting here last Saturday. On that latter occasion, there were two important developments. Firstly, the representative of the People's Republic of China proposed a neutral nations supervisory commission to assist the all-Korea Commission to hold all-Korean elections and to supervise the elections when they are held. Secondly, the representative of the Republic of Korea, Dr. Pyun, put forward a proposal of fourteen points for the unification of Korea.

Both these proposals involve some modification of the positions previously taken by the delegations concerned. Naturally, the Australian Delegation welcomes any developments which may bring the opposing views closer together.

Let me first comment briefly on the proposal of the representative of the People's Republic of China. A number of delegations, including our own, have felt the need for international supervision of elections in the turbulent and emotional conditions of Korea to-day. We believe that, in the context of the recent war and of the bitter enmities in Korea, it would be unwise, if not dangerous, to accept, as we have been invited to do, the view that the

Korean people can and will find a peaceful solution if they are left to themselves. Superficially, therefore, the agreement to accept a neutral supervisory commission might appear as a significant concession, although it would certainly need clarification in the light of the North Korean reservations that it must not interfere with the principle of no foreign interference in the internal affairs of Korea.

However, even if the proposal is for a Commission with genuine powers to supervise, the compromise is still unfortunately far more apparent than real. The original North Korean proposals remain intact. If we examine them, we see that they hinge on the proposed all-Korean Commission and that the effective functioning of this Commission is the only basis on which they can have any real meaning. It is both significant and regrettable that no satisfactory reply has been made to the enquiry by the Australian Delegation at an earlier stage in this Conference as to how the North Korean Delegation envisages the breaking of deadlocks within the all-Korean Commission and what time-limit would be placed upon the Commission completing arrangements for elections. To put it simply, on the basis of the North Korean plan, we fail to see any guarantee that there would ever be agreement to hold elections except on Communist terms. In these circumstances, the question of how such elections are to be supervised is academic, to say the least, and the proposal of a neutral commission, therefore, does not in fact reflect any significant advance towards agreement.

There is another aspect of this proposal for a neutral supervisory commission to which I feel bound to refer. The circumstances in which the suggestion has been put forward and the accompanying speeches can leave us in no doubt that the very authority of the United Nations is being challenged by the representatives of communist countries. Other speakers, both to-day and previously, have replied at length to the uncompromising attacks which have been made on the United Nations at this Conference. I should merely like to add that Australia, as a small Power which has every reason to support the principle of Collective Security, must reject this challenge to the authority and the moral significance of the United Nations. We support the principles and purposes of the United Nations Organisation and we are convinced that any settlement in Korea must be found in accordance with them.

Against this background, the Australian Delegation, while reserving until a later stage of the discussion more detailed examination of the fourteen-point programme put forward by the representative of the Republic of Korea, is of opinion that these proposals offer a much more favourable opportunity for a settlement than those made by the Democratic People's Republic of Korea. In particular, the Australian Delegation does not interpret the proposals of the Republic of Korea as inconsistent with what we would regard as the basis for any lasting solution of the Korean problem, namely, agreement to hold, within a specified period, free all-Korean elections under United Nations supervision for the unification of the country. What is urgently needed is a proposal which will lead to unification in a specified future, and we believe that the proposal of the Republic of Korea meets that requirement. In contrast, we cannot help feeling that the plan of the Communist countries, while appearing to endorse the principle of free elections, would prove in practice a means of evading the crucial test of submission to the will of the majority of the people of Korea.

For these reasons, the Australian Delegation believed that this Conference should examine carefully the proposals put forward by the Representative of the Republic of Korea, which can be said to constitute, in general, a positive advance towards a peaceful settlement of the Korean problem.

Speech by M. Molotov, Minister for Foreign Affairs of the Union of Soviet Socialist Republics, June 5, 1954

Mr. Chairman and Delegates,

The discussion on the Korean question at this Conference has already been going on for more than a month. The examination of this current international problem, which is bound up with the maintenance of peace and security in the Far East, is attracting the steadfast attention of the peoples of all countries. Particular interest in the examination of the Korean question at the Geneva Conference is being taken by the peoples of Asia, who, in common with all peace-loving peoples, are expecting this Conference to take such agreed decisions as would ensure a speedy peaceful settlement in Korea, to lead to national unification and the establishment of an independent democratic Korean State and so contribute to reducing tension in the international situation.

All this, without any doubt, places on all the participants in the Geneva Conference a great responsibility for considering the Korean problem objectively and impartially and for settling it in the interests of the Korean people and the strengthening of international peace.

At this stage it would be useful to sum up some of the results of the general discussion.

The Conference has considered proposals submitted by the delegation of the Democratic People's Republic of Korea, by the delegation of the Republic of Korea and also by other delegations. The exchange of views in connexion with these proposals has made it possible to clarify the position of the various delegations.

We may note that as a result of the exchange of views which has taken place, there have been signs of some rapprochement of points of view regarding certain basic principles on which a peaceful settlement in Korea must be based.

In this connexion mention should be made of the arguments put forward here by the head of the British delegation, which are certainly deserving of attention. I have in mind the proposal made by him on May 13, that we should lay down basic principles for reaching agreement on the Korean question. We agree that the adoption of a preliminary decision regarding the basic principles of the future agreement on Korea will ensure that we have better opportunities for completing the work we have begun.

There is every reason for singling out a few important questions, on which the Conference, in our opinion, could already come to an agreed decision since the delegations' points of view on these questions to some extent coincide.

What are these questions?

Firstly.—The participants in the Conference declared themselves in favour of the view that there should be conducted throughout the territory of Korea elections to an All-Korean National Assembly which would give the Korean people an opportunity to express their will freely and to realise their legitimate aspirations for national unification on a democratic basis. These elections must, of course, be conducted on the basis of an all-Korean electoral law, providing for universal suffrage, secret ballot and the proportional representation of the population in the all-Korean legislature.

Secondly.—In the course of the discussion, consideration has been given to a proposal that an all-Korean body should be set up to prepare for and to conduct the free general elections. It is impossible to imagine that after all that has occurred a measure of such exceptional importance for Korea as the holding of general elections could be carried out without proper preparation throughout Korean territory and without taking into account those peculiarities of an economic and political character which have arisen in the country.

Some delegations have expressed their views as to the possible nature of this body and as to the principles on which its activities should be based. The delegation of the Democratic People's Republic of Korea, for example, has proposed that an all-Korean commission, composed of representatives of North and South Korea, should be set up to prepare for and to conduct the elections and also to agree on immediate measures to restore and develop economic and cultural relations between both parts of the country.

A step forward would be made if the Conference expressed itself in principle in favour of setting up an all-Korean body for this purpose, since without such a body the holding of all-Korean elections will be practically impossible.

As regards the membership of this body, its functions and the principles on which its activities should be based, these questions could be the subject of further examination.

Thirdly.—It is recognised by the participants in the Conference that any plan for settling the Korean question must provide for the withdrawal of all foreign armed forces from Korea. The proposals submitted by the Delegation of the Democratic People's Republic of Korea on this question provide for the withdrawal of all foreign troops from Korea before the all-Korean elections are held. The question of the withdrawal of foreign troops has also been referred to in the proposals submitted by the delegation of the Republic of Korea, although they contain a reservation to the effect that withdrawal of the American forces " may start before the elections, but must not be completed until complete control over the whole of Korea has been achieved by the unified Government of Korea."

Since, in spite of the differences in these proposals, the necessity of the withdrawal of foreign troops is recognised by all the participants in the Conference, it might be regarded as a positive factor if the Conference were to declare itself, in principle, in favour of the withdrawal of all foreign armed forces from Korea. The details of the establishment of specified periods for the withdrawal of foreign armed forces from North and South Korea would have to be discussed separately.

Fourthly.—All the participants in the Conference are agreed that the all-Korean elections must be conducted under the supervision of an international body. At the Conference, however, various opinions have been expressed as to how that international body should be formed. The Delegation of the People's Republic of China has made a proposal which provides that the supervision of elections in Korea should be carried out by a Commission of neutral countries, having the same composition as the commission of neutral countries for the supervision of the Armistice in Korea. The Delegation of the Union of Soviet Socialist Republics supports that proposal and considers that it answers the purposes set before the body in question. Several participants in the Conference have spoken in favour of the idea that the supervision of the elections should be entrusted to a United Nations Commission.

In our opinion, the Conference could, in principle, settle the question of the establishment of an international commission to supervise the holding of the elections. As to the membership of that commission and its duties, on these questions there could be a further exchange of views and efforts be made to reach agreement.

Fifthly.—The participants in the Conference have noted the importance of establishing conditions which would prevent any violation of the Korean Armistice Agreement and ensure the peaceful development of the country.

In that connexion it has been argued that the peaceful development of Korea could be ensured if the States most directly concerned in the maintenance of peace in the Far East were to assume the appropriate obligations. That, in its turn, would help towards the fulfilment of the task of the national unification of Korea. The solution of this important question is provided for, in particular, in the proposals of the Delegation of the Democratic People's Republic of Korea.

It is obvious that the Conference must not pass over this serious question, connected as it is with the preservation of peace in Korea. The Conference could already take a decision in regard to the necessity of the States most directly concerned assuming the appropriate obligations to ensure the peaceful development of Korea. The question of which States should assume the aforesaid obligations and the nature of those obligations should be the subject of further examination.

Such, in our opinion, are the questions which should be considered in the first place. We should carefully discuss and endeavour to find practical ways and means of giving effect also to those principles on which the positions of the participants in this Conference substantially differ. We have not the slightest intention of belittling these differences.

Suffice it to say that these differences concern such important questions as the necessity of establishing in the near future an all-Korean body having authority for the whole Korean people, the withdrawal of all foreign armed forces from Korea, and the guaranteeing by the appropriate states of conditions for the further peaceful development of Korea.

In the opinion of the Soviet delegation the participants in the Conference must endeavour to reconcile their points of view and to reach mutually acceptable agreements regarding these principles. In this connexion, the Soviet delegation considers that the time has come to make a specific study of the above-mentioned problems of a peaceful settlement in Korea. At the same time it would be advisable to secure by an appropriate resolution the basic principles on which we might come to an understanding in the course of discussion.

In accordance with the foregoing remarks, the Soviet delegation, for its part, considers it possible to put forward the following draft resolution for the consideration of the Conference: —

The participants in the Geneva Conference have agreed on the following fundamental principles in regard to the peaceful settlement of the Korean problem: —

1. With a view to unifying Korea and to establishing a united, independent and democratic Korean State, free elections shall be held throughout the territory of Korea.

The elections shall be held within six months after the conclusion of the present Agreement.

The elections shall be conducted by secret ballot and universal suffrage.

Representation in the all-Korean legislature shall be in proportion to the population of Korea as a whole.

2. With a view to preparing and conducting free all-Korean elections and to facilitating a *rapprochement* between the Democratic People's Republic of Korea and the Republic of Korea, an all-Korean body shall be set up composed of representatives of the Democratic People's Republic of Korea and the Republic of Korea.

The composition and duties of this body shall be the subject of further examination.

3. All foreign forces shall be withdrawn from Korea within specified periods.

The periods and phases for the withdrawal of all foreign forces from North and South Korea prior to the holding of free all-Korean elections shall be the subject of further examination.

4. An appropriate international commission shall be set up to supervise the holding of free all-Korean elections.

The composition of this supervisory commission shall be the subject of further examination.

5. Recognising the importance of preventing any violation of peace in Korea, it is deemed necessary for the States most directly concerned in the maintenance of peace in the Far East to assume obligations for ensuring Korea's peaceful development, so as to facilitate the settlement of the problem of Korea's national unification.

The question of which States are to assume obligations regarding the ensuring of Korea's peaceful development and the nature of these obligations shall be the subject of further examination.

The present proposal of the Soviet delegation singles out those questions on which it is considered possible to take agreed decisions. It is clear from the text of these proposals, however, that even when these general provisions are accepted, there still remain unsolved certain questions which unless agreement is reached upon them, make it impossible to bring about the national unification of Korea. The complexity of such a situation must not be under-estimated.

In conclusion, I consider it essential to dwell for a moment on the statement of the United States representative, delivered at the meeting of May 28.

Under the pretext of defending the United Nations, the United States representative attempted to justify the American aggression in Korea and the illegal actions of the United Nations which were based on outright and repeated violation of the United Nations Charter. He attempted to represent the American aggression in Korea as carrying out the principle of collective security which, of course, cannot be maintained, except by resorting to falsification of the facts.

The American delegate went so far as to say that the Soviet Union repudiated the principle of collective security, whereas, as everybody knows, it is precisely the Soviet Union that is the most active champion of the principle of collective security, that it has advocated and still advocates the practical application of that principle. It is unnecessary to relate the well-known facts of the Soviet Union's struggle for collective resistance to aggression in the period preceding the second world war. It is well-known that since the second world war as well the Soviet Union has not ceased to carry on its struggle against the policy of splitting up the world into mutually opposed military *blocs* and groups, which is being carried out by the United States of America.

The steps recently taken by the Soviet Union for the purpose of guaranteeing collective security are well known. The Soviet Government made a proposal for the conclusion of an all-European agreement for collective security in Europe, and also declared itself in favour of Union of Soviet Socialist Republics' participation in the North Atlantic Pact, bearing in mind that the participation in that Pact of peace-loving countries like the Soviet Union would transform the North Atlantic Pact Organisation from an aggressive organisation of one group of countries, directed against another group of countries, into an organ of collective security. In addition, the

Soviet Union at the Geneva Conference declared its support of the desire to ensure collective security for all the peoples of Asia as expressed in the statement of the delegation of the People's Republic of China.

It is well known that all these steps designed to ensure the genuine collective security of peoples, regardless of the social structure of their states, are meeting with stubborn opposition from official circles in the United States of America. Such are the actual facts.

As regards the United Nations, the Soviet Union, as one of the founders of that Organisation, has never wearied of urging that the Organisation should be a genuine instrument for ensuring peace and international security, as required by its Charter and by the basic principles and purposes underlying the creation of that international Organisation. It is precisely for this reason that the Soviet Union is fighting against all attempts to turn the United Nations into an instrument of the aggressive policy of certain circles in the United States of America or other countries—against attempts which took the form, in particular, of the adoption by the United Nations of illegal resolutions sanctioning the American aggression in Korea.

The United States representatives attempt to depict themselves as the defenders of the United Nations even when they are exercising brutal pressure on that international Organisation, and when as a result of their pressure, there occur scandalous violations of the basic provisions of the United Nations Charter as, for instance, in the Korean question, or with regard to the rights of the People's Republic of China in the United Nations. But the international authority of the United Nations cannot be supported and strengthened by violations of its principles and of its very Charter. Such violations, carried out under pressure from the United States of America, undermine the foundations of the United Nations. In opposing violations of the basic principles of the United Nations Charter, the Soviet Union is defending the honour and authority of that Organisation.

Attempts have been made here to depict the ruling circles of United States of America as the champions of peace and justice and as the defenders of the rights of humanity and the guardians of the principles of morality. It has long been known, however, that words have value and meaning when they correspond with deeds and fit the facts. In the case in question, the situation is altogether different. It suffices to point out that precisely now, when the ways and means for a peaceful settlement of the Korean problem are still under discussion, the threat of a new aggression by United States of America has made its appearance—this time in the area of South-East Asia.

The United States of America representative ended his statement by giving his unconditional support to the proposals of the South Korean delegate. It is quite obvious, however, that these proposals are not in accordance with the actual situation in Korea and cannot serve as a basis for the decisions of the Geneva Conference.

For its part, the Union of Soviet Socialist Republics delegation has been anxious to include in the draft resolution submitted to your attention only such proposals as might become a basis for the decisions of the Geneva Conference on the Korean problem, should the desire for an agreement be shown. At the same time it is proposed that a further exchange of views should take place.

The Union of Soviet Socialist Republics delegation considers that the adoption of the aforementioned resolution would facilitate the subsequent work of the Conference and help towards the reaching of an agreement that would be in accordance with the interests of the Korean people, as well as with the interests of strengthening peace throughout the world.

Speech by Mr. Bedell Smith, Head of the Delegation of the United States of America, June 5, 1954

Some of my colleagues have spoken with great feeling this afternoon, as indeed the importance of the occasion warrants. As I am, I hope, the last speaker, I will exercise restraint in deference to the important statements which have been made, as well as to those who have made them.

In the first place, it is true, as Mr. Nam Il states, that the North Korean régime on April 27 made certain proposals. They proposed the establishment of an all-Korean Commission which would have the power to draw up an all-Korean election law and to establish conditions for the elections throughout Korea. Apparently, as an afterthought, because they wished to throw over this proposal the cloak of international participation in the conduct of Korean elections, they suggested the establishment of a " neutral nations Supervisory Commission " to assist the all-Korean Commission. M. Molotov to-day has spoken of an " all-Korean body " and recommended it to us. The composition and tasks of this body, he says, shall be the subject of examination. He has also referred to and recommended to us an appropriate International Commission to supervise the holding of free all-Korean elections. The composition of this Supervisory Commission, he says, shall be examined further.

Most of the delegations in this room have already pointed out quite clearly the character of such proposals. I should like to address myself to the first because its character will indicate the character of the second. Our Communist colleagues undertake to convince us that a Commission of this composition might perform an honest and impartial duty in conducting free elections in Korea. The regrettable fact is that the Communist proposal is designed to establish a kind of super Government in which the Communists would have the power actually to frustrate any efforts to achieve honest elections.

As has been many times pointed out, a spurious Commission of this kind would consist of equal numbers from North and South Korea, although the relative difference in population has also been pointed out many times. This Commission would also, I understand, have membership of so-called " social organisations "—concept with which we have had unfortunate experience in the past, when efforts were made to unify Korea in the early days after the war. This Commission is also, I should judge by previous proposals, to have the power to suppress so-called " terrorist groups " which we know, unfortunately, by experience is the communist name for any group that opposes them. A most familiar and completely significant feature is that our Communist colleagues insist that the Commission can operate only by agreement; that is, the commission will operate only if the Communists want to agree, and, of course, they will only agree on their own terms. And this is what we have known for years as the principle of unanimity, or the " built-in veto."

It is to assist this kind of Commission that Mr. Chou En-lai has felt himself obliged to suggest a so-called " Neutral Nations Supervisory Commission." Mr. Chou En-lai admitted the need for international participation, and then he made a proposal for international supervision that I regret to say seems to me to be completely fraudulent. His proposal is fraudulent because it pretends to establish an international body which we are to assume would have some authority and which could assure honest elections. As a matter of fact, such a body could do absolutely nothing, so long as the control of the entire election procedure was in the all-Korean Commission, in which the Communists have their what I have called built-in veto.

There is another spurious aspect to this so-called neutral nations Supervisory Commission. If our Communist colleagues were really sincere about impartial supervision, there is no reason in this world why they could not accept a representative of the United Nations Commission for that task. This they have categorically and repeatedly rejected, and we can only assume that they intend to perpetuate their own concept of a subservient international body. The name that they use, " Neutral Nations Supervisory Commission," is quite enough to convince most of us what they have in mind. That name, you will recall, is the name of a body established in the Korean Armistice Agreement[1]. In fact, as Mr. Chou En-lai said to-day, " Since an international organisation such as the Neutral Nations Supervisory Commission (and I am quoting) is able to supervise implementation of the Korean Armistice Agreement, there is no reason whatsoever why it cannot carry out appropriate supervision over the free elections throughout Korea."

The reason I have asked you to examine this proposal with me is because the bitter experience we have had with such a body during the Korean Armistice has given us a lesson which we will not soon forget. I have given evidence on this experience in restricted session. Mr. Nam Il's and Mr. Chou En-lai's remarks require me to testify in this plenary meeting, and it will be profitable for all of us who are not blinded by political prejudice.

Let's take a moment to examine our past and present experience with what we, of the United Nations, hopefully accepted as a so-called " Neutral " Commission set up by the Korean Armistice. That Commission, you will all recall, consists of the representatives of Switzerland and Sweden, countries whose impartiality and neutrality cannot well be challenged, and of Poland and Czechoslovakia, Soviet-satellite countries which are neutral only in the technical sense of non-belligerency, and which have certainly not shown themselves to be impartial.

The communist members of this Commission have consistently prevented the Commission from carrying out its assigned function. As a result of this obstruction the communist side has been able to violate with impunity the provisions of the Armistice. At this very time as we sit here in Geneva, the aggressors in Korea are bringing in arms and reinforcements to North Korea under conditions strictly prohibited by the Armistice and the Supervisory Commission is impotent to check these violations because the communist members of the Commission refuse to permit the Commission to act.

The situation has become so intolerable that the Swiss and Swedish representatives have repeatedly protested in writing. In these protests, which have already been made public, they have exposed the arbitrary refusal of the communist members to permit any activity by the two genuinely neutral members to carry out the solemn obligation which they assumed when they undertook their great task. I think it is worth while to review some of these reports.

In a letter of May 4, 1954, the Swedish and Swiss members of the Commission, General Mohn and General Gross, honourable and able officers, stated that " the operations of this Commission were hampered by the fact that in many instances the vote of its four members was found to be equally divided, resulting in a deadlock." Then they said, " the control activities of the fixed neutral nations inspection teams in the territory under the military control of the Korean People's Army and the Chinese People's Volunteers are not being carried out satisfactorily and in full accord with the spirit of

[1] " Korea No. 2 (1953)," Cmd. 8938.

70

the Armistice Agreement, owing to the restricted practices imposed on the activities of the teams by their Czechoslovak and Polish members."

Again, in a letter of May 7, 1954, General Mohn and General Gross said that " all effort undertaken by the Swedish and Swiss members of the inspection teams in order to increase the scope and the frequency of the spot check controls have been constantly and persistently frustrated."

To counteract these honest and impartial statements, as I have said, by the representatives of the States whose neutrality cannot be challenged, allegations have been made that the United Nations Command has repeatedly violated the Armistice. These allegations have been made formally and in writing by the Czech and Polish members of the Neutral Nations Supervisory Commission. Some of them have been repeated here in Geneva. I should like to read you the reply of the Swedish and Swiss members of the Commission to these allegations. In a letter of May 4, 1954, General Mohn and General Gross, the Swedish and Swiss members, wrote to the Military Armistice Commission as follows :—

" These are some of the comments the Swedish and Swiss members want to present in order to refute allegations which they consider to be tissue of malicious fabrications, gratuitous distortions, misleading half-truths, and delusive insinuations without foundation in reality. The methods resorted to consist largely in isolating facts and figures from their proper context and in making sweeping generalisations on the basis of premises thus distorted.

" There is no denying that the United Nations Command has laid itself wide open to inspection and observation by the Neutral Nations Inspection Teams, and has never attempted to conceal anything from the Neutral Nations Supervisory Commission, not even its mistakes and its clerical shortcomings. There is no evidence that the United Nations Command side intentionally, or even inadvertently, has violated those provisions of the Armistice Agreement, the application of which is the concern of the Neutral Nations Supervisory Commission. As far as the Swedish and Swiss members have been able to find, the United Nations Command has loyally and sincerely abided by both the letter and the spirit of the Armistice Agreement."

Gentlemen, the Neutral Nations Supervisory Commission in Korea, which is a pattern of what we have been offered today, has been completely ineffective, despite the fact that it had clear and detailed terms of reference. Its effectiveness depended on communist good faith that has been lacking. Under such circumstances, we are forced to the conclusion that this sort of a supervisory commission means, at best, no supervision at all.

Mr. Chairman, words like " free elections," and " unification " mean nothing whatever if there is no meeting of minds. The people of Korea and the peoples of the world will not be satisfied with empty words. The Communist States associated with us here are in fact willing to agree to the necessary steps, procedures and instrumentalities which would assure the concepts like " free elections " have true meaning, and assure that they can be realised for the Korean people. This can be realised only if the Communists are willing to abandon their insistence on a form of organisation which provides an automatic veto. Our objective, as Mr. Chou En-lai has said, is genuinely free elections held under conditions of genuine freedom. But, I don't think he means the same things as I mean when he says those words!

Genuinely free elections in Korea can indeed be assured if the elections are placed under the control and supervision of the United Nations. The United Nations has the competence, the experience, the authority, the impartiality and the facilities to perform this task. They could never take place under the formula proposed by Mr. Nam Il. The vast majority of us represented here know what really free, uncoerced elections are, and we are not to be deluded.

I am glad that Mr. Nam Il and Mr. Chou En-lai, and finally M. Molotov, have made the issue so crystal clear. I believe it will be equally clear to world public opinion, and in so far as my delegation is concerned, we are quite prepared to rest the case of the United Nations before the bar of world opinion, on the statements which our Communist colleagues have made today, and on those which I and my colleagues have made on this and our previous Plenary Sessions.

Document No. 22

Speech by Mr. Chou En-lai, Foreign Minister of the People's Republic of China, June 5, 1954

As early as the second day of the Geneva Conference, Foreign Minister Nam Il of the Democratic People's Republic of Korea put forward three concrete proposals for the peaceful settlement of the Korean question. These proposals have obtained the support of the delegations of the Soviet Union and of China. Any non-prejudiced person cannot but admit that the proposals made by Foreign Minister Nam Il provide broad possibilities for the Korean people to restore their national unity through genuinely free elections. In an endeavour to seek a way to agreement, on May 22 the delegation of the People's Republic of China proposed, as a supplement to the proposals of Foreign Minister Nam Il, international supervision of free elections in Korea by neutral nations, thus facilitating the progress of this Conference. But on the same day, the delegate of the Republic of Korea submitted a proposal designed to achieve the unification of Korea by the Syngman Rhee clique with foreign support. It is obvious that such a proposal cannot provide a reasonable basis for the peaceful settlement of the Korean question.

The delegates of the United States and some other countries attempted to support the proposals of the Republic of Korea by invoking the illegal resolutions of the United Nations. We have repeatedly pointed out that the United Nations and our Conference are completely unrelated. Our Conference is being held to seek other ways for the peaceful settlement of the Korean question. As a matter of fact, common ground can be found for settling peacefully the Korean question.

At our Conference no one has expressed himself against the proposition that peace in Korea should be consolidated. It is also admitted by all that the purpose of this Conference is to bring about the peaceful settlement of the Korean question. Everybody says that Korea should be unified. Most of us are of the opinion that in order to achieve the unification of Korea, free elections should be held throughout Korea. These elections should be conducted in accordance with the principle of proportional representation. Even as regards the withdrawal of all foreign armed forces from Korea within a specified period, only a few delegates have voiced different opinions in principle. As Mr. Eden, the United Kingdom delegate, pointed out on May 13, where there is so much common ground we should not despair of reaching a settlement. Some people hold that since there is no more bloodshed in Korea, the further peaceful settlement of the Korean question is no longer urgent. Therefore, they openly advocate delaying the settlement of the Korean question. We cannot share such a viewpoint. The Korean question is so closely related with peace and security in the Far East and the world, that the peaceful settlement of the Korean question permits of no delay. At the same time, since we have such common ground, we should further endeavour to seek a way to bring about a concrete solution of this question and should not allow the proposals of the delegate of the Republic of Korea to stand in our way in seeking agreement.

The delegate of the Republic of Korea claims that his Government represents the majority of the Korean people. If that were really the case, there would be no need for the Government of South Korea to be afraid of holding genuinely free elections throughout Korea in order to achieve the unification of Korea. But the delegate of the Republic of Korea is opposed to the joint setting up by the Democratic People's Republic of Korea and the Republic of Korea, in accordance with the principle of mutual consultation, of an all-Korean organ to prepare and hold all-Korean free elections. The Government of South Korea once again attempts to manipulate the Korean elections under the cloak of the United Nations. It attempts even to impose the constitution of the Republic of Korea on the Democratic People's Republic of Korea. Not only that, it is even opposed to the withdrawal, before the all-Korean elections, of the United Nations forces, which are mainly United States troops. This proves that the Government of South Korea itself does not believe that it is representative of the majority of the Korean people. The Government of South Korea is afraid to achieve the unification of Korea through genuinely free elections. It attempts to rely on the illegal resolutions of the United Nations and foreign armed forces for extending the rule of Syngman Rhee over the whole of Korea. This is not only contrary to the principle that the Korean question should be settled by the Korean people themselves, but also discards completely the democratic basis of free elections. Therefore, it is not surprising at all that even a correspondent of the *New York Times* cannot but admit in his despatch of May 28 that in the proposals of the Republic of Korea, " the real issue—giving the Korean people a chance to unify their country under a Government that they can choose by genuinely free elections—has been fogged over."

The all-Korean free elections are a matter for the Korean people themselves. Therefore, Foreign Minister Nam Il's proposal that the all-Korean Commission composed of the two sides, *i.e.*, the Democratic People's Republic of Korea and the Republic of Korea, should prepare and hold all-Korean elections is entirely reasonable. Just as Foreign Minister Molotov, of the Soviet Union, pointed out in his statement of April 29, " the solution of the Korean question is primarily a matter for the Korean people themselves. No solution imposed upon the Korean people by other countries can satisfy the Korean people or contribute to a lasting settlement of the Korean problem."

It is only because of the fact that Korea has been divided into two parts for many years, and that strained relations exist between North and South Korea as a result of the war, that we have proposed that neutral nations render assistance to the all-Korean Commission by supervising the all-Korean free elections. Some people suggest that the United Nations supervise the all-Korean free elections. That is untenable. We have already pointed out on many occasions that the United Nations is one of the belligerents in the Korean war and has long since lost the competence and moral authority to deal with the Korean question impartially. It is certainly no accident that in the Korean Armistice Agreement, the two belligerents agreed that the implementation of that Agreement should be supervised by a Supervisory Commission ·composed of neutral nations which had not participated in the Korean war, but not by the United Nations, which is one of the belligerents. In the ten months since the Korean Armistice, the Neutral Nations Supervisory Commission has played a positive rôle in

73

helping with the implementation of the Korean Armistice Agreement. The Neutral Nations Supervisory Commission has by unanimous agreement laid down effective procedures for supervising and inspecting the rotation of military personnel and the replacement of combat material entering and leaving Korea, established regular inspections at the specified ports of entry in the rear of North and South Korea, and conducted special investigations into violations of the Agreements, as requested by the two sides in accordance with the provisions of the Armistice Agreement. Although the Neutral Nations Supervisory Commission has met with some difficulties in its work, its contributions and achievements are not to be denied. Since an international organ such as the Neutral Nations Supervisory Commission is able to supervise the implementation of the Korean Armistice Agreement, there is no reason whatsoever why it cannot carry out appropriate supervision of free elections throughout Korea.

The withdrawal of all foreign armed forces from Korea is a prerequisite for the Korean people freely to express their will in the nation-wide elections without foreign interference. The delegate of the Republic of Korea repeated the views of the United States delegate and, in an endeavour to resist the fair proposal for the withdrawal of all foreign armed forces from Korea, once again slandered the Chinese People's Volunteers. These clamours of the delegate of the Republic of Korea cannot alter in the slightest the righteous character of the Chinese People's Volunteers. In fact, it is precisely the People's Republic of China and the Democratic People's Republic of Korea that have consistently advocated the simultaneous withdrawal of all foreign armed forces from Korea. Even to-day, when we are discussing the peaceful settlement of the Korean question, the Republic of Korea and the United States are still not willing to withdraw the United States forces, together with all the other foreign forces, from Korea simultaneously. Is not this ample proof that they intend to keep the United States forces in Korea to interfere in Korean internal affairs and to threaten the peace in Korea and the security of China? However, the views of the delegates of the United States and of the Republic of Korea are obviously contrary to the desire of the peoples of the various countries who have sons in Korea. On May 7, the delegate of New Zealand said that he was sure that the nations here represented were looking forward to the day when their troops would be withdrawn from Korea. On April 29, the delegate of Australia expressed his hope that on the basis of satisfactory agreements and firm commitments, it might be possible to begin withdrawals at some early date. On May 13, the delegate of the United Kingdom also said, " We have a common desire to withdraw our forces from Korea as soon as we can do so without again endangering the peace." Thus it can be seen that the desire for withdrawing foreign armed forces from Korea exists even among the countries concerned on the side of the United Nations Command.

It is said that the withdrawal of all foreign armed forces from Korea would affect peace in Korea. Such an assertion is groundless. In order to prevent the recurrence of fighting in Korea, Foreign Minister Nam Il has proposed that the nations most interested in peace in the Far East should assume the obligation to guarantee the peaceful development of Korea so as to facilitate the fulfilment of the task of the national unification of Korea. Consequently, we consider there is no reason why this Conference should not be able to reach appropriate agreements on the questions of the withdrawal of all foreign armed forces from Korea within a specified period and of guaranteeing the peaceful development of Korea by the nations most interested in peace in the Far East.

The Geneva Conference has discussed the peaceful settlement of the Korean question for more than one month already. The peace-loving peoples of various countries are all hoping that our Conference will achieve positive results. We should endeavour, on the basis of the existing common ground, to reach agreement on the peaceful settlement of the Korean question. We should not disappoint the expectations of the peoples of various countries.

FOURTEENTH PLENARY SESSION ON KOREA

Document No. 23

Speech by M. Spaak, Foreign Minister of Belgium, June 11, 1954([8])

Mr. President, Gentlemen, I apologise for speaking at this late hour and also because I am conscious that, in intervening thus, I shall repeat a certain number of things which have already been well explored this afternoon. But it seems to me that we have arrived at a decisive moment in this Conference and the very grave words uttered by Mr. Eden confirm me in this impression.

It is incontestable that the speech made by M. Molotov on June 5 last was a speech of great importance, a fact which is proved by its having led to comments which lasted throughout the whole afternoon. If, during his speech, M. Molotov had confined himself to the first part, I should have been completely happy. The second part, the comments underlining certain of his proposals and the comments also made by other delegations, have, in my opinion, lessened the importance of the proposals made to us by the delegate of the Union of Soviet Socialist Republics. Nevertheless I think we must agree that M. Molotov was right in seeking to make clear the point arrived at in our discussions. In doing so M. Molotov may have shown too much optimism. Yet, I must confess, I have not the heart to reproach him for it. We have so often reproached the delegate of the Soviet Union for emphasising the things that separate us rather than those that unite us that to-day we should rejoice when we see the delegate of the Union of Soviet Socialist Republics expressing a certain optimism.

M. Molotov has made five proposals and I think I may rightly say that an agreement in principle seems possible on a certain number of them. We have all repeatedly affirmed that we want a united Korea; that we agree to a progressive withdrawal of troops, and I should think that from no quarter whatsoever would any absolute objection be raised to the guaranteeing of a united, pacified and democratic Korea by means of special agreements concluded by the nations most directly interested in a peaceful Asia.

It is clear that these few points only represent agreements in principle and the very interesting speeches of the delegates of Canada and New Zealand have shown that, around these principles, a great number of questions have to be put forward and resolved.

What I wish to point out is that M. Molotov, in submitting his proposals, did not lose sight of this, for he said: —

" It is evident from the text of these proposals that, even if these proposals were accepted, many questions would still remain outstanding on which, if no agreement be reached, the national unification of Korea would be rendered impossible. It is necessary not to underestimate the complexity of such a situation."

([8]) Unofficial translation.

75

One thing is clear: even if we come to an agreement on the several principles we have just mentioned, there are a large number of questions to be raised, a large number of questions to be solved and we should still be far from the end of our task. But it is likewise clear that these several principles being established—principles on which agreement would appear to be not impossible—there still remains between us a divergence which is absolutely fundamental; a divergence which is not, as it might appear at first sight, a divergence in form, but a divergence which concerns a certain number of principles on which a delegation such as mine—and I am sure many others who have already said so—cannot compromise.

How are these free elections for the whole of Korea to be arranged? There are two opposite systems:

That proposed by the Communist countries, which consists in saying to us: "We are going to create a pan-Korean organism in which by parity and equally North Korea and South Korea will be represented. It is this pan-Korean organism which will have the responsibility of preparing and supervising the elections. In addition, an International Commission composed of members of neutral countries will supervise the operations."

Such, then, is the system proposed by the communists.

The system proposed by the other countries—and this is essential—envisages that it is only under the auspices and on the responsibility of the United Nations that the International Commission should be created to prepare and supervise the execution of free elections.

It is not sufficient to point out that there are two systems before us. It is necessary to say frankly and honestly why one is contested and the other approved.

We cannot accept the idea of a pan-Korean organism entrusted with the responsibility of preparing and supervising the elections. Why?

I have just heard Mr. Chou En-lai say: "Those who will have nothing to do with this pan-Korean organism are those who would deliberately help, support and favour one of the parties in Korea against the other."

That is not so.

We will have nothing to do with this pan-Korean organism because we are absolutely convinced that this organism cannot succeed in its task and that, by giving it the responsibilities suggested, nothing but disorder and chaos would ensue.

I was convinced of this before coming to this Conference. But it seems to me that all the discussions we have heard between the representative of North Korea and the representative of South Korea prove to anyone of objective and impartial mind that it is quite impossible to bring the delegates of North Korea and South Korea face to face, to disclaim all interest in their work and say to them: "Settle, then, the innumerable and most difficult questions arising by direct contact, without the intervention of an international organism." Fortunately, this afternoon the tone of the discussion has been more moderate, and we have not heard those insults which were current coin at previous meetings. Nevertheless, I have heard a delegate, when speaking of the South Korean Government, use the words: "The clique of Syngman Rhee."

I am not sufficiently conversant with Chinese to know the exact meaning of the word "clique" in Chinese, but I do know that for anyone who speaks French it must be extremely difficult to co-operate with political opponents dubbed "a clique" and that agreement must thereafter be somewhat problematic . . . . and, I would repeat, to-day the atmosphere has been excellent. . . .

I have not been able, nor have I wished, to sum up all that has previously been said on this subject. Do not therefore think that our opposition to a pan-Korean organism springs from a desire to favour one side or the other. We sincerely believe that, after the terrible war which has raged in Korea, after the development of so many political passions, to set the adversaries face to face and fancy that the questions are going to be solved, is to take up a childish position. It is more than that, it is a bad position because, I will repeat, it can only result in chaos.

Further, it has been said that the work of the pan-Korean organism will be supervised, or controlled by an appropriate International Commission, as M. Molotov said in his proposal.

I bow before the word " appropriate," which is obviously a word extremely well chosen, and I state at once that it is difficult—or that it appears at first glance to be difficult—to refuse the creation of an " appropriate " commission. If there was nothing, or if we did not know what lies behind the word " appropriate," we could no doubt register our agreement. But we know . . . . and there's the essence of the problem.

I always hope that we shall succeed in taking a step forward, but we know that in the mind of the Communist countries, at the present time, the " appropriate " Commission is, in every case, a Commission created and developed outside the United Nations.

Now, at this point, I ask my opponents to be so good as to reflect for a moment and to take note of the fact that they are asking us something to which we could never agree, something which, if we were to accept it, would have absolutely disastrous consequences in the future, as much in regard to the principle of collective security as in regard to the very existence of the United Nations.

For our opponents speak to us quite frankly and they tell us why they do not want this Control Commission to be a Control Commission from the United Nations.

They tell us: " We do not want this Control Commission to be from the United Nations because, in this matter of Korea, the United Nations are the aggressor."

Gentlemen, if we were to say " Yes," have you any idea what the consequences would be? . . . .

In the first place, for the immense majority of us, when we are told that in this matter the United Nations are the aggressor such a statement seems to us to be at the same time an untruth, and, if you will permit me to say so, almost a calumny. But, do you realise that if this Conference now gathered together were to accept such a thesis, the principle of collective security would in the future be dead? And I ask myself what would remain of the United Nations if the United Nations took note of and ratified such a proposition: acknowledging that they were the aggressors in the Korea affair.

I demand of M. Molotov, who has spoken, in eloquent terms, of collective security, and who has even said that he was defending the honour of the United Nations Organisation, not to insist and to understand that his attitude is one vital to the United Nations, and that in consequence we cannot accept it.

What then do we propose to our opponents?

We have already tried to explain this many times. We propose that the elections should be prepared and supervised by a Commission from the United Nations.

One would imagine that our opponents consider that the United Nations only and necessarily consist of the countries here represented. I did myself try to say in the first speech I made here that such is not the case. Others have confirmed this position. Mr. Eden did so again, not long ago.

The United Nations consist of sixty nations. Who can, even among the communist countries, deny that among these sixty nations there are many communist nations and many nations that, in the Korea affair, have taken up a neutral attitude? Who can deny that it would be possible to ask the United Nations to designate a Commission that would be truly an impartial international Commission?

Clearly, that could be done. It is clear that that is the only way to apply and to respect the principles of the Charter for I add to my argument that if, to-day, we were to take away from the United Nations the need to regulate a problem such as the Korea problem, we would empty the United Nations of their substance and create instead an organisation without any importance, from which we would have removed absolutely all usefulness.

What I ask then, is that our adversaries should agree to accept that the Commission for the supervising and preparation of the elections should be a Commission from the United Nations, nominated by the United Nations, but, of course, an impartial Commission which would be agreeable to the contesting parties.

What will this Commission have to do?

Will it have to ignore South and North Korea and try to resolve the problems that arise apart from the interested parties?

Of course not; that would be giving it an absurd mission. This International Commission will have to work in close collaboration with the South and North Koreans, and if one wants its mission to succeed, that is to say if one wishes it to finally succeed in creating a united Korea and organising free and democratic elections, it will not be able to act without obtaining the agreement of the two parties.

Consequently, the system we propose is a system that firstly will uphold the United Nations, who do not deserve to be condemned. It is a system that will uphold the United Nations, who, for the first time in the history of mankind, have shown that the principle of collective security could be applied, which is an essential point for all of us and for the future.

Having upheld the principle, the reputation and the responsibility of the United Nations, we naturally and willingly recognise that an impartial Commission must be created and that that Commission alone can regulate the problem.

I have tried to put into a black and white formula the idea that I have just expressed and this is what I have drawn up:—

" In order to prepare and organise free general elections for the whole of Korea, the United Nations Organisation will appoint a Commission.

Its members will be chosen impartially so that the two contending parties will have confidence in it.

This Commission will act in close collaboration with the representatives of the Republic of Korea and of the People's Democratic Republic of North Korea.

Questions relating to the final constitution and powers of this organ will be the subject of a supplementary study."

If such a text could be inserted in M. Molotov's proposals, and if we could say that the participants in the Geneva Conference have agreed that this is the principle that should be put into effect, then I believe that we will have taken an essential step.

If we are unable to agree on that, then I fear that all that will remain for us to do will be to face up to the grave and sad solution proposed by Mr. Eden.

Speech by Mr. C. A. Ronning, Acting Head of the Canadian Delegation, June 11, 1954

I should like to begin by referring to a subject which we consider very important. That is the challenge which has been made by all the representatives of communist States at this Conference to the position of the United Nations. These representatives have denied repeatedly, and even more categorically than they have done since 1950, the legality and the moral right of United Nations intervention in Korea and indeed of all the efforts made by the United Nations to bring peace, prosperity and unity to the Korean people. These are allegations which we must deny bluntly and unequivocally, with no less conviction because our rejection is not couched in the extreme terms in which the charges were made. I mention this subject here so that there can be no mistake about the views consistently held by the Canadian delegation. The majority of us at this Conference are here because we voluntarily took part in the defence of the Republic of Korea at the request of the United Nations against palpable and inexcusable aggression. This action was taken in accordance with the Charter of the United Nations and sanctioned by the vast majority of the members of that organisation. I do not wish at this point to go into the formal and constitutional justification of our position, as this has already been stated on many occasions. It is hardly necessary to do so, in fact, because the absurdity of the pretension that our actions were illegal is clear to all who are free to judge the case on its merits.

A clear attempt has been made by communist speakers to detach many of us from our devotion to the principles of the United Nations and from our belief in our own mission in Korea by referring constantly to this mission as if it were an action entirely undertaken by the United States. The United States, to its enduring credit, has undertaken by far the greatest obligations in Korea, but we other countries which have of necessity made smaller contributions are no less firmly convinced of the rightness of our mission than is the United States. Because we are a free coalition, we sometimes disagree honestly and publicly about the details of the conduct of our joint enterprise, but there should be no illusion among communist delegations that they can, therefore, drive us apart on matters of fundamental principle in which we all believe so strongly.

The attempt has been made by communist delegations to support their charges against the United Nations by arguing that the " United States," as they put it, cannot seek to impose at this Conference what it was unable to achieve by force of arms. This sordid interpretation of United Nations action and United Nations intentions is a distortion of the truth. The United Nations has not sought by force of arms to impose its will upon any country. It set out at the request of the Republic of Korea to defend the Republic of Korea from aggression, and this it was happily successful in doing. Having repelled aggression, the United Nations has resumed the effort, which it had accepted many years before 1950, to seek the unification of the two parts into which the country had been divided. It is not a question of the United Nations seeking to impose a settlement on either part of Korea but, in accordance with its practice in all disputes which have come before it, to seek by methods of conciliation to bring about a just and practical solution which will be accepted by the parties concerned.

The presence of Canadian troops in Korea and the presence of a Canadian delegation at Geneva attest Canada's unqualified support of the United Nations as the pre-eminent international agency for making and keeping peace; we have supported every step taken by the United Nations in its efforts to bring about the unification of Korea and we firmly believe that any agreement that is worked out to achieve this objective must be in accordance with the principles of the United Nations. If the Geneva Conference is not able at this stage to reach an agreement on procedures for the establishment of a united and independent and democratic Korea, the Canadian Government is confident that the United Nations will continue to seek the attainment of this objective by peaceful means and that Canada will continue to support these efforts.

I should like now to consider the resolution which has been proposed by the representative of the Soviet Union. This resolution cannot, of course, be considered apart from the explanation which M. Molotov has given, and I shall direct my attention particularly, therefore, to the points in the resolution as defined in the body of M. Molotov's presentation.

In the first place, M. Molotov spoke of free elections. M. Molotov has spoken about free elections guaranteed by a secret ballot and universal suffrage; he has, we are happy to note, repeated the North Korean representative's previous assurance that the elections to an all-Korean legislature would be based on the principle of proportional representation. This is all to the good, and we would like very much to announce mutual agreement on this point. Unfortunately, however, we must ask ourselves whether the communists and we, ourselves, do mean the same thing when we talk of free elections. Secret ballot, universal suffrage, proportional representation are essential to free elections, but they are by no means the whole story. While these three principles may be observed in elections in communist countries, we consider elections are not free unless the voter is offered freedom of choice. We believe that in the elections in the Republic of Korea the voter has had greater freedom to exercise democratic rights of choice between different parties, principles and proposals than one would have expected in a country so recently free from long years of foreign domination. There can be no question in anyone's mind, however, that the voter in North Korea has no such freedom. A situation in which voters in North Korea could feel themselves free from threats and intimidations or that Opposition leaders could feel safe to stand as candidates would come about only if the control of this country by communist armies were removed, or at any rate sufficiently relaxed to enable genuine supervision by an objective International Commission to take place. To say, therefore, that we agree on free elections would be quite false unless we had agreed also on an effective programme of supervision. That we have not agreed on an effective programme of supervision is all too clear for reasons which I shall explain subsequently.

To illustrate to M. Molotov the grave difficulties we have in stating that we agree with him on this principle, I should like to enumerate some of the questions which we must face. Do the communist representatives agree, for example, that any Korean citizen can be a candidate for the legislature, or do they intend that only candidates " approved " by the all-Korean " body " may seek election? As freedom for candidates to campaign is a vital part of free elections, are the communists prepared to agree to the terms of the fifth item of the South Korean proposals calling for full freedom of movement, speech, &c., for candidates, campaigners and their families? Under the communist proposals would the all-Korean legislature be completely sovereign within Korea and would the executive branch of the Government derive its authority from majority support in the Legislature or would the executive be separate from the Legislature? There are varying democratic solutions to these questions but it is most important in this case to know how the executive would be chosen. Is it perhaps intended that it should be chosen by the all-Korean "body" in which the Communists would retain veto power? Since the Communist representatives insist that the question of Korea's future constitution is not a matter for consideration by this Conference, do they envisage that the freely-elected legislature would be a constituent assembly empowered to draft a constitution by majority vote or do they perhaps intend that the Korean Constitution should be drawn up by the all-Korean body in which a small minority of the population would have grossly inflated representation? These are not questions which we are asking in the expectation that M. Molotov will provide us with immediate satisfactory replies, but they are questions which, although they may be considered matters of detail, are matters on which we must reach an understanding before we can be said to agree in principle.

In the second place, M. Molotov has made an interesting and not unconvincing argument for the establishment of an all-Korean body to prepare and hold the general elections. We are not prepared to reject out of hand the conception of an all-Korean Commission for the purposes mentioned by M. Molotov, but so much depends on the composition and function of this Commission that we could hardly be said to agree unless our conceptions of the Commission are more alike than they seem to be. To us it is conceivable that for certain very limited purposes of removing the present barriers even a Commission composed on a fifty-fifty basis might be acceptable. However, we would find it much more difficult to believe that there was justice in establishing a Commission to settle all the electoral details for the whole country which was composed with such complete disregard to the division of population. It is clear, therefore, that the questions of composition and function are essential components of the principle of an all-Korean Commission. They cannot be divorced from it and they cannot be left for subsequent consideration. Therefore, while we might be prepared to consider such a Commission in principle, we could not possibly do so unless we were sure that we had the same conception of its composition and functions. Unfortunately, however, everything that has been said on this subject by communist spokesmen leads us to believe that they have in mind not a Commission to assist the people of all Korea to express their will but a Commission which could be used, as such bodies have been used in other countries, to establish, if not immediate Communist domination, at least so disproportionate a representation of Communists in the Government in relation to their actual strength in the country that their programme for seizing power would be vastly strengthened and accelerated. If the communists consider that we are unduly suspicious or lacking in open-mindedness in this matter, they must ask themselves whether their record of accomplishment in Eastern Europe and of frustrated accomplishment in other countries has not given us strong reasons for scepticism.

Let me again in this connexion outline a few of the questions which must be solved before we can talk about agreement in principle. If this all-Korean body is to act only by unanimous decision, the veto power involved will be of crucial importance in connexion with the task to be carried out. What exactly do the Communists mean when they say that the body would facilitate "a rapprochement" between the two Koreas? Would this mean that it would act as an interim Government or that it would set up an interim Government of some kind, or would it be responsible for drafting an all-Korean constitution? How far will the responsibility of the body go in the preparation and conduct of the elections? Would the body be expected to rule upon the acceptability of the candidates and of parties? Would the body be solely responsible for the selection of scrutineers? Would it be responsible for establishing a police force to maintain law and order during the elections or would the International Supervisory Commission assist it

81

in this task? What other functions would the body have? If the body is to have any significant executive powers and is to be more than a negotiating agency for arranging elections, the veto power involved could completely prejudice the freedom of the elections or the establishment of a truly representative Government after the elections. It is only if we have settled some of these questions that we can determine whether M. Molotov's principle is intended to assist the democratic processes or is merely another sinister manœuvre of a familiar kind to frustrate the will of the people.

M. Molotov's proposal for an agreement on the withdrawal of forces is even more deceptive, because he has endeavoured to gloss over in a subordinate phrase the basic difference which clearly exists between us. This basic difference, which has been frequently stated, is whether the United Nations forces which came to the defence of the Republic of Korea and which want only to assist in the establishment of genuine Korean self-government in accordance with the wishes of the Korean people and then to withdraw, should be treated on the same basis as those forces which came into Korea against the wishes of the Korean people and have sought to assist in establishing in that country a form of government which the majority of the Korean people clearly do not want. As I mentioned earlier, M. Molotov has attempted to blur this issue by referring to the withdrawal of "American troops" rather than to United Nations troops. We cannot, however, reach agreement in principle by obscuring this essential matter, and so long as the communists refuse to recognise the position of the United Nations forces, it would be misleading to talk about agreement in principle.

In the fourth place, M. Molotov has raised the question of a supervisory commission. As the Canadian Secretary of State for External Affairs stated recently in the House of Commons, we believe that Korean elections " should be supervised by an international agency agreed on, if possible, by the Geneva Conference but acceptable to the United Nations." Mr. Pearson went on to say " In order to ensure maximum objectivity—and that is going quite a long way to meet the views of the other side—we felt that this supervisory agency might consist of nations which did not belong to the communist *bloc* and which did not participate in military operations in Korea." It cannot be said that our attitude on this is rigid—we are prepared to go a long way to make sure that such a commission is genuinely neutral. We believe that it is possible that countries which are accustomed to approach international problems freely and objectively can provide neutral supervision. The role played by the Indian military representatives in the Neutral Nations Repatriation Commission is a good example of the kind of assistance which can be obtained from countries of good-will. In the Neutral Nations Repatriation Commission the Indian members were by no means always in agreement with the United Nations Command, but we did not question the honesty of their intentions or their integrity. This is what we mean when we talk of international neutral supervision. Unfortunately, however, M. Molotov has betrayed what he means by supporting the proposal that the Neutral Nations Supervisory Commission which at present exists in Korea should be duplicated for the purpose of supervising Korean elections. There is little further that need be said on the subject than has been said already by Mr. Bedell Smith and in the report of the Swiss and Swedish members of the Commission on the behaviour of their Czechoslovak and Polish colleagues. If by a neutral international commission M. Molotov means a commission which includes such totally unneutral nations as Poland and Czechoslovakia, it is clear that we are not agreed in principle and should not say that we are. Furthermore, we cannot talk about agreement in principle on such a commission unless we have determined not only its composition but also its function. If we are to agree to the principle of such a commission, we would agree only on the establishing of a commission with real powers to make certain that freedom of choice exists for the electors in all parts of Korea. This question of function is in no sense a detail which could be put off for subsequent discussion, because it is basic to the principle itself.

What in this connexion do the communists mean by " supervision "? Would the commission which they envisage merely observe the elections or would it have the power and the means to correct conditions which interfere with the proper conduct of the elections? Would it be competent to appoint scrutineers? Would it assist the all-Korean body in maintaining law and order before and during the elections? In short would it be powerless execrescence or would it have an active and useful role to play in ensuring fair play and a free choice of representatives by the electorate?

In his fifth point, M. Molotov has mentioned the possibiilty of states most interested in Korea accepting obligations for its peaceful development. The Canadian delegation has listened with an open mind and not without interest to the repeated emphasis of the communist spokesmen on this theme. The possibility of some kind of guarantee of the peaceful development of Korea by other powers is one which certainly could be considered, and a determination on the part of interested powers to assist Korea to rehabilitate itself ought not to be rejected. We have noted, however, that on each of the many occasions when this subject has been mentioned, the spokesman has, after a promising introduction, retreated into extremely obscure language when he comes to defining the purposes of such a guarantee or statement of obligations. We have never been given any clear indication at all of what the representa-tives of North Korea, the People's Republic of China and the Soviet Union really have in mind. If, for example, they are interested in outside assistance to Korea in its economic development, as has been implied in several state-ments, we must point out that the United Nations accepted such an obligation in the early stages of hostilities in Korea, that members of the United Nations have contributed substantial sums to this project, and that the United Nations Korean Reconstruction Agency has established itself in Korea and has already made important contributions to the economic life of that country. It was clearly understood when the United Nations Korean Reconstruction Agency was established that its activities might be extended into North Korea. This is no partisan activity; it is intended for the benefit of all the people of that unfortunate country. It is a most substantial effort to assist in the peaceful development of Korea, and it is not the United Nations which stands in the way of its operating in the entire country. If as seems likely from M. Molotov's proposal, there is more involved than economic assistance, we can hardly be said to agree in principle when we really do not know what M. Molotov is talking about. He himself has said, " The ques-tion as to what particular states should undertake the said obligations as well as the question of the nature of such obligations should be discussed additionally." To agree in principle on this point would therefore make about as much sense as it would for us to issue a general statement that we are in favour of treaties without any indication of what kind of treaties or who were to be our partners. Once again we must emphasise the fact that the so-called details are not extraneous to the principle but essential to it.

One other matter in this connexion. In his fifth point M. Molotov has mentioned the importance of creating conditions which would prevent the violation of the Armistice Agreement in Korea. That Agreement has been approved by the General Assembly of the United Nations. Its conclusion marked the accomplishment of all that the United Nations ever undertook to do by armed force in Korea. The aggression had been repelled. Our business is to work for the establishment of a unified, democratic and free Korea and we must not be deflected from it. The Armistice Agreement is not an issue here. Its preamble clearly sets forth its objectives to " insure a complete cessation of hostilities and over all acts of armed force in Korea until a final peaceful settlement is achieved. . . ."

In conclusion, I should like to say that we of the Canadian delegation should like nothing more than to be able to register the agreement of this Conference on the principles of settling such important points as those referred to in M. Molotov's resolution. We even like the idea of trying to register at this point what limited agreements we may have achieved and then settling down seriously to solve those problems which remain, and it is a considerable temptation to do so, even on M. Molotov's terms. We have given the most careful examination to this resolution in the hope that we could find a basis of agreement, but we are led to the inescapable conclusion that to do so at the present time would be dishonest. It would mean deliberate misrepresentation to the public of the world and could lead only to charges of bad faith at a later stage. In so far as there are in the resolution some fundamental principles on which we are said by M. Molotov to agree, such as the establishment of a united, independent Korea and the ultimate withdrawal of foreign forces, these were agreed upon before this Conference began and can hardly be said, therefore, to represent an advance. M. Molotov wants us to talk about broad principles which sound easy and attractive and to leave the difficult details till later. This, however, is a method of approach which could have disastrous results. I am sure that if M. Vishinsky were here he could supply a good Russian proverb explaining what happens to carts when they are put before horses. However attractive it might be to reach agreement at this point—and no one is more anxious to reach genuine agreement than we are—nevertheless, we believe that in the long run it will be better if we squarely face the facts of our disagreement and acknowledge them than to delude ourselves with false hopes and lead the people of the world to believe that there is agreement when there is no agreement.

Document No. 25

Speech by Mr. McIntosh, Acting Head of New Zealand Delegation, June 11, 1954

The lack of progress at this Conference and the failure to arrive at some common basis upon which to begin serious negotiations are matters of deep concern and disappointment to the New Zealand Government.

The attitude of New Zealand was expressed at the outset of this Conference by the leader of our delegation when he urged a liberal approach from both sides. But it is now abundantly clear that the spirit of give and take which is the essential prerequisite for any negotiation is wholly lacking. How can we on our side be expected to consider any further compromise in the means of settlement when we have been shown no movement on issues vital to the cause the members of the United Nations have pledged themselves to uphold, a cause for which their people have sacrificed their lives.

Because we realise how important it is for the peace of the Far East and for the establishment of confidence among the countries concerned with this area that a well-based settlement of the Korean problem should be reached, the New Zealand delegation have studied with great care the series of speeches made by the distinguished representatives of the Soviet Union, the People's Republic of China, and the Democratic People's Republic of Korea.

There is a great deal with which we agree in the words and proposals contained in those speeches. It is never very difficult to agree with general principles and wide aims. But some years of experience have taught the free world to look for the realities behind words and principles. Governments, like individuals, no longer trustingly sign declarations of general principles such as one finds in manifestos or peace petitions; they study them, as they must, in their context and in their historical perspective.

It is in the context of speeches spread over six weeks and the historical perspective of the attempts to unify Korea, of the aggression upon Korea, and of the implementation of the Armistice Agreement that the New Zealand Government has studied M. Molotov's request that the Conference declare its agreement upon certain principles which are basic to any Korean settlement.

As with so many communist declarations there is much with which it should be impossible to disagree. We agree and we have already stated that Korea should be a united, independent and democratic State; we agree that elections are the best way of determining the will of the people of Korea, that these elections should be conducted on a basis of secret ballot and universal suffrage, and that they should be impartially supervised; we agree that foreign forces should be withdrawn, and that the integrity of the new Korea should be guaranteed. But what service do we give to the people of Korea and to the people of the world in declaring these things again from this Conference when we know that there is fundamental disagreement, not only about the method of translating these principles into reality but even about the meaning of the principles themselves. Even the same words have different meanings according to which of us uses them.

It would be wrong to disguise the fact that this Conference is basically divided upon the central issue of any Korean settlement, which is to ensure that the Korean people are given their right to choose their future for themselves. In practical terms this means that we are in fundamental disagreement about the preparation and conduct of elections.

For several weeks the representatives of the communist countries urged that all foreign forces should be withdrawn and that the Koreans should be left alone to settle their problems for themselves. In the abstract, this was a reasonable proposal, because if Korea is to be unified it must be through agreement between the North and the South Koreans. But, it is quite obvious that it is not realistic to expect the Koreans, who have been locked together in one of the most bitter wars in history, to sit down together and produce a workable compromise. Passions just do not cool as quickly as that. As we have been glad to see, the communist countries themselves have come to recognise that some form of outside assistance or supervision is indispensable; they proposed a supervisory or assisting body (precisely what its functions should be has not been made clear) and, having changed their position, they suddenly ceased branding outside assistance as " foreign interference." That was a welcome change, but the advance seems more apparent than real.

What an inadequate form of supervision it was that the communist countries proposed. We for our part have been advocating a supervisory system which will be genuinely impartial; one which will be in a position to supervise the actual conduct of the elections throughout the country. We consider that only in these circumstances are the Korean people likely to be able to express their will freely. The communist countries, however, merely propose that an unsatisfactory outside body should give advice to the unsatisfactory all-Korean Commission.

The faults of the proposed all-Korean Commission have already been thoroughly exposed, and it is therefore necessary only to comment upon the supervisory body advocated by the communist countries. The representatives of China and the Soviet Union insist that it should be composed exactly as is the Neutral Nations Supervisory Commission which, in theory, is supervising the armistice arrangements in Korea—that is, that it should

85

consist of four such countries as Poland, Czechoslovakia, Sweden and Switzerland. This proposal must also be looked at in historical perspective. The Neutral Nations Supervisory Commission was an experiment in international co-operation, an experiment which did not work, may prove to have been disastrous, and is not likely to be repeated. There was an even rather than an odd number on the body, thus no casting vote, and hence constant deadlock. Instead of insisting that the two communist countries be balanced by two strongly non-communist countries, the United Nations negotiators at Panmunjom agreed to the Commission being completed by two genuinely neutral countries, Switzerland and Sweden. It was taken for granted that in a vote the communist countries would always support their friends; Switzerland and Sweden were expected to vote one way or the other as the facts of each issue demanded. Thus the communists would never be outvoted and could expect at times to secure a majority. Nothing could better reflect the co-operativeness and transparent honesty of the United Nations Command than their agreement to this arrangement. In fact the communist case was so bad that they seldom appear to have secured the support of the Swiss and Swedish representatives; but at least the Polish and Czech representatives were able to frustrate action, to protect their friends, and to ensure that the extensive violations of the armistice could not be revealed through a majority vote of the Commission. The Swiss and Swedish representatives were forced to expose these violations by independent reports. The representative of the People's Republic of China at the last plenary session implied that these representatives had presented a false picture and has maintained that the version of the Polish and Czech representatives is the one to be believed.

We have long noted with concern how communist countries denounce all those others which do not give them complete support. The United Nations, in accordance with its Charter found it necessary to oppose aggression in Korea committed by a communist country; as a result, the United Nations itself has been denounced by all communist countries. The Swiss and Swedish representatives adopted an attitude of impartiality; their reports were dismissed by the communist countries as erroneous. Just as it is necessary to realise the implication of the communist attempt at this Conference to discredit the United Nations and to prevent further collective security action, so we must not blind our eyes to the implications of the rejection during past months of the facts presented by such countries as Switzerland and Sweden.

Experience thus provides a clear and negative answer to the proposal that another Four-Power "Neutral Nations Supervisory Commission" be established to assist the proposed all-Korean Commission. The will of the Korean people would never be revealed through such rigged machinery.

The problem is to find a genuinely impartial supervisory body. The United Nations is capable of providing such a body. By denying the impartiality of the United Nations and by attacking the principle of collective security the communist countries have closed promising avenues of settlement. It should be remembered that the United Nations does not consist only of countries which participated in the Korean action (though the countries which did their duty under the Charter thereby lost none of their impartiality); it consists of all 60 member countries, communist and non-communist. An organisation as broadly based as the United Nations is not merely capable of providing a supervisory body which can protect the legitimate interests of all the parties to a Korean settlement; it has a right and a duty to do so. It has this right and duty because for seven years it had been charged with the problem of Korea and because the United Nations by its Charter has an overall responsibility for the maintenance of peace and security.

The United Nations need never have become an issue in this Conference. But, it seems by deliberate plan, the communist countries have made acceptance versus denial of the United Nations into the key issue both for a Korean settlement and for the reconciliation of China with the majority of the community of nations. By abandoning their perverse atttitude to the United Nations, the People's Republic of China could open up the way for a settlement of the Korean problem and of wider Far Eastern problems also. The communist inslaught upon the United Nations makes it necessary for those of us who did our duty under the Charter to uphold its authority, and we do so with firm conviction. But our interest, which is the interest of the whole United Nations, is to promote peace, international co-operation and friendly relations among states. It can therefore be taken for granted that if the other side shows an honest desire for a settlement—if it shows a willingness to reach agreement on realities and not merely on words—we for our part can see numerous possibilities opening up. The United Nations, that body of 60 nations, is unlikely to withhold its endorsement of any supervisory arrangement that is acceptable to all the members of this Conference.

These issues then—respect for the United Nations and the principle of collective security which it embodies; the need to give the Korean people a chance to declare their will freely, and, as part of this problem, the impartiality of the United Nations and the veracity of neutral non-communist countries; the question of rigged organisations as opposed to unfettered organisations—these are fundamental. It would be a disservice to pretend that there is agreement on principles when there is no agreement on the realities.

Document No. 26

Speech by Mr. Eden, Secretary of State for Foreign Affairs, June 11, 1954

I am in complete agreement with all that has been said to-day by my Commonwealth colleagues from Canada and New Zealand.

The Debate on the Korean question at this Conference has thrown into relief two fundamental issues. The first is the question of the authority of the United Nations. The United Nations enshrine the principle of collective security, and provide the machinery by which alone it can be safeguarded. The League of Nations failed because it could not act upon its principles. The United Nations have shown in Korea that they can successfully defend the victim against the aggressor. Even before the attack of June 1950, the United Nations had long been dealing with the problem of Korea. Now, since an armistice has been concluded under their authority, the United Nations are more closely concerned than ever with the peaceful solution of the Korean question. It has been said in this room that this Conference has nothing to do with the United Nations. I cannot accept that. It is only by carrying out the principles and purposes of the Charter of the United Nations that this Conference can fulfil its mandate of finding a peaceful settlement in Korea. It has also been said here that the United Nations have lost their moral authority and their competence to deal with the Korean problem impartially. The Delegation of the United Kingdom rejects this contention. We can never agree that, by taking up arms to fulfil their obligations and resist aggression, the United Nations have thereby forfeited their rights and duties as the supreme international organisation. On the contrary, we believe that they have strengthened their authority.

The second vital issue is the question of free all-Korean elections. We all say that we agree that Korea should be unified and that this unity should be brought about by means of free elections throughout the country. We do not agree on the methods and procedures for holding the elections. This is not a superficial difference; it is a difference of principle. And we have faced it before—most recently over Germany at Berlin. On our side we maintain that the elections must be a truly free expression of the will of the Korean people. To ensure this, genuinely impartial and effective international supervision of the elections is indispensable. We have proposed that this supervision should be carried out under the auspices of the United Nations, as the most appropriate body. The members of the supervisory commission could if desired be chosen from nations which did not take part in the Korean war. But in any event it is essential that the supervisory commission should be truly impartial. It must also be so composed that it can take effective decisions, and it must command the authority to carry them out.

Other proposals have been put forward which are incompatible with these principles. These proposals provide that all foreign forces should first be withdrawn, leaving a vacuum in which the two Koreas would remain confronted, unreconciled and without mediation. They contemplate that a mixed commission should be established, composed equally of representatives of these two antagonists. This commission would act only on the basis of decisions taken unanimously. Yet it is to have responsibility not only for preparing and holding the elections but also for promoting the economic and cultural unity of the two parts of the country. The effect of this proposal would be to give a veto to the Communist North-Korean minority. It is not in dispute that differences are bound to emerge between North and South Korea. If a mixed commission which could not work effectively is to have the main responsibility, must not the result be either that elections would never be held, or that they would not be free?

On May 22 the representative of the People's Republic of China put forward a proposal for a Neutral Nations Supervisory Commission. This was to assist the proposed all-Korean Commission in preparing and holding elections. But this suggestion leaves unaltered the functions and responsibilities of the all-Korean Commission, and it is to these that we object so strongly. Moreover, this supervisory commission is to be of the same type as that which in our judgment has proved unsatisfactory in supervising the armistice in Korea. That experience has convinced us that any commission composed of members one half of whom are committed to certain positions in advance is bound to lead to deadlock. Unless we can all agree, as we have hitherto failed to do, upon a genuinely impartial commission, with effective powers, there seems no hope of progress on this issue.

On June 5 the representative of the Soviet Union asked us to consider a draft proposal of five points on which we might reach agreement in principle, leaving methods and procedures for later discussion, and the representative of the Democratic People's Republic of Korea has just endorsed that proposal. But would this really help us, when we now know that it is just on the question of methods of application that the divergence of view between us is so sharp? The careful analysis of the five points of the Soviet proposal that has been made to-day by the representatives of Canada and New Zealand has shown beyond any doubt that this is so. I will not go over the same ground again. But I must emphasise that the second of these five points embodies the proposal for an all-Korean Commission on which I see no prospect of agreement here.

Therefore, as it seems to me, two issues are now clearly before us: the authority of the United Nations, and the principle of free elections. Unfortunately, no real progress has been made to bridge our differences over either of them. We have to acknowledge candidly the position in which the

Conference thus finds itself. The delegation of the United Kingdom takes its stand firmly on the two principles which we consider essential to a solution of the Korean problem. While we are ready to explore every possible means of reaching agreement, there must be some sign that agreement is possible. If no way can be found of resolving the differences of these two main issues, then we shall have to admit that this Conference has not been able to complete its task. It is our view, as members of the United Nations, that it would then be right to report back to that organisation upon the position we have reached. This would ensure that, while the existing military armistice in any event remained in force, the search for a political settlement in Korea could be resumed whenever the right moment came.

FIFTEENTH PLENARY SESSION ON KOREA

Document No. 27

Summary of the Main Speeches in the First Part of the Debate in the 15th Plenary Session on June 15, 1954

1. *Mr. Nam Il (Democratic People's Republic of Korea)* said that the non-communist countries had shown, on June 11, that they wanted to end the discussions on Korea, reopen the war and extend the Syngman Rhee régime to North Korea. It was true that there were still important differences, but they must not relax their efforts. If nothing else, the Conference could at least try to strengthen peace in Korea and help the Korean people to pass over from a state of armistice to a state of peace. He then tabled the proposal contained in Document 28.

2. *Mr. Chou En-lai (China)* said that the Conference should continue its discussion on the basis of M. Molotov's proposal of June 5. It was a common-sense procedure first to establish points of agreement or near agreement and then to consider points of disagreement. The obstructive policy of the United States was the basic reason why the Geneva Conference had so far been unable to reach agreement. Although they were unable to reach agreement now on the peaceful unification of Korea they should still strive to reach agreement on the question of consolidating peace in Korea. The Chinese delegation therefore fully supported Mr. Nam Il's proposal.

3. *M. Molotov (Soviet Union)* recalled the five basic principles that Mr. Eden had put to the Conference on May 13 and his own draft resolution of June 5 which he thought had not differed substantially in many of its points. Yet, though supported by the Chinese and North Korean delegations, the Soviet principles had been rudely rebuffed by the United Nations side which, in a series of hypothetical speeches, had produced no alternative to them. It was now clear that the United Nations side was determined to make it impossible for a solution of the Korean question to be reached on a realistic political basis. Therefore, the only alternative was to try to consolidate peace in the best way possible. It seemed that Mr. Nam Il's proposals met this need and the Soviet delegation supported them. He believed that the States participating at Geneva should also declare their recognition of the need for peaceful development in the declaration contained in Document 28.

89

**Proposal by the Delegation of the Democratic People's Republic of Korea
tabled on June 15, 1954([9])**

The states-participants in the Geneva Conference agree that they shall
continue their efforts with the view to reaching agreement on the peaceful
settlement of the Korean question on the basis of creating a united, independent and democratic Korean state.

In the interests of ensuring peaceful conditions in Korea : —

1. To recommend to the governments of the appropriate states that
measures should be taken to withdraw from the territory of Korea all foreign
armed forces as soon as possible, with the observation of the principle of
proportionality.

The time-limit for the withdrawal of foreign troops from Korea is subject
to agreement by the participants in the Geneva Conference.

2. To reduce within the period not exceeding one year the strength of the
troops of the Democratic People's Republic of Korea and the Republic of
Korea establishing the limit of troops strength for each of the sides not
exceeding 100,000 men.

3. To form from the representatives of the Democratic People's Republic
of Korea and the Republic of Korea a Commission to consider the question
of creating conditions for gradual liquidation of the state of war, of transition
of the troops of both sides to a peacetime position and to submit to the
Government of the Democratic People's Republic of Korea and to the
Government of the Republic of Korea the proposals for the conclusion of an
appropriate agreement.

4. To recognise as incompatible with the interests of the peaceful unification of Korea the existence of treaties between one or the other part of
Korea and other states in so far as such treaties involve military obligations.

5. For the purpose of creating conditions for the *rapprochement* between
North and South Korea, to form an all-Korean Committee to work out and
implement agreed measures for establishing and developing economic and
cultural relations between the Democratic People's Republic of Korea and the
Republic of Korea (trade, settlement of accounts, transport, frontier relations,
freedom of movement of the population and freedom of correspondence,
cultural and scientific relations, &c.).

6. To recognise the necessity to ensure by the states-participants in the
Geneva Conference the peaceful development of Korea and to create thereby
the conditions facilitating the speediest solution of the task of the peaceful
unification of Korea in a united, independent and democratic state.

Document No. 29

**Proposal by the Delegation of the Union of Soviet Socialist Republics,
June 15, 1954([9])**

The States participating in the Geneva Conference have agreed that,
pending the final settlement of the Korean problem on the basis of the
establishment of a united, independent and democratic state, no action shall

([9]) Text taken from the unofficial translation.

be taken which might constitute a threat to the maintenance of peace in Korea. The participants in the Conference express their confidence that the Democratic People's Republic of Korea and the Republic of Korea will act in accordance with the present declaration in the interests of peace.

Document No. 30

Proposal by the Delegation of the People's Republic of China, June 15, 1954[8]

The states participating in the Geneva Conference agree that they will continue their efforts towards achieving an agreement on the peaceful settlement of the Korean question on the basis of establishing a united, independent and democratic Korea.

As regards the question of the time and place for resuming appropriate negotiations, it shall be decided separately by the states concerned through negotiation.

Document No. 31

Speech by M. Molotov, Soviet Foreign Minister, June 15, 1954

During the examination of the Korean problem on May 13, the Head of the Delegation of the United Kingdom declared that it was necessary for us to agree on the basic principles. He then enumerated six points on which agreement was possible, citing the following points in particular:—

Elections with a view to constituting an all-Korean Government; respect for the principle of proportional representation in the elections in North and South Korea; freedom of elections assured through universal and secret suffrage; international supervision of these elections under the ægis of the United Nations Organisation; the elaboration of the conditions which must govern the withdrawal of foreign troops from Korea.

In Mr. Eden's declaration he said " If we are agreed about these five principles I have propounded, this Conference can get down to the practical business of working out the terms and stages."

On June 5, the Soviet Delegation submitted for study by the Conference, its own proposals concerning the basic principles of a solution of the Korean problem. In a whole series of points, these proposals coincided in their essentials with the proposals of the British Delegation. The Soviet draft equally puts forward five points but in a more precise and concrete fashion, as can easily be confirmed.

The Soviet proposals are characterised by the following essentials:—

(a) The organisation of all Korean elections within a period of six months, with the principle of proportional representation for the whole of Korea being respected.

(b) The creation of an all-Korean Commission, composed of representatives of North and South Korea, charged with the preparation and organisation of free all-Korean elections.

[8] Unofficial translation.

91

(c) Withdrawal of all foreign armed forces from Korea before the beginning of the elections.

(d) Creation of an International Commission for the control and conduct of the all-Korean elections.

(e) Recognition of the necessity for certain obligations concerning the peaceful development of Korea to be undertaken by the States most directly interested in the maintenance of peace in the Far East.

In making these proposals, the Soviet Delegation also indicated the existence of a certain reconciliation between the points of view concerning the basic principles on which a peaceful solution in Korea must be based, as well as the existence of disagreement on a series of questions in suspense. At the same time it emphasised that it shared the point of view of the British Delegation, that it was opportune to define the basic principles of an agreement on the Korean problem.

What would be the significance of the adoption, with possible amendments, of the proposals which have been submitted to the Conference by the Soviet Delegation?

There is no doubt that such a decision taken by the Conference would constitute a step forward towards the re-establishment of the national unity of Korea. The adoption of the five Soviet proposals, to which the necessary corrections could be made, would, doubtless, not solve the problem of unification of Korea but they would contribute to the preparation of a decision in this sense, which might be completed in due course.

The proposals of the Soviet Delegation were fully approved by the People's Democratic Republic of Korea as well as by the People's Republic of China. However, in the examination of them they met a brutal refusal from the countries represented at this Conference who, under the flag of the United Nations Organisation, waged war for three years in Korea. As for this group of states, it is clear that at the present moment there is no desire to find a way to a concerted agreement between all the countries taking part in the Geneva Conference, even if only to take a step forward in order to facilitate the reconstitution of Korean unity. The hypocritical and the pharisaical speeches directed against the communist states cannot hide this simple fact. It is the only explanation that can be found for the fact that these states not only did not wish to recognise the just character of the Soviet proposals, but also did not wish to make any other proposals which would facilitate the re-establishment of national unity in Korea.

The principal speaker on the subject of the Soviet proposals was the representative of Canada on June 11. This speech, which contains so many passages which have nothing to do with the affair and which are quite out of place in connexion with the Soviet proposals, can only be considered as an attempt to spread confusion concerning the problem under discussion. However, the representative of Canada drew a conclusion personal to himself and of which it is easy to understand the sense. He finished his speech saying "in the long run it will be better if we squarely face the facts of our disagreement and acknowledge them than to delude ourselves with false hopes and lead the peoples of the world to believe that there is agreement when there is no agreement."

One conclusion only can be drawn from these words of the representative of Canada: that is that we must renounce all attempts to find an agreement even on certain basic principles which might lead to the solution of the present problem, since an agreement of this sort cannot be achieved. Public opinion must not be misled by the search for such an agreement.

Why then, in this case, did the representative of Canada say nothing about the proposal of the British Delegation on May 13, a proposal which equally contained the idea of agreement on the basic principles and which considered such an agreement to be extremely desirable?

If the representative of Canada made allusion to the fact that one should not mislead public opinion by proposals which would show that certain dispositions are not recognised by all the countries taking part in the Geneva Conference, one must ask whether he would include the proposals on basic principles put forward by the British Delegation. To be convincing one should stick to a certain logic.

On June 11, the Head of the French Delegation associated himself with the representative of Canada's statement. However, he, himself, made a proposal concerning the Korean problem, a proposal which contained five principal points. The majority of these points resemble, more or less, the proposals of both the Soviet Delegation and the British Delegation. However, the French Delegation, as well as the Canadian Delegation, consider that it is not inopportune to allude to the adoption by the Geneva Conference of general principles concerning the Korean problem.

One might ask if the French Delegation takes its own five points concerning the general principles of the Korean problem seriously.

The Head of the Belgian Delegation, M. Spaak, has just said that the proposals of the Soviet Delegation would result in terrible consequences for the United Nations Organisation, that they would even be fatal for this Organisation.

All these frightening statements were made only because the Soviet proposal concerning the creation of an International Commission for the control of all-Korean elections did not propose that this Commission should be nominated by the United Nations Organisation. However, M. Spaak seems to forget that when the Geneva Conference, in which he is participating, was convoked, we acted without the United Nations Organisation. Now none of us considered, nor do we consider, this to be acceptable.

In his statement of June 11, the Head of the British Delegation no longer remembered the five essential principles of the Korean problem which he announced on May 13. As he said he concerned himself then only with two problems: The authority of the United Nations Organisation and the principle of free elections.

It is clear that none of those who participate at the Geneva Conference would deny that a great price should be attached—and that not only in terms of words but also in deeds—to the authority of the United Nations Organisation, even as much as to the necessity of respecting the principle of free elections in Korea.

A certain number of other delegations also called for the rejection of the proposals of the Soviet Delegation, setting themselves up on their own authority as defenders of the United Nations Organisation.

It only remains for me to draw the attention of the Conference once more to the fact that there are different ways of defending the authority of the United Nations Organisation and that not every defence employed to that end enhances this authority.

In the course of the Korean war, the flag of the United Nations Organisation was used, under pressure from aggressive circles in the United States, to the detriment of the principles of the Charter of the same Organisation. Now, it is impossible to strengthen the authority of this International Organisation by means of this kind. The Soviet Union has always considered—and does so still—that the authority of United Nations should not be undermined by violations of the United Nations Charter and should not be debased by the use of this International Organisation in the interests of any aggressive group of states.

As far as the principle of free all-Korean elections is concerned, the Soviet proposals fully assure respect for this principle. None of those who have spoken against the Soviet proposals have been able, in any measure, to lessen the justice of these proposals as far as the principle of freedom of elections is concerned.

The most violent attacks have been directed against the proposal to create an all-Korean Commission composed of representatives of North and South Korea in order to prepare for and to organise these elections.

However, the fact of opposing the creation of an all-Korean organism for the organisation of these elections shows a lack of respect for the rights of the Korean people, since an undertaking such as all-Korean elections, must clearly be in Korean hands—in the hands of the Korean people themselves.

Whatever the motives given for such a refusal, they constitute an attempt to impose on North Korea the régime of Syngman Rhee existing in South Korea, a régime which, as everyone knows, has taken three years to establish itself. In consequence the refusal to create an all-Korean Organisation for the good conduct of free elections in Korea constitutes an artificial means of undermining the possibility of proceeding to all-Korean elections.

The attempts made to refer the question of all-Korean elections to the United Nations Organisation, which has acted in Korea as a belligerent and which in consequence has no moral right to function as an impartial organisation for the solution of the Korean problem, are clearly without justification. These attempts cannot rid of their responsibility, those who do not wish to make even a first step for the preparation of national unity in Korea, a unity based on acceptable conditions for the whole population both in the North and in the South.

The discussion has shown that at present the majority of countries participating in the Geneva Conference make an agreement on the first measures to be taken to re-establish national unity in Korea impossible. Nevertheless the Soviet Delegation will continue to attempt to ensure that no possibilities will be neglected for reaching an agreement on the peaceful settlement of the Korean problem based on the creation of a united, independent and democratic Korean state.

We consider that in the present conditions, that which will contribute the most towards the re-establishment of national unity in Korea will be the creation of the necessary conditions for the strengthening of the peaceful development of North and South Korea. The proposals which have been made to-day by the Delegation of the People's Republic of Korea are in conformity with this object and are designed to create durable conditions of peace in Korea.

In consequence the Soviet Delegation supports both the proposal which would establish as short a delay as possible for the withdrawal of all foreign armed forces from Korea and the proposal designed to reduce the strength of the armed forces of North and South Korea. Such proposals may be displeasing to the supporters of Syngman Rhee in Korea but there is no doubt that these proposals are in conformity with the interests of the Korean people and that they serve the cause of the consolidation of peace between nations of the world.

The Soviet Delegation equally supports the proposal that a Commission composed of representatives of the People's Democratic Republic of Korea and of the Republic of Korea should be formed to examine the problem of the progressive abolition of the state of war in Korea, and of the maintenance of the armed forces of the two parties in peacetime.

The adoption of such a decision would result in not only the improvement of the economic situation of the Korean people, both in the North and

South, but would also be of great importance to the strengthening of peace throughout the Far East.

Equally, the Soviet Delegation fully supports the demand of the People's Democratic Republic of Korea that the Government of the United States of America and of other countries should abolish the illegal measures of blockade and embargo directed against the People's Democratic Republic of Korea, and which run counter, not only to the elementary rules of international law, but also constitute a crime against the Korean people.

It would be completely right that the Conference should recognise as incompatible with the work of the peaceful unification of Korea, the existence of agreements between one or other party in Korea and other states—agreements involving military obligations. In this respect it is impossible not to observe that the Treaty of so-called " mutual defence " concluded between the United States of America and South Korea is completely contrary to the interests of the Korean people. This agreement provides for the maintenance of American armed forces on the territory of South Korea for an indefinite period. In other words, this agreement signifies a military occupation of Korean territory by foreign troops. This agreement is designed, not to permit a peaceful settlement of the Korean problem, but to facilitate aggressive plans designed to launch Korea into new military ventures. One can only admit that the aggressive circles in the United States are transforming South Korea into a spring-board for a new war in the Far East. The incompatibility of agreements of this kind with the interests of the Korean people is clear. At the same time the Soviet Delegation supports the proposal for the creation of an all Korean commission for the preparation and execution of concerted measures designed to establish and develop economic and cultural relations between the People's Democratic Republic of Korea and the Republic of Korea.

To deny the necessity of measures of this kind is to be opposed to a *rapprochement* between South Korea and North Korea and makes it more difficult to prepare the conditions necessary for the reconstitution of the unity of the Korean people. It is important that the states taking part in the Conference at Geneva should make a special declaration by which they recognise the necessity of the peaceful development of Korea. There is no doubt that international assistance of this kind would receive a favourable welcome and general support from the Korean people. This recognition by other states would help to create the necessary conditions for a more rapid solution of the problem of the peaceful unification of Korea, and of the creation of a united, independent and democratic state.

In order to complete the proposals which have been put forward to-day by the People's Democratic Republic of Korea, the Soviet Delegation submits for study by the Conference, the following draft of a joint declaration by all the countries taking part in the Conference:—

" Declaration on the Korean Question

The States taking part in the Geneva Conference have agreed that, pending the final settlement on the Korean question on the basis of the establishment of a united, independent and democratic Korean state, no action of any kind shall be taken which might constitute a threat to the maintenance of peace in Korea.

The participants in the Conference express their confidence that both the Democratic People's Republic of Korea and the Republic of Korea will act in accordance with the present declaration in the interests of the people."

The Soviet Delegation considers that every measure taken by the Geneva Conference to strengthen the eventual peaceful development of Korea is of great importance and at the same time will permit the reduction of international tension and the strengthening of universal peace.

Document No. 32

Summary of remaining Speeches, June 15, 1954

Mr. Bedell Smith (United States), referring to the draft declaration proposed by the representative of the Soviet Union, recalled that the Korean Armistice Agreement, and paragraph 62 in particular, contained specific provisions for its continuance. The General Assembly resolutions of August 28, 1953, approved the Armistice Agreement. The Armistice Agreement and the United Nations resolutions supporting it provided in much more formal and exact terms for the maintenance of peace than did M. Molotov's proposal.

2. *Mr. Casey (Australia)* said that Mr. Nam Il's six-point proposal reflected a familiar communist technique of putting forward proposals appearing on the surface designed to achieve peace, which would in fact deliver the country concerned bound and gagged to communism. He believed and thought that many of his colleagues would believe that the proposal did not represent a basis on which further discussions would be fruitful. It put the sovereign and lawful Government of the Republic of Korea on a par with the communist aggressor régime in the north. The Conference should not agree to strip the Republic of Korea of its defences in the face of aggression. Mr. Nam Il's proposal sought in effect to isolate the Republic of Korea from its treaty access to its friends, while implying no close treaty link between the Government of North Korea and the Government of the People's Republic of China. He believed the proposal was designed to confuse world opinion and to make the peoples of the world forget that the communists had frustrated the purpose of the Conference by refusing to agree to the unification of Korea on a just and honourable basis, in accordance with United Nations principles. He did not believe that it contained anything new which could justify the reopening of discussions. He would find it difficult to accept the second part of M. Molotov's proposal, which called for a declaration that the participants in the Conference expressed their confidence that both the People's Democratic Republic of Korea and the Republic of Korea should act in accordance with the present declaration in the interests of peace. He thought all could be reasonably certain that that sentiment applied to the Republic of Korea, but he would not like to take responsibility for its applicability to the Government of the People's Democratic Republic of Korea.

3. *Mr. Garcia (Philippines)* said that the speeches and declarations just heard from the delegates of Communist countries contained nothing new. They were still insisting on the so-called all-Korean Commission. They also insisted that the United Nations had no authority to intervene in Korea, they called the exercise by the United Nations of the world police power to repel aggression in Korea an illegal act of belligerence, and they insisted that the resolutions of the United Nations on the Korean question were illegal. As a matter of fact, all propositions, old and new, by all communist countries, were premised on the repudiation of the authority of the United Nations to exercise its fundamental function in achieving world collective security. The position of the Sixteen nations, on the other hand, had

clearly been that to achieve the unity and peace of Korea it was essential that recognition of the authority of the United Nations to maintain collective security should be upheld, and that the legality of all its resolutions and actions in Korea should be fully recognised and accepted. He expressed willingness to continue negotiations as long as desired. But further negotiation would serve no useful purpose unless the communist countries accepted the fundamental principles of respect for the United Nations and free elections.

4. *M. Spaak (Belgium)* said that three points made in the speeches from the Communist countries required to be taken up: first, that the only aim of the Sixteen was to subject North Korea to South Korea; secondly, that they wished to put an end to the Conference; and thirdly, that M. Molotov's proposals had not been seriously considered. On the first point, the intention was to provide means for the Korean people to express their will freely in accordance with democratic principles. Secondly, it was better for the peace of the world, and perhaps for the success of a future conference, at times to have the courage to face the facts. Thirdly, the meeting on June 11 had been devoted to an examination of M. Molotov's proposal and to refuting certain of the ideas which it contained. At that meeting two fundamental questions had been put (the authority of the United Nations and free elections). The Sixteen nations could not conceive of the unification of Korea without free elections. The speeches heard that afternoon had given no reply or clarification on the two questions. He was convinced that at the present time what was at stake was the possibility of the continuation in the world of a policy of collective security and, what was more, the very existence of the United Nations. Hopes had been completely disappointed, and the Conference had made no progress. He would not reply to the new proposal made by Mr. Nam Il, which he thought even worse than the earlier proposals. The representatives of the United Nations at the Conference could not agree to settle the question of the withdrawal of forces without any guarantee for the political future of Korea. Therefore, one of the Sixteen would read shortly a declaration which would be considered as a final declaration of the Conference. The intention of the Sixteen must be clearly understood. They did not consider that the negotiations on Korea were finally and completely broken off and that there was no hope of reaching an agreement. But first, they wished to report to the United Nations. Public opinion must not think that the failure of the Geneva Conference meant the resumption of fighting in Korea. He had noted with real satisfaction the supplementary proposal made by the delegate of the Soviet Union at the end of his speech and thought that this declaration would make a good impression on the world. He would have been ready to vote in favour of this resolution if the representative of the United States had not shown that the object in view was better covered by the Armistice Agreement. It was better to refer to the Armistice Agreement than to try to find a new wording. But he was glad in any case that M. Molotov's proposal, either textually or in spirit, should receive the unanimous approval at the Conference. Finally, he thought we should not separate without declaring that nothing had been lost. He thought that in course of time the participants would be able to meet again and that the work of the past weeks would not have been completely useless. Certain principles had been elaborated which required further reflection. All this would not have been unfruitful, and he hoped that soon there would be the possibility of a further meeting to re-examine the conditions in which the wish of all at the Conference could be realised: A unified, independent and democratic Korea.

5. *Mr. Pyun* (*Republic of Korea*) said that the three communist speeches that afternoon had put forward specious plans which aimed at the perpetuation of the division of the country.

6. *Prince Wan* (*Thailand*) then read the text of the Declaration of the Sixteen (Document No. 30).

7. *M. Molotov* (*Soviet Union*) said that the Sixteen nations had refused to accept the Soviet Union's proposals and at the same time were unable to put forward other proposals on the general principles on which the Conference should reach agreement. Moreover, the proposals which these delegations had previously put forward had suddenly disappeared from circulation. They were no more seen, no more heard. He did not know for what reason, but it was an important fact which should be noted. From the course of the discussions it appeared that the Sixteen delegations had sought to use the Geneva Conference to impose the anti-popular South Korean régime on North Korea. These attempts had not succeeded. Therefore they did not wish any agreement on this question. The Conference had also examined a second problem, the strengthening of peace in Korea. The Six-Point Proposal presented by the People's Democratic Republic of Korea, which had this as its aim, had been turned down by the representative of the United States and by those who supported him. The meaning of Mr. Casey's declaration was clearly that he would not study any question the reply to which might constitute a step forward and might contribute towards an improvement in the conditions of peace in Korea. He only wanted to bury the Korean question as quickly as possible. Mr. Bedell Smith had asked why the Soviet delegation's draft declaration was necessary in view of Article 62 of the Armistice Agreement. But there was not only an Armistice Agreement, but also a Geneva Conference, which has the task of examining the Korean problem and trying to solve it. The participants in the Conference declared officially that they were in favour of the Armistice Agreement. That they wished the armistice to be enduring and stable, and that they were all in favour of the maintenance of the armistice. In view of bellicose statements from South Korea, preaching an offensive against the People's Democratic Republic of Korea, it was not surprising that the Soviet delegation had spoken in favour of the consolidation of peace in Korea. To the declaration of the Sixteen, the Soviet delegation replied that that declaration did not contain any reply to the question whether its authors really wished to contribute to the re-establishment of the national unity of Korea. There was not one word in the declaration which could be considered as favourable to the cause of peace. The Soviet Union had always been, and would continue to be, on the side of the democratic forces of the Korean people, who wished for early unification in conditions of independence and democracy. It was true that the Soviet Union did not accept that the unity of Korea should be brought about on the conditions dictated by Mr. Syngman Rhee. It was true that the Soviet delegation was ready to work with other delegations and governments for the democratic evolution of Korea, for the true unification of Korea in the interest of the people in the country, and for the consolidation of peace in Korea.

8. *Mr. Chou En-lai* (*China*) said that his delegation could not agree to the attitude and position manifested in the declaration by the Sixteen. Since the Conference had been convened on the basis of the Agreement of the Berlin Conference, it had nothing to do with the United Nations. The People's Republic of China had been deprived of its legitimate rights and rightful place in the United Nations. The declaration of the Sixteen categorically announced the intention to terminate the Conference. The Chinese delegation

could not but feel deep regret at this. The Chinese delegation fully supported M. Molotov's proposed declaration. It was their deep regret that even such a proposal to express the common desire of the Conference had been rejected by the United States delegate. To attempt to justify rejection of the proposal by paragraph 62 of the Korean Armistice Agreement was untenable because the Armistice Agreement bound only the two belligerent States in Korea, whereas the Geneva Conference had been convened on a broader basis and must have its own agreement. The United States delegate and his followers were not only bent on obstrucing the peaceful unification of Korea, but were also intent on preventing the Geneva Conference from reaching any agreement on the question of the preservation and consolidation of peace in Korea. The Chinese delegation considered that despite that situation the Conference still had the obligation to reach certain agreements on the peaceful settlement of the Korean question. It should be the common desire of the Conference to continue their efforts towards an agreement on a peaceful settlement of the Korean question on the basis of establishing a united, independent and democratic Korea. For this reason the Chinese delegation made the following proposal: —

"The states participating in the Geneva Conference agree that they will continue their efforts towards achieving an agreement on the peaceful settlement of the Korean question on the basis of establishing a united, independent and democratic Korea. As regards the question of the time and the place for resuming appropriate negotiations, it shall be decided separately by the states concerned through negotiations."

If even such a proposal were to be rejected, such a spirit of refusing to negotiate, of refusing to make conciliations, would leave a most unfavourable impression.

9. *Mr. Nam Il (Democratic People's Republic of Korea)* said that all the proposals put forward by the People's Republic of Korea had been rejected without justification. This showed that the only object was to put an end to the negotiations. It amounted to a rejection of every proposal designed to re-establish peace in Korea. The responsibility for the rupture of the negotiations rested with the Sixteen Powers which had published the declaration. In conclusion, the delegation of the Democratic People's Republic of Korea fully supported the proposal just put forward by the representative of the People's Republic of China.

10. *Prince Wan (Thailand)* denied and rejected categorically the statement that the Sixteen had taken the initiative in breaking off the Conference. They would continue to work for the peaceful unification of Korea on the basis of the two fundamental principles set forth in the declaration.

11. *M. Spaak (Belgium)* said that the two proposals put forward by M. Molotov and Mr. Chou En-lai were in no way contradictory to the declaration of the Sixteen. None of the Sixteen intended that any action should be undertaken which could call in question the conditions of the Armistice or which could lead to the rupture of the Armistice, with the resumption of hostilities in Korea. M. Molotov's declaration was contained in the Sixteen Nation declaration and did not have to be repeated. The same was true of Mr. Chou En-lai's proposal. He had already said that if the participants in the Conference separated, it should not be considered a final separation, and that, on the contrary, it was to be hoped that they would meet again to discuss their common aim in better circumstances. The fact that M. Molotov's and Mr. Chou En-lai's proposals had not been agreed to did not amount to any sort of rejection of the ideas which they expressed. These ideas were contained in the declaration of the Sixteen.

12. *M. Molotov (Soviet Union)* gave full support to Mr. Chou En-lai's proposal.

13. *Lord Reading (United Kingdom)* regretted that it had not been possible to make more progress, but as the declaration issued by the Sixteen showed, they had done everything possible to produce a favourable result. If that result had not been attained, that did not mean that hope was abandoned for the future. The sentiments expressed by M. Spaak on the possibility of more propitious development in the future were common to all his colleagues who had put their names to the declaration which had been read.

14. *Mr. Chou En-lai (China)* did not agree that his last proposal was included in the Korean Armistice Agreement. There was there no provision that agreement should be reached by the States participating in the Geneva Conference to express their desire to continue their efforts for a peaceful settlement of the Korean question. The delegation of the People's Republic of China had brought with it the spirit of negotiation and conciliation to participate for the first time in this international Conference. If the last proposal which they had put forward was to be rejected by the states concerned on the side of the United Nations, the Chinese delegation could not but regard that fact with the greatest regret.

15. *The Chairman (Mr. Eden)* said that he would say a few words and try to give a ruling, to which perhaps all could adhere. He suggested that the Conference could not adopt any of the various drafts that had been submitted as representing the collective agreement of the Conference; but they, together with the statements which had been made, would now form part of the record of the Conference. That was the ruling which he suggested should be adopted. It seemed the only thing to be done, since in the Conference there was no voting. He thought it met the points that had been made. If there were no objection, he would only like to repeat once more his own personal hope that the day might come soon when the Conference's task, its joint task, could be carried through to a successful conclusion.

16. The Chairman then declared the meeting closed at 8·40 p.m.

Document No. 33

Declaration by the Sixteen Nations, June 15, 1954

Pursuant to the Resolution of August 28, 1953, of the United Nations General Assembly, and the Berlin communiqué of February 18, 1954, we, as nations who contributed military forces to the United Nations Command in Korea, have been participating in the Geneva Conference for the purpose of establishing a united and independent Korea by peaceful means.

We have made a number of proposals and suggestions in accord with the past efforts of the United Nations to bring about the unification, independence and freedom of Korea; and within the framework of the following two principles which we believe to be fundamental :—

1. The United Nations, under its Charter, is fully and rightfully empowered to take collective action to repel aggression, to restore peace and security, and to extend its good offices to seeking a peaceful settlement in Korea.

2.   In order to establish a unified, independent and democratic Korea, genuinely free elections should be held under United Nations supervision, for representatives in the National Assembly, in which representation shall be in direct proportion to the indigenous population in Korea.

We have earnestly and patiently searched for a basis of agreement which would enable us to proceed with Korean unification in accordance with these fundamental principles.

The communist delegations have rejected our every effort to obtain agreement.   The principal issues between us therefore are clear.   Firstly, we accept and assert the authority of the United Nations.   The communists repudiate and reject the authority and competence of the United Nations in Korea and have labelled the United Nations itself as the tool of aggression. Were we to accept this position of the communists, it would mean the death of the principle of collective security and of the United Nations itself. Secondly, we desire genuinely free elections.   The communists insist upon procedures which would make genuinely free elections impossible.   It is clear that the communists will not accept impartial and effective supervision of free elections.   Plainly, they have shown their intention to maintain communist control over North Korea.   They have persisted in the same attitudes which have frustrated United Nations efforts to unify Korea since 1947.

We believe, therefore, that it is better to face the fact of our disagreement than to raise false hopes and mislead the peoples of the world into believing that there is agreement where there is none.

In the circumstances we have been compelled reluctantly and regretfully to conclude that, so long as the communist delegations reject the two fundamental principles which we consider indispensable, further consideration and examination of the Korean question by the Conference would serve no useful purpose.   We reaffirm our continued support for the objectives of the United Nations in Korea.

In accordance with the Resolution of the General Assembly of the United Nations of August 28, 1953, the member states parties to this Declaration will inform the United Nations concerning the proceedings at this Conference.

Geneva, June 15, 1954.

For Australia :

R. G. CASEY.

For Belgium :

P. H. SPAAK.

For Canada :

C. A. RONNING.

For Colombia :

FRANCISCO URRUTIA.

101

For Ethiopia:
>Z. G. HEYWOT.

For France:
>JEAN CHAUVEL.

For Greece:
>JEAN KINDYNIS.

For Luxembourg:
>J. STURM

For the Netherlands:
>A. BENTINCK.

For New Zealand:
>A. D. McINTOSH.

For the Philippines:
>CARLOS P. GARCIA.

For the Republic of Korea:
>Y. T. PYUN.

For Thailand:
>WAN WAITHAYAKON.

For Turkey:
>M. C. ACIKALIN

For the United Kingdom:
>ANTHONY EDEN.

For the United States of America:
>WALTER BEDELL SMITH.

PART II

INDO-CHINA

INTRODUCTION

In the communiqué issued by the Foreign Ministers of the United States, France, the United Kingdom and the Soviet Union at the end of their Conference in Berlin between January 25 and February 18, 1954([2]), they announced their agreement that the problem of restoring peace in Indo-China would be discussed at the Conference to be convened in Geneva on April 26. Representatives of the United States, France, the United Kingdom, the Union of Soviet Socialist Republics, the People's Republic of China and other interested States were to be invited to this phase of the Conference.

The Conference opened in Geneva on April 26 and, following preliminary consultations on the question of the other participants to be invited, the first plenary session on the Indo-China question was held on May 8. Nine Delegations took part in the meetings. To date there have been seven plenary sessions of the Conference and a larger number of restricted meetings have also been held. On May 29, as a result of proposals the Secretary of State for Foreign Affairs had put forward in restricted session, the Conference announced that talks between the military representatives of France and the Democratic Republic of Viet Nam would begin at once.

Part II of this White Paper contains a selection of speeches made and documents tabled in the Indo-China plenary sessions of the Conference. The proceedings at restricted sessions are of a confidential character.

Foreign Office,
June, 1954.

([2]) " Miscellaneous No. 5 (1954)," Cmd. 9080.

LIST OF COUNTRIES REPRESENTED AT THE INDO-CHINA PHASE OF THE GENEVA CONFERENCE

Cambodia.

Democratic Republic of Viet Nam.

France.

Laos.

People's Republic of China.

State of Viet Nam.

Union of Soviet Socialist Republics.

United Kingdom of Great Britain and Northern Ireland.

United States of America.

Document No. 1

Speech by M. Bidault, Foreign Minister of the French Republic, May 8, 1954

Mr. Chairman, at the outset of this Conference I should like to describe its dramatic prelude and the most cruel battle in a fight that has been carried on for seven years. This broke loose after Berlin on February 18. The Conference of Four Ministers of Foreign Affairs had adopted a resolution which brought about the first light of hope for the restoration of peace in Indo-China.([2]) The decisive assault of a deplorably unequal fight, which lasted for fifty-five days, took place on the very eve of the date which had been earmarked for this meeting in Geneva, and the prospect for which alone should normally muzzle the guns. Thus, that bloody event takes place between two meetings both of which are to be placed under the sign of the relaxation of tension. We have already had an experience of sudden slaughter immediately after such peaceful negotiations—an experience that actions can so cruelly disprove words. And it is- not on our side that was wanted, when the peace was spoken about, a hardening of the fight, going so far as preventing the wounded being evacuated contrary to the laws of war and to the principles of the civilised world. The outcome of the Battle of Dien Bien Phu had been announced yesterday by the Commander-in-Chief in these words: " The garrison of Dien Bien Phu has fulfilled its task which has been given to it by the command." The French Delegation cannot conceal here its deep emotion and its pride in the face of the heroism of the soldiers and the troops of France, of the Viet Nam, and ot all of the French Union who have resisted beyond human endurance.

Such events dictate imperiously to the French Delegation its line of behaviour and conduct in the negotiations which are about to start. These negotiations are pre-conditioned by two terms of equal firmness: To insure the restoration of Indo-China to peace, which would be both lasting and fair; and to accompany this peace with the necessary guarantees so that peace could not be threatened afresh.

The responsibilities that we have assumed, the part we take in the conflict which had been imposed upon us in Indo-China, the close ties by which we are united with the peoples and the independent Governments of Viet Nam, Cambodia, and Laos, those are our titles to open this debate, which is of such paramount importance to peace, and from which we hope an acceptable solution will stem, and a solution acceptable to all. We have met here in order to try to obtain results that will be both practicable and concrete, and also in order to put an end to hostilities. No effort will be spared on our part in order to obtain solutions that would be based on reason and equity which are to be found if one genuinely and really wishes, as issued in the Berlin communiqué, the restoration of peace.

If we wish to discover the elements and the prospects of such settlement it is necessary, in the first place, that we should consider the over-all problems. Once those have been delineated I shall say how the French Delegation considers that we should work, if this Conference wishes to obtain results that would be speedy; that we all wish, so that bloodshed should stop at long last.

We have heard repeatedly about Asia in the course of the general debate on Korea. I may say that the way in which certain delegations consider this problem appears to me unilateral in its nature. We have heard statements

([2]) "Miscellaneous No. 5 (1954)," Cmd. 9080.

here to the effect that Asia—a scene of upheavals, the scope and magnitude of which can be noted by all—had now been engaged on the path upon which it had been thrown by the Revolution of 1917 in Russia. If I understand it correctly, this means that inevitably the peoples of Asia will be led to establishing régimes similar to that of the Soviet Union. If this point of view is really that which is being held by some of my colleagues, it seems to me that such a view would be rather bold, or, to repeat, expressions that we have already heard, one which is contrary to facts—the facts show, in fact, that the peoples of Asia, who enjoy independence, have been able to accede to it with the agreement and in accordance with the decision of Powers which are being paradoxically described as imperialists. On the contrary, everywhere where the so-called " popular régime " had been installed it can be established only as a consequence of several wars, or as a consequence of occupation by foreign armies. I believe that this ought to be recalled rather than distort history. It is highly desirable, in fact, that this Conference should avoid engaging in too ideological discussions, which would merely serve as a prevention to the obtaining of possible solutions and would merely strengthen and harden the specific positions. If, indeed, we refer to agreement and at the same time accept only unilateral solution; if, in order to obtain the triumph of that solution and of that solution alone, the war is being pursued which has no independence as its goal, since independence has already been completed, but it is rather for the purpose of domination and oppression; if, finally, at the very time when the hope of a pacific and peaceful negotiation appears, the fight is being intensified with the support of more considerable armament from a well-known source, obstacles are being accumulated on the road towards justice, freedom and peace.

In order to solve this problem correctly, I believe it is necessary that I should recall certain facts and certain circumstances. On the eve of the Second World War the States and the countries of Indo-China had been in all respects in the processes of development. The population had risen gradually from 16 to 26 million inhabitants in the course of the last 30 years. The efforts that have been made in order to develop the country have brought about an increase in the production of the main goods through the construction of a network of communications, hydro-electric plants, processing industries, &c. Two million hectares of fallow land have thus been turned into fertile fields in Cochin-China. The production of rice exceeded six million tons. Considerable work had been done in order to save the population from natural scourges and from a period of epidemics. Indo-China thus stood on the way toward modern civilisation which called, within necessary solidarities, for full sovereignty and independence.

The world war slowed down that development and the Japanese coup in 1945 stopped it altogether. As war came to an end and on the departure of those troops which had been called upon to disarm the Japanese, we could have hoped that peace would be rapidly restored and that progress should be renewed. But a plot took place.

In the beginning of August, 1945, in North Viet Nam and under the chairmanship of Ho Chi-Minh, a committee of 10 members had been set up, all of them belonging to the Communist Party and which a few days later had set up in Hanoi a provisional government through the adjunction to minor positions of certain foreign people who were not members of that party.

France, desirous of favouring the return of peace, had in the course of 1946 negotiated with the Vietminh in the spirit of complete and constant good faith. However, by the end of 1946 the break which would have been wanted by the Vietminh, first of all, resulted in slaughter and then in fight. The war had started in Indo-China. That war, the Vietminh had alleged, had started under the guise of independence. However, France had asserted as early as

1945 its will that the people of the peninsula should succeed to independence and to freedom. Without the war Cambodia and Laos have been able to develop normally and under the very best conditions. As early as 1946 both of these countries have been able to adopt democratic constitutions. They passed general elections. Their independence has been consecrated by treaties which have been signed with France.

In Viet Nam, and in spite of the war, France has been able to keep its promises and full independence has been recognised and has become effective. Thirty-five free countries, by recognising those three States, and a number of international organisations by accepting them in their midst, have consecrated that independence. The national Government of Viet Nam has been able to set up an administration to organise its finance, to develop its economy, to establish diplomatic relations with the main free countries. It built up an army. All those elements mean sovereignty.

However, the war that Vietminh had stated it leads for the independence of Viet Nam is continuing. It has now spread to the neighbouring States. Cambodia and Laos, who were living peacefully under the authority of Governments that their population had freely elected, have been already for one year the subject of characterised aggression on the part of the foreign troops of Vietminh.

On April 2 last, that is on the very eve of this meeting of the Conference at Geneva, the new aggression committed against Cambodia took place. The increasing assistance given by the Communist countries to the Vietminh army has allowed for developing without ceasing their spirit of domination.

The true nature of the war in Indo-China no longer appears as clearly as before. The independence of those States is not at stake. The attempt at present is made to grab the resources and to rule the peoples of Asia. The free nations cannot be deceived. They know that the free States of Indo-China and France are fighting for the cause of liberty. On our side, we are thinking in terms of defence and not of a crusade. And that is why the will of peace of France and of the Associated States has not waited for the meeting of a Conference in Berlin in order to manifest itself. Long before that date, and for the last time as soon as the prospects of an Armistice in Korea had become a likelihood, the French Government had expressed a desire to see to it that that peace should spread through contagion and that it should not be concentrated in one particular point in Asia. It was necessary, however, to wait still for many months; it was necessary that great efforts and patient efforts had to take place before decisions be made and that a Conference be convened which would be entrusted with, not in order to examine all the problems of the world as it was proposed but rather to bring a real positive contribution to peace through trying to find a solution to the problem of Korea and putting an end to the hostilities in Indo-China.

The French Government is thus confident that it has done everything in its power to put an end to the conflict. Not only has it removed all reason for this conflict to exist by recognising fully and unreservedly the independence of Viet Nam, Laos and Cambodia but, furthermore, the French Government has manifested for a long time its readiness and its desire of obtaining a reasonable settlement which would allow for the hostilities to be brought to an end. This is the main and primary task assigned to this Conference.

As to the political problems, the Governments of the three States competent in this regard will have to tell us how they visualise the solution of the problems where they arise once the war has been terminated.

In order to get out of the present war situation, the French Delegation, sure that it is responding to the profoundly felt feelings of the peoples cruelly tried, and by all peace-loving countries, believes that it is our duty to suggest the following method which seems to us the most appropriate with a view to bringing about a rapid agreement along the lines desired.

We propose that the Conference should, first of all, declare that it adopt the principle of a general cessation of hostilities in Indo-China based upon the necessary guarantees of security, these terms of the principles thus enunciated being inseparable in our mind and in our resolution.

The necessary guarantees are required to preserve the security of the troops of the parties involved and for the protection of the civil populations from abusive exploitation of the suspension of hostilities. The measures of implementation will have to be established once this principle has been adopted. It will immediately be seen that the situation does not present itself in exactly the same way to the States concerned. And it will be wise, therefore, to take account of these differences. In two of these States, Laos and Cambodia, the problem is clear. There, there is no civil war but an invasion, without motive and without a declaration of war, an invasion which furthermore threatens the neighbouring countries.

The solution consists therefore in agreeing upon the withdrawal of the invading forces and the restoration of the territorial integrity of those States. In order that the implementation of this agreement may be uncontested and in order that the application of it may go forward without hindrance, a system of International Supervision is called for. On such bases, the Conference can in a very short time ensure, on conditions in conformity with equity, the restoration of peace in Laos and Cambodia.

In Viet Nam the situation is very different and more complex. There, there is a civil war in reality. For France, there is a Viet Nam State of which the unity, territorial integrity and independence must be respected. With the presence at this Conference of a party which, in order to fight against this State, has organised armed forces, has been admitted as a necessity with a view to bringing about a cessation of hostilities, this presence must not be interpreted as implying on our side any kind of recognition. The situation thus defined makes it necessary to provide for a transitional phase in the course of which, hostilities having ceased, political problems may be progressively resolved. The elements of this solution depend, first and foremost, in our opinion, upon the opinion which will be expressed by the Government of Viet Nam. I shall confine myself here to indicating that the most just solution of the political problem can be found and finally assured only when the population is in a position to express in complete freedom its sovereign will by means of free elections. For the present moment, I repeat, the problem is that of bringing about a cessation of hostilities and the guaranteeing of that cessation. These guarantees, in our opinion, must be of two kinds.

These guarantees, as I say, in our view should be of two kinds. On the one hand, while the other armed forces are disarmed the regular forces of the two parties would be brought together in clearly demarcated regrouping zones. On the other hand, the implementation of the agreement should be placed under the supervision of International Commissions. As long ago as March 5, last the head of the French Government stated his views regarding the implementation of such a decision. These points and many others, too, will, of course, have to be cleared up between us. The essential thing is to know whether these principles are recognised by all the participants as being the principles which must govern the settlement which the Geneva Conference is called upon to bring about.

It is desirable, and indeed normal, that the agreement that it is our duty to obtain here both as to the settlement at Laos and as to the settlement at Cambodia and as regards Viet Nam should be guaranteed in appropriate conditions by the States participating in the present Conference. That, in its main lines, is the method which is proposed by the Delegation of France.

Our conception of the problem and of the solution is inspired by the desire to bring about a settlement which can be counted upon to last. Experience teaches us that without solid guarantees, agreements of this kind are essentially fragile. Instead of consolidating peace they represent only brief interludes, or ill-respected armistices.

In the case now under consideration, the consequences of a breach would be unpredictable. We have not the right to run such a risk.

I have thus defined the conception of the French Government with regards the cessation of hostilities. The imperious duty of the French Government, of attending to the security of the forces which are in Indo-China under French command, will always remain present in our thoughts in the course of the negotiations. But the French Delegation will also be guided, while giving necessary attention to all legitimate interests, by the desire to put an end as rapidly as possible to the sufferings and sacrifices that are going on and to put an end to a conflict, the length and aggravation of which constitute a danger for the peace of the world.

It is in this spirit that the French Delegation has the honour to submit to you, Mr. President, a series of proposals inspired by the considerations which I have just stated. The French proposal is as follows: —

I. *Viet Nam*

1. All regular units to be assembled in assembly areas to be defined by the Conference on the basis of proposals by the Commanders-in-Chief.

2. All elements not belonging either to the army or to the police forces to be disarmed.

3. All prisoners of war and civil internees to be released immediately.

4. Execution of the above provisions to be supervised by international commissions.

5. Hostilities to cease as soon as the agreement is signed

The assembly of troops and disarmament of forces as above provided to begin not later than x days (the number to be fixed by the Conference) after the signature of the agreement.

II.—*Cambodia and Laos*

1. All regular and irregular Vietminh forces which have entered the country to be evacuated.

2. All elements which do not belong either to the army or to the police forces to be disarmed.

3. All prisoners of war and civil internees to be released immediately.

4. Execution of the above provisions to be supervised by international commissions.

III. These agreements shall be guaranteed by the States participating in the Geneva Conference. In the event of any violation thereof there shall be an immediate consultation between the guarantor States for the purpose of taking appropriate measures either individually or collectively.

This, Mr. President, is the proposal submitted to the Conference on the responsibility of the French Delegation and by that Delegation. Thank you, Sir.

Speech by M. Pham van Dong, Head of Delegation of the Democratic People's Republic of Viet Nam, May 8, 1954

Mr. President and Gentlemen: The task of the Conference is to examine the problems, and to put an end to the hostilities and to restore peace in Indo-China. This task is an extremely important one. Upon it depends the destiny of the peoples of Indo-China and the peace and security of the people of South-Eastern Asia and the peace of the world as a whole.

The peoples of Indo-China desire a cessation of hostilities and the restoration of peace in Indo-China. They are prepared, by negotiation, to assert their national rights. The peoples of France and nearly all the political circles in France call for the restoration of peace in Indo-China. The peoples in Indo-China and of France desire the restoration of friendly relations between France and the peoples of Indo-China. The people of South-East Asia and Asia want to put an end to the war and to re-establish peace in Indo-China, since the war in Indo-China constitutes a threat to the peace and security of South-East Asia and Asia.

At present, this threat has become more serious and pressing because of those who intend to prolong and extend the war in Indo-China. That is why the peoples of South-East Asia and Asia demand ever more energetically, the cessation of hostilities and the re-establishment of peace in Indo-China.

The people of the whole world want to put an end to the war and to re-establish peace in Indo-China, in order to reduce international tension and to consolidate peace in the whole world.

Enjoying the approval and support of the people of the whole world, this Conference is under favourable conditions to achieve the successful settlement of this problem of the re-establishment of peace in Indo-China. We welcome everything that helps us to realise this task. And one should not miss this opportunity under any pretext whatever.

In the same spirit, expressing the sentiment of the three peoples of Viet Nam, Khmer, and Pathet Lao, the delegation of the Democratic Republic of Viet Nam proposes to the Conference that it invite the official representatives of the Government of resistance of Khmer and of the Government of resistance of Pathet Lao to take part in its work. We submit this proposal having in mind the following: —

The peoples of Indo-China, the people of Viet Nam as well as the people of Khmer and Pathet Lao are greatly concerned about the question of the cessation of hostilities and the re-establishment of peace in Indo-China. For a long time, the people of Khmer and Pathet Lao, closely tied with the people of Viet Nam, fought for peace, independence and democracy. In the course of this struggle, the peoples of Khmer and Lao established the Government of resistance of Khmer and that of Lao. Under the leadership of these Governments of resistance of the peoples of Khmer and Pathet Lao, the peoples of Khmer and Pathet Lao have liberated vast areas of their national territory. The Governments of resistance have exerted all their efforts in creating a democratic Power and in raising the living standard of the population in liberated areas. That is why the Government of resistance of Khmer, as well as that of Pathet Lao enjoy the support and warm affection of the population in liberated areas, and they enjoy great prestige and influence among the population of both countries.

These Governments represent the great majority of the people of Khmer and Lao, the aspirations of whom they symbolise. Therefore, the presence of the official representatives of these Governments is necessary at this Conference, the task of which is the settlement of the problem of cessation of hostilities and of the re-establishment of peace in Indo-China. The peoples of the governments of resistance of Khmer and Pathet Lao, as well as the people and the government of the Democratic Republic of Viet Nam are bent upon using negotiations in order to put an end to the war and to re-establish peace in Indo-China, and at the same time to achieve their national rights which are independence, unity, and democracy.

In the second part of March of this year, the Ministers for Foreign Affairs of the governments of resistance of Khmer and Pathet Lao declared that they support the resolution of the Berlin Conference regarding the Geneva Conference. In conformity with the aforesaid, the delegation of the Democratic Republic of Viet Nam is convinced that the presence of the official representatives of the governments of resistance of Khmer and Pathet Lao, who will bring to the attention of the Conference the aspirations and proposals of the peoples they represent, instead of being an obstacle, on the contrary will be a guarantee of the success of our Conference. Such is the will not only of the Indo-China peoples, but also of the peoples of the whole world, as well as all the peace-loving peoples who are really anxious to settle the problem of the cessation of war and that of the re-establishment of peace in Indo-China.

Alas, the delegation of the Democratic Republic of Viet Nam proposes to the Conference that it adopt the following resolution:—

" In view of the present situation of the countries of Indo-China and in the interests of the thorough and objective examination of the question of the cessation of hostilities and the re-establishment of peace in Indo-China, the Conference recognises the necessity to invite the representatives of the governments of resistance of Khmer and Pathet Lao to take part in the work of the Conference in regard to the question of the re-establishment of peace in Indo-China."

Having submitted this proposal to the Conference, I would ask the President of this meeting to authorise me to continue my statement when the Conference has discussed the proposal that I have submitted.

Document No. 3

Speech by Mr. Bedell Smith, Head of Delegation of the United States of America, May 8, 1954

The United States delegation takes this opportunity to recall that at Berlin, the United States joined with France, the United Kingdom, and the Soviet Union in agreeing to organise a Conference at Geneva to consider the problems of Korea and Indo-China. Subsequently, the same four Powers reached agreement as to the composition as to the Indo-China phase of the Conference. That agreement reflected, in the presence here to-day of the nine delegations in this hall, as in the case of the Korean phase, that there are only four Inviting Powers: the United Kingdom, France, the Soviet Union and the United States. Therefore, if, as has been stated in the press, the invitation issued to the so-called Democratic Republic of Viet Nam appears in the name of both the Soviet Union and the Communist Chinese régime, that invitation is in its form at variance with the clear understanding of the Foreign Ministers present at Berlin last February.

Assuming the press reports to be accurate, the United States delegation can only regret that the Indo-China phase of this Conference should be initiated by a procedural evasion of previously-reached agreements.

At Berlin, we also agreed that the problem of restoring peace in Indo-China would be discussed at this Conference, to which representatives of the United States, France, the United Kingdom, the Union of Soviet Socialist Republics, the Chinese People's Republic and other interested states will be invited.

At Geneva, the four Inviting Powers have agreed that in addition to the participation specified at Berlin, there should be representatives at this Conference of the Governments of Laos, Cambodia and the Viet Nam. The United States cannot agree to the suggestion which has just been made that non-existent, so-called governments or states, such as the so-called Pathet Lao or Free Cambodians, can in any way be considered as qualified for invitations to this Conference under the Berlin Agreement.

The United States proposes that any idea of inviting these non-existent, so-called governments be rejected. If there is opposition to this United States proposal, the United States suggests that this meeting be adjourned after the delegate who has just been speaking has completed his presentation, in order to allow for further discussion on this point between the four Inviting Powers.

Document No. 4

Extract from Speech by M. Molotov, Foreign Minister of the Soviet Union, May 8, 1954

Mr. Chairman and Gentlemen: This Conference is proceeding to discuss the problem of the re-establishment of peace in Indo-China. From the weighting of this agenda item, it follows that the Conference must discuss the problem of re-establishing peace in all the three States of Indo-China, in Viet Nam, Khmer and Pathet Lao. It is quite obvious that in order to make the work of our Conference successful, all the parties concerned must take part in it.

With respect to Viet Nam, this has already been recognised by the participants of the Conference, with the result that we have among us the representatives of the Democratic Republic of Viet Nam. It is known, however, that a war of national liberation is being waged, not merely in Viet Nam, but also in Pathet Lao and Khmer. The peoples of these countries, like those of Viet Nam, are fighting for their national independence, national unity and freedom.

In the course of this struggle, there have been formed in Khmer and Pathet Lao, democratic governments which heeded the struggle for national liberation for peoples of these countries. Considerable areas of Pathet Lao and Khmer are now under the control of these democratic governments.

The delegates of the governments of Khmer and Pathet Lao which are collaborating with the French authorities have already been invited to this Conference. This being so, there is no ground whatsoever for denying to the delegates of the governments of Pathet Lao and Khmer, which head the national liberation struggle of the people of these countries, the right to take part in our Conference.

Document No. 5

Extract from Speech by Mr. Sam Sary, Head of the Delegation of Cambodia, May 8, 1954

If there is a Free Government of Free Khmer, we do not know of that government, and I would submit that it has been created for a particular purpose. The representative of the Democratic Republic of Viet Nam has

114

said that the peoples of Free Khmer have liberated vast territories and improved the standard of life of the populations inhabiting those territories. I would like to say, Mr. President, that I do not know anything about these various territories. There have been territories occupied for a few days by these forces previous to the arrival of the regular troops of Cambodia. When these troops arrived, the occupying forces took flight and took refuge in the mountains.

But what is the position with regard to the so-called Free Khmer Government? In the first place, it has no territory. I showed in the first part of my statement that such territory as it can be said to have is very small, is elastic, varying in size, and doubtful with regard to its future. In other words, it is not clearly demarcated territory of a state. Secondly, as regards regular troops, I have already said that the troops of the Free Khmer movement are not regular troops at all. They are more in the nature of bandits, partly under the control of Vietminh. They are engaged in pillage and they are not regular troops at all. Thirdly, as regards the regularity of the government, as I said in the first part of my statement, there is no government here. If there is anything that can be called a government at all it existed only since April 3, and it consists of only two or three persons; in other words, a body invented and created by our enemy. Those are the conditions which are required if a state is to exist, and which are not fulfilled in the present case.

What is it that the so-called Free Khmer represent? They represent only themselves. There are only a very few of them and they represent only themselves. Three times there have been general elections in Cambodia and these people have never been elected to office. They, therefore, do not represent any department or locality in Cambodia.

Finally, these Free Khmers are foreigners who are being manipulated by a foreign *bloc,* a foreign *bloc,* incidentally, which has always worked to the harm of our country. The real Free Khmers are the real nationalists who love peace, who have already rallied to the Government of Cambodia. These acts of submission and support took place recently in connexion with Chantarangsei and Savang Vong.

What is left is not a body of Free Khmers at all but a few slaves. And these are the people that you want to invite to this Conference.

Finally, Mr. President, the delegation of Cambodia would appeal to the members of this Conference to reject the proposal made by the delegation of the Democratic Republic of Viet Nam. Or if the question must be studied, we would ask for the adjournment of the meeting so that the four Inviting Powers can study it.

Document No. 6

Speech by Mr. Phoui Sananikone, Head of the Delegation of Laos, May 8, 1954

Mr. President, with regard to the proposal of the Democratic People's Republic of Viet Nam that we should invite Khmer and Pathet Lao to take part in the Conference, I must say, surprised me very much. If I may I would like briefly to say what Pathet Lao is. The transformation of the Kingdom of Laos into an independent democratic state has been completed and it was completed with the participation of all the citizens of Laos. The movement Laos Issarak in Pathet Lao existed until 1949. The members of that movement desired to await certain guarantees before giving their approval to the reorganisation, the conversion of the Kingdom into the new state. These guarantees were given in 1949 and they satisfied the members of the

Laos Issarak movement. The movement, therefore, dissolved itself voluntarily and its participants returned to the free territory of Laos at the time when, with the French Government, the agreement was signed setting up the free Laos. The representatives of Laos Issarak were consulted and they were present at this time of the setting up of the free state.

The members of the Laos Issarak movement returned to the territory and participated in the life of the country, co-operating in the government. Two Ministers of the Royal Government, including the President of the Council of Ministers, belonged formerly to the movement. And I repeat that the movement dissolved itself voluntarily on October 24, 1949. Its dissolution was complete and final and the majority of the members of the movement returned to the territory and took part in the national life.

Thus, Mr. President, in the Kingdom of Laos there is complete unanimity. When in April, 1953, there was invasion of Laos by these foreign regular forces, the Government and people of Laos learned with great surprise of this so-called government of Pathet Lao under the leadership of Prince Souphanugvong. That Prince left Laos when he was only of school age, and he took part in the Laos Issarak movement in 1946. He was excluded from it in May, 1949, because of his complete dependence upon foreign elements and powers.

As I have already said, the movement was dissolved in 1949, and its members returned to Laos and rallied to the Government. Prince Souphanugvong, however, remained abroad where he formed links with Vietminh. He is not entitled in any way to say he represents Free Laos. He has no mandate from Laos. He cannot in any way represent the aspirations of the people of Laos, who simply do not know him.

Where is he? Where has he his administration? Where is his government, if there is such a thing? He may indeed have found a few of the population in certain frontier zones, but these dupes will return to Laos as soon as the Prince goes abroad again, across the frontier.

This so-called Pathet Lao represents absolutely nothing. It would be almost comic to recognise him as representing anybody. If that were done, all local leaders and party leaders and leaders of movements in all countries would consider they had the right to form governments and represent states.

Finally, let me say the delegation of Laos will oppose the invitation of the so-called Pathet Lao.

SECOND PLENARY SESSION ON INDO-CHINA

Document No. 7

Proposal by the Delegation of the Democratic Republic of Viet Nam regarding Viet Nam, May 10, 1954[11]

1. The sovereignty and independence of Viet Nam over the whole territory of Viet Nam to be recognised by France as well as the sovereignty and independence of Khmer and Pathet Lao.

2. An agreement for the withdrawal of all foreign troops from the territories of Viet Nam, Khmer and Pathet Lao to be concluded within a period to be fixed by agreement between the belligerent parties. Before the withdrawal of such troops, agreement must be reached on the question of assembly areas for the French troops in Viet Nam, and special attention must be given in this connexion to reducing the number of these assembly areas to the minimum. It is understood that the French troops shall refrain from interfering in the affairs of the local authorities in the districts where they are stationed.

[11] French text supplied by the Delegation of the Democratic Republic of Viet Nam.

116

3. Free general elections to be organised in Viet Nam, Khmer and Pathet Lao, with a view to the formation of a single government in each country, Advisory Conferences composed of the representatives of the governments of the two parties respectively in Viet Nam, Khmer and Pathet Lao to be convened to prepare for and organise the free general elections. These Conferences will take the necessary steps to ensure freedom of activity for the patriotic social parties, groups and organisations. No foreign interference will be allowed. Local committees will be set up to supervise the preparation and organisation of the elections.

Pending the establishment of single governments in each of the Indo-Chinese countries and subsequent to the conclusion of a settlement in accordance with the agreement on the cessation of hostilities, the governments of the two parties respectively will administer the districts under their control.

4. The delegation of the Democratic Republic of Viet Nam to declare the intention of the Government of the Democratic Republic of Viet Nam to examine the question of the Democratic Republic of Viet Nam's association with the French Union on the basis of free consent, and the conditions for such association. Similar declarations will be made by the governments of Khmer and Pathet Lao.

5. The Democratic Republic of Viet Nam, and also Pathet Lao and Khmer, to recognise the fact that France has economic and cultural interests in those States.

After the constitution of single governments in Viet Nam, Khmer and Pathet Lao, those states' economic and cultural relations with France must be regulated in accordance with the principles of equality and mutual interest. Pending the constitution of single governments in the three States, economic and cultural relations between Indo-China and France will remain provisionally unchanged, as they are at present. In those districts where trade and communications have been disrupted, however, they may be re-established by agreement between the two parties.

Nationals of each party shall enjoy a privileged status, to be determined later, with regard to domicile, movement and economic activity on the territory of the other party.

6. The belligerent parties shall undertake to refrain from any action against persons who have collaborated with the opposing party during the war.

7. Prisoners of war to be exchanged.

8. Before the measures listed in paragraphs 1 to 7 are carried out hostilities in Indo-China must cease and to this end agreements must be concluded between France and each of the three countries. Each of these agreements must provide for the following: —

(a) A complete and simultaneous cease-fire throughout Indo-Chinese territory by all the land, sea and air forces of the belligerent parties. With a view to stabilising the armistice, the two parties opposed shall proceed, in all three countries of Indo-China, to a readjustment of the zones they occupy, and for this purpose neither party shall hamper the passage across its territory of troops of the other party endeavouring to reach the zone occupied by the latter party.

(b) The complete cessation of all movement into Indo-China of fresh troops, whether military, naval or air force, and of all types of arms and ammunition.

117

(c) The establishment of supervisory machinery to ensure implementation of the provisions of the agreement on the cessation of hostilities, and the creation for this purpose of joint committees of representatives of the belligerent parties in each of the three countries.

Document No. 8

Extract from Speech by Mr. Pham van Dong, Head of Delegation of the Democratic People's Republic of Viet Nam, May 10, 1954

Mr. Chairman, the delegation of the Democratic Republic of Viet Nam submits to the Conference the following proposals for the re-establishment of peace in Indo-China : —

One, recognition by France of the sovereignty and independence of Viet Nam throughout the territory of Viet Nam, and also recognition of the sovereignty and independence of Khmer and Pathet Lao.

Secondly, conclusion of an agreement on the withdrawal of all foreign troops from the territory of Viet Nam, Khmer, and Pathet Lao within the time limits to be agreed upon by the belligerents. Pending the withdrawal of troops, the regrouping of French troops in Viet Nam shall be agreed upon—particular attention being paid to limit to the minimum the number of their dislocation points. Provision shall be made that the French troops should not interfere in the affairs of local administration in the areas of their dislocation.

Thirdly, holding of free general elections in Viet Nam, Khmer, and Pathet Lao with a view to constituting a single government in each country, convening of Advisory Conferences of the representatives of the governments of both sides in Viet Nam, Khmer, and Pathet Lao—in each of the States separately and under conditions securing freedom of activity for patriotic parties, groups, and social organisations; the preparation and the holding of free general elections to establish a unified government in each country. Interference from outside should not be permitted. Local commissions will be set up to supervise the preparation for, and the carrying out of the elections. Prior to the establishment of unified governments in each of the above-mentioned States, the governments of both sides will specifically carry out the administrative functions in the districts which will be under the administration, after the settlement has been carried out, in accordance with the agreement on the termination of hostilities.

Fourthly, the statements by the delegation of the Democratic Republic of Viet Nam on the readiness of the Government of the Democratic Republic of Viet Nam to examine the question of the entry of the Democratic Republic of Viet Nam into the French Union in conformity with the principle of free will, and on the conditions of this entry corresponding statements should be made by the governments of Khmer and Pathet Lao.

Fifthly, recognition by the Democratic Republic of Viet Nam, as well as by Khmer and Pathet Lao, of the economic and cultural interests of France in those countries. After the establishment of unified governments in Viet Nam, Khmer, Pathet Lao, the economic and cultural relations of these states with France should be subject to the settlement in conformity with the principles of equality and mutual interest. Pending the establishment of the unified governments in the three states, the economic and cultural relations of Indo-China with France will temporarily remain without a change such as they exist now. However, in the areas where communications and trade ties have been broken off, they can be re-established on the basis of understanding between both sides. The citizens of both sides will enjoy their privileged status to be determined later in matters pertaining to domicile, movement, and business activities on the territory of the other side.

Sixth, the belligerent sides undertake not to prosecute persons who collaborated with the other side during the war.

Seven, there shall be mutual exchange of prisoners of war.

Eight, implementation of measures that are referred to in paragraphs one through seven should be succeeded by the cessation of hostilities in Indo-China, and by the conclusion to this end of appropriate agreement between France and each of the three states which should provide for a complete and simultaneous cease-fire throughout the whole of the Indo-Chinese territory by all armed forces of the belligerent sides, ground, naval, and air forces. Both sides, in each of the three states of Indo-China, for the purpose of strengthening the Armistice, will carry out a necessary settlement of territories and of the areas occupied by them, and it should also be provided that (a) both sides should not hinder each other during the passage, for the purpose of the above-mentioned settlement, by the troops of the other side over the territory occupied by the other side; (b) the complete termination of transportation into Indo-China from abroad of new ground, naval, and air units or personnel, or of any kind of arms or ammunition; (c) to set up control over the implementation of the terms of agreements on the cessation of hostilities, and to establish for this purpose, in each of the three states, mixed commissions composed of the representatives of the belligerent sides.

The delegation of the Democratic Republic of Viet Nam is convinced that its proposals would be supported by the governments of resistance and the peoples of Khmer and Pathet. It is common knowledge that for the re-establishment of peace in Indo-China it is necessary to stop the deliveries by the United States of arms and ammunition to Indo-China: to recall the American Military Missions, advisers and instructors, and to cease any intervention of the United States in the affairs of Indo-China.

In the proposals submitted by the Delegation of the Democratic Republic of Viet Nam, the question is raised about the establishment of the economic and cultural relations between France and the Democratic Republic of Viet Nam. This means that the Democratic Republic of Viet Nam is ready to establish close economic relations with France, to develop trade relations with France; to utilise, if necessary, the French Merchant Marine; and to maintain under certain conditions French cultural conditions in Viet Nam.

The above-mentioned proposals submitted by our delegation pursue a triple aim: The first is to cease war and to establish peace; the second is to ensure the re-establishment of peace on the basis of the recognition of the national rights of the peoples of Indo-China; the third is to establish friendly relations between the countries of Indo-China and France. It is necessary to emphasise that the main point of this proposal is the settlement of the question of the re-establishment of peace on the basis of the recognition of the national rights of the peoples of Viet Nam, Khmer and Pathet Lao. The solution of this fundamental question, as well as the solution of the question of the relations between the peoples of Indo-China and France, will ensure the establishment of stable and lasting peace in accordance with the principles of justice and honour.

Another point which is to be emphasised is that our proposal has as its aim the re-establishment of peace in the whole of Indo-China. The lessons of history prove that war, as well as peace, are indivisible on the whole territory of Indo-China. From this it follows that the cessation of hostilities and the re-establishment of peace in Indo-China should be carried out simultaneously in the three countries of Viet–Khmer–Lao in accordance with common principles, methods and procedures and respecting the principle of the national sovereignty while taking into account the conditions prevailing in each country. Thus the settlement of the questions relating to the re-establishment of peace in Indo-China requires the participation of all parties concerned without any exception.

We are convinced that our proposals are in conformity with the requirements of the present-day situation, the re-establishment of peace on the basis of the recognition of the national right of the Indo-Chinese peoples and the establishment of friendly relations between the countries of Indo-China and France. We are convinced that the entire population of Viet Nam, Khmer and Pathet Lao, loving their motherland and anxious to see independence, unity, democratic freedoms and peaceful life established on their native soil will wholeheartedly support our proposals.

We are convinced that the vast strata of the French people, various political circles and public opinion of France desiring the cessation of war and the establishment of friendly relations between France and the countries of Indo-China share our views.

We are convinced that the peoples of South-East Asia, the peoples of Asia who are menaced by the extension of the war in Indo-China, the peoples of the world who, after the termination of the war in Korea, urged the cessation of the war in Indo-China will be on our side. In this spirit we present to this Conference our proposals, realising that they provide a basis for discussion, contributing to the peaceful settlement of the Indochinese question.

Mr. Chairman, I have finished my statement. Now I should like to say a few words regarding the statement of the French Delegation. First of all, inasmuch as the statement of the French Delegation relates to the recent developments in Indo-China and to the developments of the remote past, my statement provides the documentation for a more objective and just appreciation of what has taken place in Indo-China, particularly as far as the relations between the countries of Indo-China and France are concerned. In this connexion, no person of good faith can deny the fact that almost a century has elapsed since the time when France seized the countries of Indo-China and established their colonial domination; that, in the course of the Second World War the French authorities in Indo-China surrendered to the Japanese, that after the capitulation of the Japanese people, the people of Viet Nam rose in rebellion, seized the power and established the Democratic Republic of Viet Nam.

But France signed treaties with this Democratic Republic of Viet Nam, treaties which were subsequently violated by the colonisers who wanted to wage the war for the reconquest of our country, that the resistance of the peoples of Viet, Khmer and Lao is becoming more and more victorious; that for the last few years this war has been carried out due to the intervention of the American imperialists; and that at present the advocates of this war, in agreement wih the American interventionists, are seeking by all means to prolong and extend this war.

Then with regard to the proposal of the French Delegation, it is necessary to make the following remark. Since this proposal does not take into consideration the facts, including the military developments in Indo-China, it cannot serve as a serious basis for a satisfactory solution of the problem of the cessation of hostilities and of the re-establishment of peace in the whole of Indo-China. For such a solution should include military and political matters. It proceeds from the outworn imperialist colonial conception, which does not correspond to the actual situation in Indo-China and in the world.

And contrasted to the French proposal, the proposal of the Democratic Republic of Viet Nam takes into account the situation as it exists in the free

countries of Indo-China and provides a wide basis for a positive solution of
the question of re-establishing peace in Indo-China. It contributes to a
satisfactory solution of this question, that is to the re-establishment of a stable
and lasting peace in conformity with the principles of justice and honour.

Document No. 9

Proposal for a Cease-fire, Submitted by the Cambodian Delegation, May 10, 1954

1. All regular and irregular Vietminh forces which have invaded the
country since April 2, 1954, or which penetrated into it before that date to
be completely evacuated.

2. All elements which do not belong either to the army or to the police
forces to be disarmed.

3. All prisoners of war and civilian internees to be released or exchanged.

These three operations to begin immediately after the conclusion of the
general agreement on the cessation of hostilities and to be completed within
two months at the latest after the date of the signing of such agreement.

4. Execution of the above provisions to be supervised by International
Commissions, the members of which shall be proposed by the Conference and
chosen as far as possible from States which have not taken part in the fighting
in Indo-China.

Other measures will be proposed in due course by Cambodia according
to the solution to be adopted for Viet Nam, its immediate neighbour, with
which it has lived a life in common for almost a century and whose destiny
is bound to affect the Khmer country.

Document No. 10

Extract from Speech by Mr. Phoui Sananikone, Head of Delegation of Laos, May 10, 1954

I have already stated the conditions in which the Free Laos Movement
had rallied to the legal, Royal Government as early as 1949, and I have already
stated how all of its members had entered back into the country.

This peaceful evolution, unhappily, failed to be lasting. Bands coming
from outside, and provided for by foreign countries, have been able to
sporadically upset certain areas in our country where police operations have
been necessary. Then, in April 1953, the frontiers of the Kingdom were
violated by regular units which started war operations on the national territory. They were contained, and then forced back by the National Army,
with the assistance of the forces of the French units. These foreign regular
units have unsuccessfully since applied pressure on the Kingdom, and some
provinces in the Kingdom have been occupied by these forces.

These have once more invaded our country, in the month of December
last, bringing war in a territory where previously order and peace had
prevailed.

The Laotian Government does not believe, naturally, that the Kingdom
is in a position alone to face such dangers. It is a firm partisan of international solidarity, and it considers for its part that security, just like peace, is
indivisible.

To an unprovoked attack, Laos has replied with the determination of
defending itself with the assistance of its friends. France, to whom we are
related by an association treaty, has assisted us with military forces, and has

121

thus prevented the territorial invasion of our country and the installation there of a foreign power. Thus, there is no civil war in Laos; rather, there has been a characterised foreign invasion.

The peace that must come now must respect this independence and this freedom. The end of the fighting can mean for us the withdrawal of the invader from the national territory. Its troops must return to their own country, and leave ours. All prisoners must be returned. The civil population which has been deported must be repatriated. The control of the implementation of those provisions on which there would have been agreement could be entrusted to observers appointed by the Conference. These would receive from our government all facilities in order to accomplish their task. Thus, conditions of peace and security would be re-established in the Kingdom. Laos would then find it again possible to pursue its evolution toward progress and freedom, together with all other peoples with whom it would feel solidarity.

Document No. 11

Speech by Mr. Eden, May 10, 1954

Mr. Chairman, I listened with close attention to the speech of the representative of the Democratic Republic of Viet Nam. No doubt we shall all have comments to make upon his detailed proposals later. Meanwhile, I have one or two observations I must make. I am prepared to credit him with believing all he said about the national aspirations of those he represents, but I must tell him that in what he said about the United States he has painted a picture of the United States which no one who knows that country —its people or its Government—can possibly recognise. It is a picture which distorts American history and its long and generous tradition. It is a travesty of the truth to suggest that the United States threatens the liberty and independence of other nations. It is true that the United States is strong, but they have used their strength to support the independence of free countries and the welfare of all people. At least this statement cannot be challenged: " No one in the world has been enslaved by the United States."

The representatives of the Governments of Laos and Cambodia who have just spoken have dealt with many of the claims in the speech of the representative of the Democratic Republic of Viet Nam, and I thought that in what those spokesmen said (and they represent Governments which have been recognised by more than thirty states)—I thought that what they said was, in effect, a reply in respect to some of the charges made against the endeavours of France and her contributions in Indo-China.

Mr. Chairman, I don't propose myself to go into the rights and wrongs of the past. It would be easy to spend a great deal of the time of the Conference in that way, but that is not what we are here to do. Our purpose is to reach a settlement.

Now it seems to me that the proposals which M. Bidault laid before us the other day are a constructive effort to try to meet what is admittedly a most difficult situation. He has himself explained that they constitute merely an outline. Many details will have to be settled by negotiation. But there can be little doubt that the principle of an armistice on specific conditions, with provision for control and enforcement, is the right practical and first step. Whichever side in the Indo-China struggle we happen to champion, all of us around this table must face certain facts: There is no clear, recognisable battlefront in Indo-China. There is no existing line on which the opposing forces can simply remain standing. Therefore, a simple cease-fire would be quite impracticable and could not possibly lead to a peaceful solution.

There must be arrangements to separate the opposing forces and to withdraw them into distinct and clearly-defined zones. There must also be agreed measures to insure that the armistice is respected, and that there can be no misunderstanding about its provisions.

I hope, therefore, that the Conference will be ready to make an immediate study of these proposals and to work upon them. If we can do that this week it should soon be possible for us to have a practical and detailed plan to consider. That seems to me, Mr. Chairman, to be the best way so far proposed at this Conference to enable us to set about our anxious and important task.

THIRD PLENARY SESSION ON INDO-CHINA

Document No. 12

Proposals by the Delegation of the State of Viet Nam for the Restoration of Peace throughout the National Territory, May 12, 1954

The Berlin Conference recommended the restoration of peace in Indo-China[2]. Such restoration implies:—

(A) a military settlement, to put an end to hostilities, and

(B) a political settlement, to establish peace on real and lasting foundations.

A.—*Military settlement*

1. The Delegation of the State of Viet Nam declares itself ready to consider any working document submitted for this purpose to the Conference, provided such document represents a serious, positive effort, made in good faith and is calculated to lead to a satisfactory military settlement.

2. It must include adequate guarantees for the ensurance of a real and lasting peace and the prevention of any possibility of further aggression.

3. It must not involve any division, whether direct or indirect, definitive or temporary, *de facto* or *de jure*, of the national territory.

4. It must provide for International Supervision of the cease-fire terms.

B.—*Political settlement*

As regards relations between the State of Viet Nam and France :

Such relations must be regulated on the basis of the joint Franco-Viet Nam Declaration of April 28, 1954, which provides for the signature of two fundamental treaties: the first of these treaties recognises the complete independence of the State of Viet Nam and its full and entire sovereignty; the second establishes a Franco-Viet Nam association within the French Union based on equality.

As regards the internal political settlement of Viet Nam :

1. By reason of the political and territorial unity of Viet Nam, recognition must be accorded to the principle that the only State entitled to represent Viet Nam legally is the State of which His Majesty Bao-Dai, Head of State, is the embodiment. In this State alone are vested the powers deriving from the internal and external sovereignty of Viet Nam.

[2] Miscellaneous No. 5 (1954), Cmd. 9080.

2. Recognition must be accorded to the principle of a single army for the whole territory. That army is the national army under the control and responsibility of the State of Viet Nam.

The status of the soldiers of Vietminh within the framework of the legal army of the State of Viet Nam shall be regulated in conformity with the above-mentioned principle and in accordance with methods to be determined.

Application of the aforesaid regulation shall be carried out under International Supervision.

3. Within the framework and under the authority of the State of Viet Nam, free elections shall be held throughout the territory, as soon as the Security Council determines that the authority of the State is established throughout the territory and that the conditions of freedom are fulfilled. International Supervision must be exercised under the auspices of the United Nations so as to ensure the freedom and genuineness of the elections.

4. A representative Government shall be formed under the ægis of His Majesty Bao-Dai, Head of the State of Viet Nam, after the elections and in accordance with their results.

5. The State of Viet Nam shall undertake to refrain from any prosecution of persons who collaborated with Vietminh during the hostilities.

6. The political and territorial integrity of the State of Viet Nam shall be guaranteed internationally.

7. Assistance shall be furnished by the United Nations towards the development of the national resources of Viet Nam and raising the standard of living in the country.

Document No. 13

Extract from Speech by Mr. Chou En-lai, Head of the Delegation of the People's Republic of China, May 12, 1954

Mr. Chairman and Fellow Delegates, the Chinese people have maintained for a long time a profound friendship with the Indo-Chinese peoples. In the last hundred years, subjected similarly to colonial aggression, the Chinese people and the Indo-Chinese peoples have sympathised with each other in their respective movements for national liberation. This is only natural.

After the founding of the People's Republic of China, the Democratic Republic of Viet Nam established formal diplomatic relations with the People's Republic of China. The Governments of the two countries have also established normal economic and cultural relations under the principle of equality and mutual benefit. Such friendly relations are developing the common desire of the Governments of the People's Republic of China and the Democratic Republic of Viet Nam as mutual respect for each other's independence and sovereignty and non-interference in each other's internal affairs, and the safeguarding of peace in Asia and the world.

For the sake of safeguarding peace in Asia and the world, the Chinese people honestly hope that the war can be stopped and peaceful life restored in Indo-China at an early date. Not only the Chinese people but other Asian peoples as well are in favour of a peaceful settlement of the Indo-China question. The demand for the termination of war in Indo-China has been continuously voiced in India, Indonesia, Burma, Pakistan, and other countries.

The recent conference held in Colombo by the Prime Ministers of five Asian States has also expressed its concern about the restoration of peace in Indo-China. The peoples of Europe and other continents are no less desirous of ending the fighting in Indo-China than are the peoples of Asia. Moreover, even among the American statesmen, not every one of them is in favour of embarking upon military ventures in Indo-China or South-East Asia.

In this connexion, special reference should be made to the peace policy of the Union of Soviet Socialist Republics. The Government of the Soviet Union and the Soviet people have insisted all along on a peaceful settlement of the Indo-China question, and have consistently stood for the national rights of the Indo-China peoples at various international conferences.

Mr. Chairman, the Indo-China peoples have fought for nearly a century for the sacred cause of national liberation. In order to enable this Conference to have a better understanding of the aspirations of the people of Viet Nam and other peoples of Indo-China, I would like to suggest that we read the Declaration of Independence issued by the Democratic Republic of Viet Nam on September 2, 1945.

It may surprise some gentlemen that the Declaration of Independence of the Democratic Republic of Viet Nam begins with the following sentences which paraphrase the Declaration of Independence of the United States of America, of 1776:—

" All men are born equal. They are endowed by nature with certain inalienable rights, among which are life, liberty and the pursuit of happiness."

The Declaration of Independence of the Democratic Republic of Viet Nam then quotes the French Declaration of the Rights of Man, of 1789:—

" Men are born and remain free and equal in rights."

The Declaration of Independence of the Democratic Republic of Viet Nam then states:—

" A people who have courageously opposed the French domination for more than eighty years, a people who have courageously fought on the side of the Allies against fascism during the past several years, this people should be free, this people should be independent."

Gentlemen, can it be said that these demands of the Indo-Chinese people are excessive? I think that the Governments of those countries which had issued the two great Declarations, of 1776 and 1789, should recognise that the peoples of Indo-China, like the peoples of the United States of America and France, must be fully entitled to the rights of independence, liberty and equality.

The Delegation of the People's Republic of China hopes that this Conference will consider in a most serious manner the statement and proposals made on behalf of the Viet Namese people by Mr. Pham van Dong, head of the Delegation of the Democratic Republic of Viet Nam, with respect to the restoration of peace in Indo-China and the achievement of national independence, national unity, and democratic liberties for Viet Nam, Khmer and Pathet Lao.

We are of the opinion that the statement and proposals of the Delegation of the Democratic Republic of Viet Nam truly expresses the will of the Indo-Chinese peoples to fight for peace, independence, unity and democracy as well as their legitimate demands. These proposals, in the view of the Chinese Delegation, have already opened the way for the peaceful settlement of the Indo-Chinese question.

However, M. Georges Bidault, chief of the French Delegation, in his statement of May 8, still maintained the attitude of a colonial ruler. He continued to ignore the existence of the Democratic Republic of Viet Nam which the

French Government had recognised, and the fact that the Government of the Democratic Republic of Viet Nam enjoys the support of the broad masses of the people of Viet Nam. He refused participation by the representatives of the resistance governments of Khmer and Pathet Lao at this Conference. He let aside the political basis for the restoration of peace in Indo-China, and acted like a victor laying down unilateral terms for cessation of hostilities and demanding their acceptance by the peoples of Indo-China.

This line of action is unrealistic, unreasonable and inconsistent with the principle of negotiating with equal rights.

Mr. Chairman, now that we are assembled here to examine and study the ways of restoring peace in Indo-China, it is essential, in accordance with the existing situations in Indo-China and in Asia, and on the basis of recognising the national rights of Indo-China peoples, to seek terms that will be considered honourable, fair and reasonable by the two sides concerned, and to take effective measures so as to achieve at an early date an armistice in Indo-China and restore peace there. If all the delegates to this Conference are genuinely desirous of restoring peace in Indo-China, I believe that there exists the possibility of reaching agreement in this Conference.

The Delegation of the People's Republic of China expresses its full support for the statement and proposals made by Mr. Pham van Dong, head of the Delegation of the Democratic Republic of Viet Nam, and feels that these proposals can serve as the basis for this Conference to discuss the termination of war and the restoration of peace in Indo-China, and to adopt appropriate resolutions thereupon.

These proposals, in our view, are consistent with the wishes of the Indo-Chinese peoples for peace, independence, unity, and democracy, and are in the interests of peace for the French people and the peoples of other nations of the world.

Document No. 14

Speech by Mr. Eden, Secretary of State for Foreign Affairs, May 12, 1954

I would like to say a few sentences on behalf of the Government of the United Kingdom.

I shall not follow some of the previous speakers in the re-writing of history or the passing of historical judgments, because I know we here are most unlikely to reach any agreement on such things.

But we for our part will certainly not change our judgments, nor our friendships.

If we differ on history, I hope that does not mean that we must disagree on what should be done now. I should like to attempt some clarification of the position our Conference seems now to have reached, and to put some practical questions which we must, I think, resolve.

As I understand it, we are agreed that the first step is to get the fighting stopped in an orderly manner. If that is so, a number of questions arise which require urgent answers.

I assume that arrangements are in hand at Dien Bien Phu for dealing with the wounded. Here are the remaining questions.

1. Are we all agreed that all troops on both sides shall be concentrated in determined areas?

2. Is it accepted that Laos and Cambodia are in a special category and that Vietminh forces will be withdrawn from them?

3. Who is to work out the areas of concentration for Viet Nam? Is it to be the Commanders-in-Chief with, I suppose, reference back to the Conference here?

4. Do we agree that when all troops have been concentrated in determined areas any irregulars shall be disarmed?

5. Are we in favour of international supervision? If so, in what form? We are in favour of United Nations supervision. And I would mention here that the five Asian countries, whose Prime Ministers recently met in Conference at Colombo, expressed themselves at the end of their Meeting as favouring the use of the good offices and machinery of the United Nations for the furtherance of the purposes of the Geneva Conference and the implementation of its decisions on Indo-China.

When we say United Nations, we do not mean the combatants or necessarily any of us round this table. There could be an agreed panel of countries from whom these United Nations countries could be drawn.

I hope that my colleagues will consider these questions helpful, and will be willing to express their views upon them.

FOURTH PLENARY SESSION ON INDO-CHINA

Document No. 15

Extract from Speech by M. Molotov, Minister for Foreign Affairs of the Union of Soviet Socialist Republics, May 14, 1954

There is a growing danger of an extension of the war in Indo-China.

The more insistently the peoples demand that an end be put to the war in Indo-China, the more frequent are the statements made by influential circles in the United States of America on the necessity of open-armed intervention by the United States of America in the war in Indo-China. Strenuous efforts are now being made to find at least the appearance of a pretext of any kind for such intervention. Particular care is being taken that the United States of America should not find itself absolutely isolated in carrying out the relevant new plans for aggression in Asia.

Of late we have witnessed persistent attempts to form for these purposes a certain *bloc* with the participation of the United States of America, France, Great Britain and some other States. As the time for the Geneva Conference drew nearer, these attempts became more persistent than ever. No less a person than the United States Secretary of State, on the eve of the Geneva Conference, began strenuously to advocate extending United States intervention in the Indo-China war. This time there was talk of creating another " defence community " although here again it was, of course, not at all concerned with the defence of the United States of America, France, Great Britain or any other State, but with forming a new military *bloc* for combating the national liberation movement of the peoples of Indo-China and South-East Asia.

It is obvious that the creation of the new aggressive *bloc* also serves definite military-strategic aims. It means the establishment of new American bases in this area, which cannot be viewed with indifference by those states whose safety is affected in connexion with the plans for the creation of the aforesaid *bloc* and the extension of American intervention in Indo-China.

It is said that the planned new *bloc,* as well as American intervention in Indo-China, was necessary in order to protect the peoples of South-East Asia against some sort of danger from outside. Leaving aside the question as to where the real threat to the peoples and independence of these countries comes from, it is legitimate to ask—is it proper to proclaim oneself the protector of the peoples of these countries, which, as is well known, have not requested the United States to do so? Is it not at least immodest to take upon oneself the role of self-styled protector of the peoples of South-East Asia, when these peoples want only one thing—peace, national independence and freedom.

At present, as you are aware, work is going on behind the scenes on the formation of this new aggressive *bloc*. The purpose of this *bloc* is to unite States interested in maintaining colonial régimes and prepared for this reason to extend the war in Asia.

The Geneva Conference is taking place at the very moment when efforts are being made to extend the war in South-East Asia instead of restoring peace in Indo-China. That will be the outcome of the new aggressive plans now being worked out by influential circles in the United States of America, about which so much has been said and written of late.

In recent years, the United States of America has intervened increasingly in events in Indo-China, following here also a policy of supporting the colonial system. It will suffice to quote the figures relating to the financial aid given by the United States to France and the Indo-Chinese Governments associated with France over the past few years. The relevant figures for the past few years are as follows: in 1952–53—314 million dollars, in 1953–54 —more than one thousand million dollars, which amounts approximately to four-fifths of the total expenditure on the war in Indo-China. For the 1954–55 financial year, the estimate for these appropriations is 1,133 million dollars. And, as we know, he who pays the piper calls the tune.

These ever larger appropriations made by the United States of America were devoted mainly to financing the colonial war being waged in Indo-China. At the present time, one can already speak of direct American intervention in the Indo-Chinese colonial war.

American intervention in Indo-China is now increasing steadily, taking the form of the supply of arms and war materials, and the dispatch of military advisers, instructors, technicians, &c. This constitutes the main obstacle to the restoration of peace in Indo-China. Moreover, the result of this intervention is to extend the scale of military operations in Indo-China, with all the attendant consequences.

This intervention, further, shows the desire of the United States of America to establish its domination in Indo-China as a matter of fact. There, much has already been done to replace the colonial domination of one country by the colonial domination of another.

The intervention of the United States of America in Indo-Chinese affairs is, in addition, evidence of its desire to bring about a conflict between the peoples of Indo-China fighting for their freedom and independence, and other peoples of Asia; and to exploit the conflicts between the peoples of Asia for its own ends.

All this testifies to the fact that, in the East as well, intensified preparations are being made for a new world war.

Explaining the significance of these American plans in the Far East, the United States Secretary of State, on January 13 this year, made the following statement:—

" The interest of the United States in that part of the area is, from a strategic standpoint, very closely tied in to what is commonly called the offshore island chain. The offshore island chain has, in essence, two land bases: At the north, the Korean mainland; and in the south, we would hope in Indo-China. Then in between are the islands themselves —Japan, the Ryukyus, embracing Okinawa, Formosa, the Philippines,

128

Australia and New Zealand. The United States has a security tie, of one sort or another, with each of these areas, not formalised in some cases, in the form of a treaty, but nevertheless very real and very actual."

It is clear from this statement by the United States Secretary of State that the rights and destinies of the peoples of Indo-China or of the other peoples of this area are of no concern whatever to the persons engaged in working out the strategic plans of the United States of America. On the other hand, it is evident that these American strategic plans, which are preparing to extend the war in this area, constitute a serious threat to the peaceful development of the peoples of the whole of this extensive region. It is not yet certain whether the United States will succeed in building up a military *bloc* with the participation of various states in order to carry out their plans; but these plans are obviously calculated to support colonial régimes in Asia by all and any means.

A great responsibility is incumbent on the Geneva Conference as to whether it will fulfil its obligation to oppose these aggressive plans for extending the war in South-East Asia. Only decisive counter-action to these plans will fulfil the purpose of the Geneva Conference, the aim of which was and continued to be to restore peace in Indo-China.

What is meant by helping to restore peace in Indo-China? The Geneva Conference cannot interpret this task as meaning that the cessation of military operations in Indo-China should become, as it were, a cunningly devised respite for one of the parties, intent on exploiting this breathing-space for preparing to extend the war in Indo-China. The task of the Geneva Conference should be understood as meaning that it must bring about a cessation of the fighting in Indo-China as soon as possible, and at the same time reach such an agreement as would enable the legitimate claims of the Indo-Chinese peoples to be satisfied in regard to securing their national independence and democratic rights.

The Head of the delegation of the Democratic Republic of Viet Nam has at this Conference made proposals which provide a basis for the settlement of the Indo-Chinese question, and a possibility of securing the restoration of peace in Indo-China. So far, we have heard here neither any justified criticism of these proposals nor any willingness to accept any particular points in them.

In the opinion of the Soviet delegation, the gist of these proposals, if we select the most important points, is as follows: —

1. France shall ensure recognition of the sovereignty and independence of Viet Nam, and also of Khmer and Pathet-Lao.

At the same time, there shall be an agreement for the withdrawal of all foreign troops from the territory of Viet Nam, Khmer and Pathet-Lao within a period to be fixed by agreement between the two parties.

2. Free general elections shall be held in Viet Nam, Khmer and Pathet-Lao, and a single democratic government shall be set up in each of these States as the result of these elections.

Prior to these elections, advisory conferences of the representatives of both parties shall be held in Viet Nam, Khmer and Pathet-Lao, and freedom of activity for the patriotic parties, groups and social organisations shall be ensured.

3. The Government of the Democratic Republic of Viet Nam, and also the governments of Khmer and Pathet-Lao, shall declare their readiness to examine the question of these States entering the French Union in accordance with the principles of free consent.

129

In addition, the Governments of Viet Nam, Khmer and Pathet-Lao shall recognise the fact that France has economic and cultural interests in these states, and the relevant questions shall be regulated in accordance with the principles of equality and mutual interest.

4. The implementation of the above measures and the execution of the other measures mentioned in the draft of the Democratic Republic of Viet Nam must be preceded by the cessation of military operations in Indo-China and the conclusion of appropriate agreements completely stopping the movement to Indo-China, from outside, of any fresh troops, arms and military supplies of any kind.

In addition to the points I have enumerated, agreement will also have to be reached on a number of other questions: exchange of prisoners of war; undertaking to refrain from action against persons who have collaborated with the opposing party during the war, &c. It is also essential that the four points mentioned above should take due account of the legitimate desires of both parties in reaching agreement on both political and military questions.

These aims are fully attainable provided that both parties show a real desire to establish a genuinely stable and lasting peace in Indo-China.

The aim of the proposals made by the Democratic Republic of Viet Nam is to reach an agreement with France. These proposals are founded on the expediency of mutual recognition of the principles of justice and honour, on the basis of which it is perfectly possible to establish new friendly relations between the peoples of Indo-China and France. These proposals may perhaps not satisfy the advocates of the colonial policy, with their clinging to old, obsolete ideas. These persons, by rejecting the possibility of reaching an agreement on the Indo-Chinese question, are furthering not national interests but the interests of those foreign aggressive circles who are anxious to extend the war instead of to restore peace in Indo-China.

At our first meeting, the French delegation put forward its proposals for the settlement of the Indo-Chinese question. In the meantime, we have had an opportunity to make a close study both of the French plan and of the proposals submitted by other delegations.

A defect of the French proposals is that they do not deal at all with political problems. But everybody realises that the cessation of the protracted war in Indo-China cannot be divorced from the solution of some at least of the problems of that nature.

The French draft reveals an under-estimation of the struggle for national liberation that has widely developed in Laos and Cambodia. Yet the question of the situation in Indo-China cannot be narrowed down simply to events in Viet Nam.

Moreover, the French draft also refers to guarantees for the agreements reached at this Conference. The draft reads:—

" These agreements shall be guaranteed by the States participating in the Geneva Conference. In the event of any violation thereof there shall be an immediate consultation between the guarantor States for the purpose of taking appropriate measures either individually or collectively."

The Soviet Union delegation cannot entirely agree with this proposal. It recognises however the acceptability, in principle, of the French proposal that the agreements reached at this Conference should be guaranteed by the States participating in the Geneva Conference, and that in the event of any violation of the agreements there should be consultations between the guarantor States. The object of these consultations should be the adoption of collective measures to implement the agreements. It would be desirable for the other participants at this Conference to make known their attitude with regard to this important proposal of the French delegation.

It is also pointed out that the draft of the Democratic Republic of Viet Nam provides for the establishment of supervisory machinery to ensure implementation of the provisions of the agreement on the cessation of hostilities only by joint committees of representatives of the belligerent parties in each of the three countries. In this connexion it is emphasised that the draft does not provide for supervision by international bodies of any kind.

In view of the great importance of reaching agreement on this matter, the Soviet Union delegation suggests an addition to these proposals. It would be possible to come to an agreement that supervision of implementation of the provisions of the agreement on the cessation of hostilities should be entrusted to commissions composed of representatives of neutral countries. No insuperable difficulties should be encountered in determining the composition of these commissions.

The Soviet Union delegation accordingly submits the following addition to the above-mentioned draft proposals. (*See Document No. 16.*)

In connexion with the Geneva Conference, France is faced with the important problem of deciding what course to adopt in Indo-China. One alternative is to go on with the war in Indo-China, which involves extending the war on behalf of foreign aggressive plans and bodes no good for the satisfaction of French national interests. The other alternative is negotiations, first of all with the Viet Namese people, and further steps of a similar nature to bring the war to an end and establish peace in Indo-China as speedily as possible. Adoption of the latter alternative would make it possible to establish mutual understanding and friendly relations between France and the peoples of Indo-China.

The Geneva Conference must do everything in its power to promote this peaceful settlement of the Indo-Chinese question.

The Soviet Union delegation will, of course, make known its attitude with regard to all the questions asked by the United Kingdom representative at the last meeting. It must be stated even at this stage, however, that it would be inappropriate to narrow the matter down to these questions and to by-pass those problems of a military and political character that have already been raised by events in Indo-China.

The Soviet Union delegation, like the delegation of the Chinese People's Republic, attaches great importance to the proposals made by the representative of the Democratic Republic of Viet Nam. It associates itself with those proposals and hopes that they will receive all due attention. At the same time, the Soviet Union Delegation expresses its confidence that the Geneva Conference will also examine any other proposals that will really help to establish peace in Indo-China.

The Soviet Government believes that a settlement of the Indo-Chinese question, due regard being paid to the national interests of the peoples of Indo-China, would constitute an important contribution not only to the cause of strengthening peace in Asia, but to that of strengthening peace throughout the world.

Document No. 16

Proposal by the Delegation of the Union of Soviet Socialist Republics for a supervisory commission, May 14, 1954

In order to help the parties to implement the conditions of the agreement on the cessation of hostilities, the agreement must include provisions for the setting up of a supervisory commission composed of neutral countries.

**Extract from Speech by M. Bidault, Minister for Foreign Affairs of France,
May 14, 1954**

Mr. Chairman,

The French delegation has studied with close attention the statement made here on the 10th of this month by Mr. Pham Van Dong. It has done so in the spirit of the final communiqué of the Berlin Conference, which states that the problem of restoring peace in Indo-China will be discussed at the Geneva Conference. No flights of eloquence can further our common concern, no polemics can help us to accomplish our task. The general discussion which is now going on is valuable only to the extent that it enables delegations to express their views clearly and to expound the conclusions they have reached. So long as it is conducted in this spirit, it provides the necessary groundwork for the negotiations proper, which must bear on specific points.

For these reasons I shall not reply to the whole of Mr. Pham Van Dong's statement. I have already told you what I thought about a particular way of writing—or rewriting—history, and there is no need whatever for me to revert to the subject. Of this statement, then, I will comment only on the first sentence and the proposals with which the statement concludes.

Mr. Pham Van Dong tells us that Vietminh's fundamental position is: peace, independence, unity and democracy. All of us here, I think, can subscribe to these words, and the French delegation has no hesitation in doing so. Peace, as I recently recalled, has been, ever since Berlin, the very purpose of our Conference. Independence is the final goal of a process of development which began immediately after the Second World War and which has already been achieved, a fact proclaimed in this very place and in the most precise and detailed manner by the representatives of the three states. Unity, in the case of Viet Nam, is not open to question: the French delegation, at any rate, considers that the territorial unity of Viet Nam, and the inviolability of its frontiers, must be respected in any future settlement. Lastly, democracy is a principle which is common to all the nations of the free world. To our mind it must find expression in the normal exercise of civic rights and human freedoms. If all the delegations here present accept these four terms in their authentic connotation, our task will be greatly simplified.

The French delegation feels that the proposals made by Mr. Pham Van Dong at the end of his statement call for more substantial comment.

These proposals are striking, first, for their monumental character. Their amplitude is due to the fact that they include everything, all mixed up together. They deal with Laos, with Cambodia, with Pathet Lao and the Khmer Issaraks, with cultural and economic relations between France and Viet Nam, with the French Union, and finally with means of restoring peace in Indo-China. I suppose it was Mr. Pham Van Dong's desire to paint a broad picture of the problems concerning the three countries of Indo-China. I am also of opinion that a number of these problems are outside the competence of our Conference. I shall say first which and for what reasons.

I have already expressed our astonishment at the insistence with which Vietminh constitutes itself the spokesman of Laos and Cambodia, or more particularly of Pathet Lao and the Khmer Issarak movement. On these two groups I can add nothing of value to the very pertinent remarks already made by the delegations of Laos and Cambodia. On Vietminh's competence to speak for the three movements, I shall say only that I see in it an unexpected survival of a distant past. I recollect the insistence with which Mr. Ho Chi Minh, in 1946 and even later, rejected federation for Indo-China. Does he perhaps now want to restore it for the benefit of Vietminh?

I hasten to add that if ever the three States one day wished to re-establish in any form this Indo-Chinese community whose disappearance they desired, the decision would rest with them and with them alone. The French Government, at any rate, has taken their wishes into account. It has recognised the independence of Laos and Cambodia. In the exercise of this independence, both States have adopted constitutional democratic institutions, and have consequently proceeded to free elections. Both Governments have negotiated agreements regulating relations between their countries and France, on a bilateral basis, and in complete equality. These negotiations are complete in the case of Laos, and will shortly be completed in the case of Cambodia. It seems, therefore, that the problems referred to in paragraphs 1, 3, 4 and 5 of the Vietminh proposals[12] are disposed of in the case of Laos and Cambodia, and that there is absolutely no reason why our Conference should discuss them further. In the case of Laos, and in the case of Cambodia, the only question to be dealt with is that of the invasion of their territories by foreign forces, and the foreign forces are those of Vietminh. Now I note that Mr. Pham Van Dong's proposal evades this fundamental problem, unless there is an implied reference in paragraph 2, which provides for an agreement on the withdrawal of all foreign troops from the territories of what are called " Khmer " and " Pathet Lao."

As has been clearly stated here by the delegations of Laos and Cambodia, the Laotian problem and the Cambodian problem consist in first obtaining, and then supervising, the withdrawal of the Vietminh forces. This withdrawal and this supervision imply specific measures of the kind referred to in paragraphs 2, 6, 7 and 8 of the Vietminh proposals. These measures, however, must not be confused with those required in the infinitely more complex question of settling the present situation in Viet Nam, precisely because the problem of Laos and the problem of Cambodia, which are distinct one from the other, must also not be confused with the problem of Viet Nam, which is quite different: the arrangements for disposing of them must be considered separately. That is why in the French delegation's basic proposals, while Viet Nam is dealt with in Chapter 1, the special provisions relating to Laos and Cambodia are brought together in Chapter 2, and the provisions of Chapter 3 apply to all the settlements to be reached.

The French Government stands by these proposals. It will gladly supplement them in the sense advocated by the delegations of Laos and Cambodia. Finally, even though it hardy seems to it that French troops in countries associated with France can be considered as " foreign " in the usual sense of the term, the French Government is ready, subject to the opinion of the governments concerned, to withdraw its own troops if the invading forces are themselves withdrawn. On this particular point it accepts in advance the views of the Governments of Laos and Cambodia.

From the foregoing observations it follows that the questions relating to these two States are simple, that they are independent of the question of Viet Nam and that they can be disposed of without delay. The French Government hopes that they will be disposed of at once. It depends on the goodwill of Vietminh whether so desirable a development is possible. All that is needed is for Vietminh to recognise the facts for what they are.

I now come to what in my view is the essential part of the statement by Vietminh, namely, the problem of peace in Viet Nam.

Here again, I must make a preliminary observation. The Vietminh proposals pay scant regard to facts and events. I would remind you first of all that there does exist a Government of the State of Viet Nam. That Government is the government of His Majesty, Bao Dai, which is recognised by thirty-five states, is a member of various international organisations, and

(12) Document No. 7.

133

which is represented here in the eyes of all those who have recognised it. This Government is fully and solely competent to commit Viet Nam. With it the French Government has conducted a series of negotiations which, as I mentioned at the beginning of this statement, led to the joint declaration and to the conclusion of two treaties which the delegation of Viet Nam read to the Conference on the 12th of this month. The sovereignty and independence of Viet Nam are therefore recognised by France over the whole territory of Viet Nam, a fact which demonstrates the superfluity of paragraph 1 of the Vietminh proposals. The association of Viet Nam with the French Union on the basis of free consent, and the conditions for such association, are therefore already determined. Paragraph 4 of the Vietminh proposals is accordingly pointless.

With regard to paragraph 2, I must point out that movements of French troops in Viet Nam territory are governed by the conduct of the war, and will continue to be until peace is restored. Once peace is restored the French Government has no intention of keeping any forces in Viet Nam against the will of that country's legal government. It is therefore for that government to say whether it considers it advisable, in the light of its own security requirements, to maintain or to modify the agreements on this subject. The French Government, at any rate, does not intend to make the re-establishment of peace in Indo-China conditional on any undertakings whatever on that point.

The recognition by Viet Nam of the fact that France has economic and cultural interests in that State, referred to in paragraph 5 of the Vietminh proposals, is already the subject of agreements or of negotiations still in progress with the Government of the State of Viet Nam. I may add that, here again, the French Government has never thought of making the cessation of hostilities in Indo-China conditional on the conclusion of these negotiations.

Paragraph 3 of the Vietminh proposals is in a different category. It deals with the conditions for the establishment of democratic institutions to ensure Viet Nam's political unity.

For a long time now the French Government has been devoting considerable thought to this problem as it affects Viet Nam, in the same way as in relation to Korea and other countries. It is convinced that only by applying these two principles of democratic institutions and political unity will it be possible to efface the political consequences of the war, and consolidate the re-establishment of peace. But the lesson of experience is that, without the indispensable measures of supervision, so-called free elections can spell the death of freedom. The plan proposed by the Vietminh delegation is so similar to plans we have heard elsewhere and are still discussing, that at first glance its purpose seems obvious. The sole purpose of the method proposed is to ensure, even before the elections are held, that Viet Nam shall be completely dominated by Vietminh. That is not the way to find a real solution to the problem before us. Arrangements must be made for safeguards and inspection. We know from Mr. Nguyen Quoc Dinh's statement that it is also the Viet Nam Government's desire that freedom of choice for the electors at the general elections should be ensured by the provision of a suitable system of inspection.

The Plan it has already submitted constitutes a useful basis for discussion in that connexion. Since it would be impossible in practice to provide the indispensable safeguards and to carry out an election in motion before the cessation of hostilities has had time to exercise a pacifying effect, the French delegation does not think that an agreement on the political settlement ought to precede, and thus delay, the application of a military settlement. While not unmindful that the two are connected, it feels that the former should be not a precondition of but should follow from the latter.

134

There is nothing in paragraphs 6 and 7 of the Vietminh proposals to which the French delegation can object, since the first goes without saying and the second is partly taken from our own proposals. While agreeing on the principle, the French delegation reserves the right to examine the methods of application. As regards prisoners of war and civil internees, it has, as everyone knows, proposed that they should be set free immediately hostilities cease.

Paragraph 8 is obviously essential, since it deals with the cessation of hostilities in Indo-China.

The first sub-paragraph of this paragraph is ambiguous. Does it mean that an agreement on the measures listed in paragraphs 1 to 7 must *precede* the cessation of hostilities? Or does the Vietminh delegation agree that the political aspects of the general settlement it is proposing if they have not been dealt with already, can be dealt with after the cessation of hostilities? The French delegation is convinced that, if concrete results are to be speedily achieved, solution of the political problem cannot be a condition of the end of hostilities.

The French delegation notes that the Vietminh proposals envisage, to secure the restoration of peace, a settlement for each country. As I have already said that is also the view of the French Government. But in the case of Laos and Cambodia, there can hardly be a Franco-Laotian and a Franco-Cambodian settlement because France, as we all know, is not at war with either of those States. The Viet Nam settlement, on the other hand, should be reached by means of an agreement between the opposing Commands in accordance with terms decided upon by this Conference.

Sub-paragraph (a) provides for a complete and simultaneous cease-fire throughout Indo-Chinese territory. While it has no objection of principle to this procedure the French delegation does not, however, think it necessary to bind itself to what looks like a rigid and precise formula but is in fact a very vague one: for in the first place a cessation of hostilities can undoubtedly be much more easily achieved in Laos and Cambodia than in Viet Nam, and can therefore take place earlier on Laotian and Cambodian territory than on Viet Nam territory, and secondly, for Viet Nam proper a gradual region to region method has been suggested. The French delegation sees no reason why the two Commands should be prevented from examining this suggestion.

The French delegation listed, in section I of the basic proposals it submitted to the Conference on the 8th of this month, the safeguards which would have to be provided in any agreement concluded before the cessation of hostilities.

It observes that the Vietminh proposals take up the idea of assembly areas and of a readjustment of those areas contained in paragraph 1 of section I of the French proposals, that is, the part of those proposals which relates to Viet Nam. It considers that the method by which these operations are to be carried out should be carefully and clearly defined; that the troop movements involved in the assembling should be regulated by agreement between the Commands. The French delegation feels that sub-paragraph (b) of paragraph 8 of the Vietminh proposals requires more detailed explanation on a number of points.

It notes that the Vietminh proposals do not provide for the disarmament of elements not belonging either to the army or to the police forces. On this point it confirms the proposal contained in paragraph 2 of section I of its text of May 8.

Lastly, the French delegation observes that the provision concerning supervisory machinery is taken up in sub-paragraph (c) of paragraph 8 of the Vietminh proposals. The nature of this machinery is, however, different from what was proposed in its text of May 8, which mentioned International

Commissions. The Vietminh text of May 10 merely refers to joint committees. The French delegation considers the establishment of international supervisory machinery to be an indispensable guarantee for the proper implementation of the agreements.

It also points out that, according to section III of the French proposals of May 8, the agreements would be guaranteed by the States participating in this Conference, and notes that the delegations of the United Kingdom, the United States of America, and of Viet Nam, Laos and Cambodia have already given their consent to the principle of international supervision and guarantee of the agreements.

And now, having concluded this comparison of the texts of the French and Vietminh proposals, the French Delegation wishes to reply to the very pertinent questions put by the Head of the United Kingdom Delegation on the 12th of this month:—

Question 1.—France considers that in Viet Nam the troops on both sides should be concentrated in determined areas.

Question 2.—France has proposed that the Laotian and Cambodian problems should be dealt with separately, and proposes that the Vietminh forces should be withdrawn from the territories of those countries.

Question 3.—As regards Viet Nam, France considers that it is for the Conference to work out the areas of concentration, on the understanding that the respective Commanders-in-Chief would be consulted by both sides. The Commanders-in-Chief would be responsible for the details of the concentration.

Question 4.—France has proposed the disarmament of irregular forces. In Viet Nam the procedure for this disarmament will have to be decided in the light of the arrangements for the concentration of regular troops.

Question 5.—France has proposed international supervision. She is prepared to consider any proposals that may be made regarding the composition of the Commissions and the method of supervision. If the principle of international supervision is accepted, then in Viet Nam joint bodies might be employed, the terms to be settled by mutual agreement, to work under the International Commissions and assist them in their task.

The French Delegation puts these views before the Conference in the belief that it will thereby be helping in the task to which we must all devote our energies. It hopes they will be studied in the same objective and constructive spirit as that in which they are made. Its primary concern, I repeat, is to prepare the way for concrete negotiations, which it hopes will not be long delayed. It is accordingly prepared to consider any methods of procedure calculated to expedite our work.

Document No. 18

Communiqué issued by the Conference on May 29

Following is text :—

" In order to facilitate the early and simultaneous cessation of hostilities it is proposed that:—

(*a*) Representatives of the two commands should meet immediately in Geneva and contacts should also be established on the spot.

(b) They should study the dispositions of forces to be made upon the cessation of hostilities, beginning with the question of regrouping areas in Viet Nam.

(c) They should report their findings and recommendations to the Conference as soon as possible."

FIFTH PLENARY SESSION ON INDO-CHINA

Document No. 19

Speech by M. Bidault, Minister for Foreign Affairs of France, June 8, 1954

After six weeks' Conference and a month's debate on Indo-China, the French Delegation feels that the time has come to see how far our discussions have got, to define the points of agreement, to recall the problems still pending and, finally, to bring out the important questions on which it has been impossible so far to reconcile the opposing views.

To go back to the beginning, I would remind you that it took two weeks to establish the list of members of the Conference. As a result of exchanges of views between the French Delegation and the Soviet Delegation, the list was finally settled with the agreement of the nine participants, subject to the reservation included in the Berlin communiqué that "neither the invitation to, nor the holding of, the above-mentioned Conference shall be deemed to imply diplomatic recognition in any case where it has not already been accorded."

At the very first meeting of the Conference, on May 8 last, the French Delegation set out its views, in a plan which has been communicated to you all, on the conditions and method of application of a cessation of hostilities in Indo-China. Four public meetings enabled the other delegations to explain their position in turn and some of them to submit, like my delegation, proposals on several points. Bearing in mind these first indications on May 14 I made a second general statement in which on two important points—machinery of supervision and withdrawal of French forces from the three countries of Indo-China—I was at pains not to reject but even to meet halfway the stated terms of the opposing party.

Once this first phase was concluded, the Conference decided to hold restricted meetings, which it did from May 17 onwards. An immediate decision was taken, at the request of the French Delegation, to begin with a study of the military aspects of the cessation of hostilities. So long as blood is being shed in Indo-China, these aspects take priority, the final political settlement obviously depending on what can be done to end the fighting. That proposal was accepted by all. It has enabled us to make some progress, which is far from negligible.

This procedural point having been settled, the French Delegation would have liked the Conference to deal first of all with the case of Laos and that of Cambodia.

In this connexion, it pointed out that these two cases were both different in nature from that of Viet Nam, and more easily settled. It was not a question, as in Viet Nam, of civil strife but of an invasion of two States by foreign forces. To put an end to hostilities in those two territories, all that was necessary was to secure the evacuation of those forces. Such a decision could be taken rapidly and peace thereby restored over vast areas. In order to facilitate such a desirable result, my Government was prepared, subject to its contractual engagements and to the opinion of the Governments concerned, to withdraw its own troops.

This proposal, which was supported by five delegations, and first and foremost by the representatives of Laos and Cambodia, was not accepted. The reply to our argument was that peace is indivisible since the war is indivisible. It was maintained that the three countries constituted a single theatre of operations and that a cessation of hostilities was impracticable unless it applied to all parts of that theatre. It was argued that the same principles applied to all places, although it was agreed that their application might differ in each of the three States. It was agreed, moreover, to proceed in the first instance with an examination of the conditions peculiar to Viet Nam, considered, in the words of Mr. Pham Van Dong on May 24, as "the most important theatre of operations."

Purposely overlooking the fact that this statement contradicted the argument about the war's indivisibility, the French delegation accepted that procedure. It holds that it is our duty to restore peace wherever possible and as soon as possible. That is why we preferred not to delay, by arguing the question of simultaneous operations, the study of the conditions for the restoration of peace throughout the whole of the territories in question. I am obliged, however, to note that, while the study of general principles has led to some appreciable progress, and while further progress, likewise not without value, has been realised in connexion with Viet Nam, the cases of Laos and Cambodia have so far been discussed only intermittently. Indeed, on those two cases practically everything remains to be said.

With regard to Viet Nam then, on May 24 the French delegation put before the Conference a concrete proposal, a seven-point plan of work. This plan was not incompatible with the five-point plan submitted at the same time by M. Molotov. The two together have served as a basis for the discussions which have been going on since. In order to avoid any confusion, I shall, if you permit, go over what is common to both as well as what is peculiar to each, and shall consider with you the stage we have now reached in our work.

On May 8 the French delegation asked the Conference to adopt the principle of a general cessation of hostilities in Indo-China. Of this all members of the Conference have now acknowledged the necessity. The Soviet, Chinese and Vietminh delegations have also insisted that the cease-fire should be simultaneous in the three countries. On this question other delegations have expressed the same reservations as the French delegation, but all have stated unequivocally that in fact they agreed to a simultaneous cease-fire. This common viewpoint, resulting from the conciliatory spirit shown by the majority of the Conference, has made unanimous agreement on the first general principle possible.

Six of the nine delegations have pointed out that this problem only arose in Viet Nam, since in Cambodia and Laos all that is needed is to obtain the withdrawal of the Vietminh forces.

In the case of Viet Nam, the French plan of May 8, as amplified and clarified on May 14, proposed that the two parties' regular units should be regrouped in areas the limits of which would be fixed by the Conference, after consultations with the High Commands. In the course of his substantial statement on May 12, the Viet Nam representative endorsed these principles. Mr. Pham Van Dong, too, on May 10, proposed a readjustment of the areas. The clarification of his views furnished by his statement on May 25 was particularly interesting in that it provides evidence of a clear evolution in Vietminh thinking during recent days.

In these circumstances the Conference felt that it was fruitless to continue further with the general debate and that the representatives of the High Commands should be invited to meet in Geneva to study the assembly areas in Viet Nam, as I had proposed on May 14. In the course of a procedural debate on May 27, 28 and 29, various draft resolutions, including a French draft, were examined; the text proposed by Mr. Eden on May 29 was finally adopted. Before its adoption the various delegations expressed both their support and their reservations. As far as the French delegation is concerned its comments, as my colleagues will recall, were two-fold: the problem of regrouping only arises in the case of Viet Nam and the principle of the unity of Viet Nam is not open to question. The French delegation is happy to recall that the Chairman of the Conference, on that day M. Molotov, clearly proclaimed this principle on behalf of his colleagues, at the meeting on May 29.

The agreement reached in this way is a positive achievement, since it has enabled the representatives of the High Commands to meet in Geneva since Wednesday, June 2. Their work must go on in the strictest secrecy, and I shall therefore make no comment on it. I should only like to express the French delegation's hope and desire that the military discussions will progress so that the Conference may soon be in a position to examine specific recommendations including the assembly areas marked on the map. That is a prerequisite for further examination of the cessation of hostilities in Viet Nam and, more especially, of the subsequent measures linked with the establishment of the assembly areas, such as administration of the areas, economic and financial provisions, irregulars, practical arrangements for supervision, &c. Finally, the resolution of May 29 provides for meetings on the spot between representatives of the High Commands; the purpose of these meetings, for which arrangements are now being made, is to enable the necessary further studies and the conclusions decided on at Geneva to be carried out.

We note with satisfaction the progress achieved with the second item of the agenda. But, let us not disguise the fact, the problem of assembly areas is a complex one and will require a good deal of unremitting effort.

The delegations of Viet Nam and France have stressed the importance of this problem on several occasions. More than a third of the Vietminh forces belong to the category of what are called irregulars. It would be remarkable if the decisions of a Conference whose task it is to restore peace in Indo-China left a substantial part of one of the adversaries' forces entire freedom of action in the territory in which they happen to be. The prospects of restoring peace would be jeopardised. The Conference will have to consider this question carefully once we have made sufficient progress with the assembly areas. Certain of Mr. Pham Van Dong's words on May 25 do not exclude possibilities of agreement in this field.

An armistice, we have been told time and again, must contain an undertaking by each of the parties not to increase its total military strength.

It is obvious, although it has not always been stated, that such a clause is only conceivable as applying equally to the two parties.

I repeat that it should also cover war supplies manufactured locally. It implies strict supervision of the land and sea frontiers of Viet Nam, without which the undertaking would be illusory and the guarantee fraudulent. Most delegations have not yet had time to give their views on the problem. I shall merely note that agreement on the principle of such an undertaking in Viet Nam does seem possible.

There has been no objection to the release of prisoners of war and civil internees immediately after the cessation of hostilities. Agreement between members of the Conference appears to be complete.

All those who hate war can only welcome this with a feeling of satisfaction for the present and hope for the future.

The last three restricted meetings of the Conference have been devoted to supervision and, to a lesser extent, guarantees. Our discussions on these subjects have, up to the present, been very thorny, even disappointing.

The problem is three-fold. To begin with, there is one principle that must be clearly established right at the start—the principle of neutral international supervision covering all the clauses of the armistice. In Indo-China, men have been fighting for eight years. Whatever the value of the agreements we reach, they will be difficult to carry out and there is a danger of clashes.

Unless neutral and impartial supervisers, umpires or observers are empowered to deal with the differences and disputes likely to arise between parties which have been at war for so long, violations and perhaps serious incidents are to be feared. Without neutral supervision, there is a danger of the agreements losing all real force, and any chances of peace killed by perpetuating the atmosphere of mistrust.

As long ago as May 8, the French delegation proclaimed the principle of international supervision. Five delegations have expressed the same conviction. At the three restricted meetings devoted to supervision, I three times stated the position of the French delegation. On June 2, I circulated the written text of our observations to the members of the Conference. On June 4, I submitted a specific plan containing a detailed study of the duties and structure of the International Supervisory Commission and of the joint bodies to be attached to it as working instruments. That is the second element of the problem.

Under this plan, the International Commission will supervise the execution of the clauses of the agreements. It will install throughout the country, on its own responsibility, a complete supervisory system, partly fixed and partly mobile, and equipped with modern transport, communications and observation facilities. It will not be a Commission of just a few members scattered here and there over an immense territory, but a solid organisation, numerous and flexible enough to meet changing needs. Finally, the International Commission will have at its disposal, for specified duties, a number of joint commissions, composed of representatives of the two commands acting under its authority and in accordance with its instructions. In the event of any violation, directly it is clear that the parties cannot reach agreement and that consequently the joint commissions are powerless, the International Commission will deal with the dispute and enforce its decisions. Decisions of the Commission will in all cases be taken by a majority vote.

That is the system proposed by the French delegation. It establishes a logical and practical link between various bodies and so covers the whole subject.

On May 10, Mr. Pham Van Dong submitted a counter-proposal. Supervision should, in his view, be ensured by a joint Commission composed of representatives of the two parties. The experience of 1946 has taught us what to think of this kind of arrangement which, against all commonsense, is based on the principle that the same person is both judge and party.

Following M. Molotov's speech of May 14, his position was slightly modified. Provision for a neutral commission was added to the original Vietminh proposals. The main duty of this neutral Commission would be to supervise the entry of foreign supplies into Indo-China. On this point, we entirely agree with Mr. Dong. But as regards the other clauses of the armistice, in the most difficult cases, those where the two parties come face to face in the course of movements of regular troops on either side of the dividing line between the assembly areas, &c. Mr. Dong wishes to entrust the primary responsibility for supervision to the joint Commission. The French delegation has not yet been able to fathom in what circumstances that Commission would have to intervene. Under our plan, the joint commissions would be working instruments, subordinate to the International Commission. Mr. Dong and the Union of Soviet Socialist Republics and Chinese delegates after him, expressed his opposition to this system. There is a serious divergence here which will have to be bridged.

The third element of the problem is the membership of the International Commissions. In the French view the qualifications for selection are simple: objectivity, impartiality and efficiency. Any country possessing these qualifications is acceptable. As Mr. Eden very rightly remarked, if the

International Commission is the political counterpart of the joint commissions it will be paralysed in the same way. The proposal put forward by M. Molotov would have precisely this effect: four neutral powers, selected two by two for their particular sympathies, would be reduced to impotence. A supervisory body composed on this basis would be no guarantee for anyone. All that we, for our part, are trying to secure is the certainty that firm decisions will be taken whenever necessary.

Finally, there is the problem of the authority to which the International Control Commission is to be responsible. Unless the Commission has proper backing there is a danger of its decisions remaining a dead letter for lack of a court of appeal. Some body must be set up or selected to which the International Commission can appeal if circumstances so require. This body in turn would appeal to the guarantors. In our view, the guarantors should be the members of the Geneva Conference, that is the signatories of the future agreements. The problem of guarantees has not yet been seriously studied by the Conference. Only the principle has been accepted. All I need say to-day is that it must be impossible for the guarantees to be paralysed by any right of veto.

To end now, a statement which I would have liked to have been shorter, we have to record that the Conference has already achieved appreciable results. It has chosen an appropriate working method in agreeing, as the French delegation requested, to devote its present efforts to the military aspects of the problem of the cessation of hostilities. It has accepted the principle of a complete cessation of hostilities to apply, if possible, simultaneously throughout the whole of Indo-China.

In Viet Nam, it has adopted the principle of regrouping in assembly areas and entrusted the study of it to the competent persons. In the field of supervision, it has agreed to international commissions. We have already advanced several stages along the road that leads to peace.

I will not go so far, however, as to say with M. Molotov that the principles put forward in the Chinese proposal have met with the unanimous agreement of the Conference. Unfortunately, as I have already shown, serious differences of opinion have come to light during our debates on essential points. And, whatever spirit of conciliation we may show, there are limits beyond which we cannot go without infringing essential principles. In each case, the French delegation has endeavoured to be conciliatory; this has been particularly evident in the field of supervision.

I will merely recall that, on three main subjects, either we have not yet completed our examination or have not yet reached our conclusions.

The case of Laos and that of Cambodia have still to be discussed. We have explained in what they consist. In the circumstances I have described, it has not been possible for us to embark on a thorough discussion of them. It is clear, and it is precisely the argument of the Soviet, Chinese and Vietminh delegations, that we cannot restore peace in Viet Nam and leave Vietminh forces operating on its flank beyond its frontiers.

The military experts are getting on too slowly with their work which should lead to the establishment of the assembly areas. They have, however, to deal with concrete facts, and are not concerned with the political aspects. We hope that the geographical definition of the military agreement will be speeded up.

Finally and especially, it is an imperative necessity for all of us to reach agreement on the methods of application of supervision. I will not repeat what I have said on this subject. There are some problems of structure which are very important. There is the question of which countries should be chosen to carry out the supervision and that choice is crucial. Without effective supervision, I see no way out. Without the power of rapid decision, there would be disorder and all the risks attending the unforeseen.

Difficulties await us and we must not close our eyes to the fact that they are still extensive. I trust we may overcome them quickly. Efforts have been made and some progress has been achieved. The results obtained point the way to future agreements. We must neglect nothing in an endeavour to complete our work. The edifice that has only been started must be completed. It is on the completion of our work and not just on its beginning that depends the accomplishments of our task, which is the restoration of peace.

Document No. 20

Proposal by the Cambodian Delegation for the settlement of the Cambodian problem, June 8, 1954

1. A cessation of hostilities shall be proclaimed in Cambodia, if possible at the same time as a cessation of hostilities in Laos and Viet Nam. In case of an agreement on a simultaneous cessation of hostilities, the three plans for Cambodia, Laos and Viet Nam respectively shall be put into effect simultaneously.

2.—(*a*) All regular and irregular Vietminh forces shall, on the date of the cessation of hostilities, be evacuated from Cambodian territory and regrouped, in Viet Nam territory, in the assembly areas assigned to the Vietminh command by agreement between the French, Viet Nam and Vietminh commands.
For this purpose, the Cambodian and Vietminh commands shall meet on the spot to fix the method of execution of the evacuation.
(*b*) All armed elements belonging neither to the army nor to the police forces shall, on the date of the cessation of hostilities, be disarmed and dispersed. Foreign non-national elements shall be returned to their country of origin.

3. Prisoners of war and civil internees shall be released or exchanged after agreement between the Cambodian and Vietminh commands.

4. A system of international supervision by neutral countries or a system of supervision by the United Nations shall be established to supervise the execution of the above agreements. This system of international supervision must be installed and ready to operate on the date of the cessation of hostilities.

Document No. 21

Speech by M. Molotov, Minister for Foreign Affairs of the Union of Soviet Socialist Republics, June 8, 1954

Mr. Chairman, Delegates:
The restoration of peace in Indo-China is an important task for the Geneva Conference. The peoples of Indo-China are pinning their hopes on the Geneva Conference, in the expectation that it will contribute to ensuring peace, independence, freedom and unity for the peoples of Viet Nam, Laos and Cambodia. The sympathies of the peoples of the whole world are on the side of the national liberation movement of the peoples of Indo-China. Their struggle for national independence and freedom must receive recognition from this Conference. To those taking part in the Geneva Conference falls the responsible task of helping to bring about as soon as possible the cessation of hostilities and the establishment of a sure and stable peace in Indo-China.

142

Nor must the fact be overlooked, however, that evidently not all the participants in this Conference have the self-same understanding of their tasks. That is plain from what is going on at this Conference, and also round about it and concurrently with it. The impression is being created that not all the participants in the Conference are interested in restoring peace in Indo-China as soon as possible. Indeed, it is possible to take part in the Geneva Conference, but to see one's task as being not to restore peace in Indo-China but to prove the impossibility of reaching agreement on the question of ending the war in Indo-China. But those who are striving to prove the impossibility of reaching agreement are not only going the right way to drag out the war in Indo-China; they are in fact preparing for a further extension of the war, with all its dangerous consequences.

There is evidence to show that it is the intention of certain governments, instead of restoring peace, to pave the way for a further widening of the war in Indo-China and an extension of the number of those taking part in it. We cannot fail to reckon with such plans, with which the State Department of the United States is very closely connected.

That is shown by such facts as the continuing hullabaloo over the creation of the military *bloc* of so-called " South-East Asia," under the leadership of the United States of America and including certain colonial Powers and their most amenable satellites. It is also shown by the fact of the military talks going on in Washington between the United States of America, the United Kingdom, France, Australia and New Zealand. To this class of facts must be related the attempt by the Government of Thailand to impede settlement of the Indo-Chinese question at the Geneva Conference, a step clearly taken at the bidding of foreign aggressive circles. Thailand's proposal to establish, under the Security Council, a commission to observe the situation on the Indo-Chinese frontier is an attempt to prepare the ground in advance for some pretext or other for interference, in form by the United Nations but in fact by the United States of America, in the internal affairs of Indo-China; its purpose is to undermine confidence in the Geneva Conference, which is dealing with specific questions relating to the restoration of peace in Indo-China.

We cannot neglect the fact that in aggressive circles in certain countries there are apprehensions on account of the possibility of some positive results being achieved at the Geneva Conference with regard to a peaceful settlement of the Indo-Chinese question. In these circumstances, the Soviet delegation considers it essential to stress the great responsibility which rests on this Conference for ending hostilities and restoring peace in Indo-China.

The Soviet Union, for its part, regards the cessation of hostilities in Indo-China, not as a short breathing-space before further continuation, and possibly extension, of the war, but as the establishment of a lasting peace. For this very reason, we regard it as essential for the Geneva Conference to consider both military and political questions.

I.—*The Question of a Cessation of Hostilities*

When we took up consideration of the Indo-Chinese question, agreement was reached that we should begin with military questions, and go on later to consider questions of a political settlement in Indo-China. The time has now come to sum up some of the results of the past four weeks' consideration of military questions and to postpone no longer the consideration of questions of a political settlement, the more so since the discussion has confirmed the fact that these two categories of questions are closely inter-related.

Proposals relating to the cessation of hostilities in Indo-China have been submitted both by the delegation of the Democratic Republic of Viet Nam and by the French delegation. In the course of the discussion the delegation

143

of the People's Republic of China submitted its proposals concerning the basic principles of an agreement on the cessation of hostilities. Consideration of these proposals has shown that on a number of questions there have been signs of a *rapprochement* between the viewpoints of the participants in the Conference.

First and foremost among such questions is that of the need for the simultaneous cessation of hostilities throughout Indo-Chinese territory by all the armed forces of the belligerents. Although certain reservations were made here in this connexion, we have none the less, as is well known, reached agreement on this question.

In view of the complicated military situation in Indo-China, settlement of the question of assembly-zones for the forces of the two sides is a necessary condition of a cessation of hostilities. This question cannot be settled otherwise than by direct negotiations between the two sides, and in accordance with the decision taken by the Conference on May 29, their military representatives have already established contact, here in Geneva. The need is also recognised for similar contact to be established on the spot in Indo-China. Consideration of the question of zones and of the corresponding dispositions of the troops of both sides has already begun, and this is an important step towards settling the Indo-Chinese question.

In the course of the discussion it has also been established that all the participants in the Geneva Conference agree in principle to the proposal of the Democratic Republic of Viet Nam that the cessation of hostilities in Indo-China should be accompanied by a ban on the movement into Indo-China from outside of fresh troops and military personnel of all kinds, and also of every type of armaments and military supplies. And that is understandable, since any agreement on the cessation of hostilities can be turned into a mere scrap of paper unless care is taken to prohibit the movement of troops, armaments and military supplies into Indo-China from outside. If that is not done, the cessation of hostilities could be used as a short breathing-space for massing strength and renewing the war, possibly on a still larger scale.

Nor have any doubts been aroused in the participants in the Conference by the proposal to set up joint commissions of representatives of the two sides to supervise the implementation of the terms of the Agreement on the cessation of hostilities. The role to be played by such commissions is an important one, if only because the main responsibility for carrying out the said Agreement should fall precisely on the parties directly concerned and because, in the event of the parties not endeavouring to observe the compact arrived at, no one else will be able to ensure that the Agreement which has been signed has the consequences which it should have.

The question of the need for establishing international supervision of the carrying out of the terms of the Agreement on the cessation of hostilities in Indo-China has been given specially detailed consideration. All delegations have agreed that to put such international supervision into effect requires the creation of an appropriate, authoritative international body. I shall have to dwell further on this question, since there are serious divergencies between the various delegations' views concerning it.

As is known, the Soviet delegation has also adopted a positive attitude towards the French proposal that the participants in the Geneva Conference should assume obligations to guarantee the implementation of the Agreement on the cessation of hostilities in Indo-China. Other delegations, too, have spoken in favour of the necessity of guarantees, although not all aspects of this question have been sufficiently examined.

There are, however, questions on which there exist divergencies of view between the various delegations.

What are these questions?

First of all it is necessary to dwell on the question of International Supervision of the carrying out of the Agreement.

As is known, the Soviet Union has proposed the establishment of a Neutral Nations' Supervisory Commission, composed of India, Poland, Czechoslovakia and Pakistan. Two of these countries—India and Pakistan—have diplomatic relations with the one side, namely with France, and two of the others—Poland and Czechoslovakia—have diplomatic relations with the other side, namely with the Democratic Republic of Viet Nam. The Soviet delegation considers that an international commission with this composition would have the necessary authority and could ensure that there was no one-sidedness or partiality to either side in the work of this international body. Objections to the participation in this commission of countries such as Poland and Czechoslovakia, on the pretext that ideological considerations prevent them from taking a neutral attitude in this matter, are completely unfounded. Such objections can be raised to no less an extent against capitalist countries. In this connexion, it is obviously forgotten that this argument is a two-edged sword, a fact on which it is surely hardly necessary to enlarge. Nor must it be forgotten that in the Korean armistice agreement also a Neutral Nations Commission was set up, including representatives of Poland and Czechoslovakia. The present attempts to discredit this Korean Commission are plainly worthless and can only be regarded as denoting a desire to prevent agreement from being reached on an important question

Nor has the necessary agreement yet been reached with regard to the tasks and functions either of the International Supervisory Commission or of the joint commissions composed of representatives of the two sides. The relationship of these bodies to one another must be determined by differentiating their functions.

The main task of the Commission of Neutral States is:—

to ensure that there shall be no movement into Indo-China of troops and personnel of all types, and also of any kind of armaments and military supplies;

to supervise the implementation by both sides of the decisions regarding the fixing of military demarcation lines and the establishment of demilitarised zones;

to supervise the transfer of military units, carried out with a view to readjustment of the zones;

to supervise the work of both sides in repatriating prisoners of war and civilian internees;

at the request of a joint commission or of either side in such a commission, to investigate cases of breach of the Agreement of the cessation of hostilities in the demilitarised zones and to submit proposals to both sides for eliminating the breaches in question.

The task of the joint commissions is to ensure that specific measures are taken on the spot with regard to carrying out the terms of the Agreement on the cessation of hostilities. These measures will relate to:—

supervision so as to ensure that the cease-fire is simultaneous and general;

execution of the plan for readjustment of zones, and regrouping of the armed forces of both sides;

settlement of other questions, connected with a breach of the terms of the Agreement, by negotiation between military representatives of the two sides.

The question arises, what will happen if agreement is not reached on some question or other within these commissions or between them. In other words, where is the body to which appeal should be made in the event of a difference of opinion in the commission? It is not difficult to answer this question if one takes as a basis the proposal I have already referred to, that certain states should become guarantors for implementation of the Agreement on the cessation of hostilities in Indo-China. That means that the guarantor states are the body to which appeal should be made when necessary. On them will rest an obligation to take the proper agreed steps to eliminate any breach of the appropriate Agreement or the threat of any such breach.

It is impossible not to recognise that the question of the character and functions of supervision to ensure the implementation of the terms of the agreement on the cessation of hostilities in Indo-China requires further consideration. If we all agree to certain basic premises, however, there will be no specially serious obstacles to reaching agreement on this important question.

During consideration of the problem of restoring peace in Indo-China the question has arisen whether a decision on the cessation of hostilities and on the establishment of suitable conditions for an armistice should apply to all three Indo-Chinese States. In this connexion, differences of opinion have appeared among the participants in the Conference. The Soviet delegation bases itself on the premise that our task is to restore peace in Indo-China as a whole, and that is, moreover, what is envisaged in the Berlin Communiqué.

In this connexion it must be borne in mind that the events in all three Indo-Chinese States—Viet Nam, Cambodia and Laos—have the same basic causes. The events which have developed in Indo-China show that in Viet Nam, as well as in Laos and Cambodia, what is taking place is a struggle for national liberation against a foreign colonial power. Those taking part in this struggle are not only particular armed forces, but also the peoples themselves. Only this can explain the scope and the strength of the national liberation movement in Indo-China.

Naturally, the differences in the national liberation movement in the separate Indo-Chinese States cannot be ignored.

Thus, in Viet Nam three-quarters of the country's territory is not under the control of the official authorities of the Bao Dai Government. It is well known that vast tracts of Viet Nam territory in the north, as well as in the centre and the south, of the country are administered by organs of the Government of the Democratic Republic of Viet Nam. As regards Laos, here too approximately half the territory of the country is not under the control of the official governmental organs. In Cambodia the extent of territory which is not under the control of the official authorities is less than in other districts of Indo-China, but even here the struggle for national liberation is developing. It would therefore be wrong to deny the existence of a struggle for national liberation either in Laos or Cambodia and to explain what is going on there by the influence of some outside factors or other, such as interference by the armed forces of Viet Nam. The head of the delegation of the Democratic Republic of Viet Nam has convincingly refuted assertions of that type.

The representatives of Laos and of Cambodia who are present here hold a different opinion on this subject. But then the representative of the Bao Dai Government who is present among us is also prepared to deny the existence of a national liberation movement in Viet Nam, although the hollowness of these assertions is obvious. It can be said with every justification that statements of that kind bear witness to the fact that neither the real situation nor any real connexion with the people of the country is reflected in them and that widely known facts are denied without any supporting evidence.

Some participants in the Conference have attempted to persuade us that the problem of establishing the independence of the Indo-Chinese States of

Viet Nam, Laos and Cambodia has already been fully settled and that the national demands of these countries have already been satisfied. In this connexion the representative of Cambodia referred to the agreements with France of 1949 and 1953. The representative of Laos referred here to the agreement with France of 1949. Finally, the representative of the Bao Dai Government referred to the recent agreement with France which, however, still remains unsigned and therefore unpublished. None of these declarations is of a nature to inspire confidence, since they did not guarantee nor do they guarantee real independence of the Indo-Chinese States. In this situation it is understandable why scarcely a single State in Asia, including India, Pakistan, Indonesia and Burma, attaches any serious importance to such declarations. Only in this way is it possible to explain why the countries of Asia do not wish to have diplomatic relations either with Viet Nam or with Laos or Cambodia. Moreover, reference could be made, for example, to statements by prominent statesmen and social leaders in France and the United States of America, who are devoting considerable attention to Indo-China; these statements contain definite acknowledgements of the existence of a national liberation movement in all three countries of Indo-China and at the same time point out the necessity of the independence of Viet Nam, Laos and Cambodia being ensured at last by France.

The war in Indo-China has already been going on for eight years. Great efforts have been made by the Government of France to achieve its aims by military measures, but to no effect.

Since the Democratic Republic of Viet Nam was first formed, there have been a good many plans aimed at defeating its army and crushing the Democratic Republic of Viet Nam in order to restore the colonial régime. This has cost the peoples of Indo-China heavy sacrifices. At the same time, the war in Indo-China has inflicted on the French people heavy losses in lives and material resources.

After initial successes, achieved as a result of a sudden attack on the Democratic Republic of Viet Nam, the French expeditionary force began year after year to suffer defeats, in spite of all the deliveries of American arms: tanks, aircraft, military supplies and other war equipment and material, the amount of which has been steadily increasing in recent years. It is appropriate here to give some of the figures concerning the losses of the French expeditionary force in Indo-China, which have become widely known from the statements made in the National Assembly of France. These losses are considerably more than 100,000 killed and wounded, and they are steadily increasing. The Indo-Chinese war has cost France over 2,000 milliard francs. According to the data published in the American magazine *Reader's Digest* for May 1954: "The 8-year War has cost France almost as much as she has received from the United States in economic and military aid."

Quite recently high praise has been given to the plan of General Navarre, in connexion with which the United States of America Secretary of State, said last year that the war in Indo-China would be successfully ended in the course of the coming year, that is in the course of 1954. In another statement made in February 1954, a representative of the State Department said: "We have put our signature to General Navarre's plan and we believe that it will bring success." It did not take long before hopes for the success of such plans had to be given up. It must be admitted that this fact is an instructive one.

II.—*The political problems of Indo-China*

I have been obliged to touch upon military events in Indo-China, as well as upon their consequences. It must be recognised, however, that the restoration of peace in Indo-China is not concerned only with military questions.

It is quite obvious that the task of establishing lasting peace in Indo-China requires a settlement of political problems. This has been repeatedly pointed out by the Soviet delegation, when it spoke in support of the proposals submitted by the Democratic Republic of Viet Nam for the consideration of the Conference.

In this connexion, two fundamental problems are of great importance. The first relates to the mutual relations between France and the States of Indo-China. The second concerns the internal political situation in the Indo-Chinese States.

The Soviet delegation considers that the position of the Democratic Republic of Viet Nam, which has been set forth here, in regard to mutual relations with France, provides the essential pre-requisites for an amicable settlement of this problem between the parties concerned, should France also desire such a settlement.

We have heard here statements to the effect that France has expressed its willingness to recognise the independence of Viet Nam and the other Indo-Chinese States and to give the requisite guarantee of their sovereignty and national interests. On the other hand, we know that the Government of the Democratic Republic of Viet Nam has expressed its willingness to examine the question of the Democratic Republic of Viet Nam joining the French Union in accordance with the principle of voluntary association. Since both sides declare that the question of mutual relations can be settled on the basis of recognising the principles of national freedom and independence, it would seem that the settlement of this problem should not encounter any insurmountable obstacles.

The official representatives of the King of Cambodia and the King of Laos have stated here that the question of the independence of these kingdoms has been fully settled almost since 1949. The representative of the Bao Dai Government, in his turn, referred to and quoted the text, which has not been signed by anyone and, apparently, is still in his pocket. The unconvincing nature of these statements has already been mentioned. It can be said that these statements do not inspire confidence anywhere.

Here, for instance, is what is said in the report of May 12, 1953, of the Special Mission of the House of Representatives of the United States of America to Pakistan, India, Thailand and Indo-China on the question of the situation in Indo-China: "Despite French statements of intent to grant independence, many Indo-Chinese say that the unrest and failure to develop stronger support of their Government is because the people do not have the necessary confidence in their rulers nor in the willingness of the French to grant genuine independence . . . ." This statement was made in the spring of last year. In another report of the Special Mission of the House of Representatives of the United States of America, dating back to January 29, 1954, on the results of its visit to the countries of South-East Asia, further reference was made to the Indo-Chinese States' lack of "political independence."

These statements of American missions relating both to the past and to the present year are deserving of attention, since they record facts, although actually they are imbued with a spirit of hostility towards the national liberation movement in Indo-China.

But much greater significance attaches to those simple and well-known facts which relate to the position in Indo-China.

Who will deny that the defence of Dien Bien Phu was carried out in the main, not by the forces of the French or the forces of the Vietnamese, but by the forces of all kinds of foreigners brought together there? In the troops of Dien Bien Phu garrison, the overwhelming majority consisted of men who had no connexion whatever either with France or with Viet Nam. And these men, you see, were defending the interests of Viet Nam, although the Vietnamese people had not asked them to do so.

In regard to the troops of the Democratic Republic of Viet Nam the situation is altogether different. Its troops consisted only of Vietnamese. All attempts to put abroad rumours about the presence of foreigners in these troops proved to be a falsification obvious to everybody. Does this not show on whose side the Vietnamese people stand? Attempts to belittle the significance of the national liberation movement break down against facts of this kind.

Take another recent example.

A short while ago, in May, the Bao Dai Government carried out the mobilisation of Vietnamese men in order to increase his army. You know how the matter ended. Only 10 per cent. of those called up put in an appearance. Ninety per cent. did not want to go into the army of the Bao Dai Government. It is worth while recalling also a communication published two days ago in the English newspaper *The Observer*. According to this communication: " The Vietnamese Army of Bao Dai is now losing more recruits through desertions and passive resistance than it can effectively raise through new call-ups." Do not these current facts show that the people are not on the side of the present Bao Dai authorities and that the Vietnamese people are following an altogether different path, giving more and more active support to its own Democratic Republic?

In these circumstances what is the meaning of the continuation of the colonial war in Indo-China? It cannot mean anything else than a further deepening of the differences between France and the peoples of Indo-China. Yet the statements of the Government of the Democratic Republic of Viet Nam and those of the Government of France both bear witness to the possibility of finding a common language for setting the mutual relations between France and Viet Nam, as well as between France and the other Indo-Chinese States. If the Government of France is really anxious to establish the independence of the States of Indo-China, then in the present circumstances there are no grounds for continuing the war in Indo-China, since important pre-requisites for an amicable settlement of these mutual relations have been brought about. This settlement has now become possible on honourable terms for both sides. In any case, nobody is going to prove that the continuation of the war in Indo-China is required by the national interests of France. On the contrary, to refuse or evade negotiations on this question with the real representatives of the Vietnamese people is, in our opinion, contrary to the national interests of France.

Great importance attaches also to the settlement of the internal political situation in Viet Nam and in the other Indo-Chinese States.

We have listened here to the claim of Bao Dai representative on the subject of the internal political settlement in Viet Nam. The Bao Dai Government, it appears, also speaks of free elections on the territory of Viet Nam. But, according to his proposals, only such elections would have to be held and only at such a time in Viet Nam as would ensure the maintenance of the present Bao Dai régime, whose complete lack of authority is a matter of common knowledge. But in fact general elections are not necessary to such a régime. Elections are a danger to it. Such a régime does not rest on the people but on foreign bayonets.

In this connexion it may be appropriate to recall what was said in the French National Assembly on March 5, 1954, concerning the Bao Dai Government by such an authoritative French statesman as M. Daladier: —

" This Government does not have the confidence of the people. This is shown by the fact that it could have recourse only to a caricature of municipal and provincial elections: in a region such as Hue, for example, where there are 250,000–300,000 inhabitants, the right to vote was given only to 7,000–8,000 persons, and even they did not vote for the candidates of His Majesty Bao Dai."

In this connexion I will also mention that the English weekly *The Spectator* recently stated: " Free elections in Viet Nam would undoubtedly result at the present stage in the victory of Ho Chi Minh over Bao Dai."

The foregoing is clarified to some extent by the comments of the French newspaper *France-Observateur* on June 3, which gave the following appraisal of the present situation in Viet Nam:—

" The hostile attitude to Bao Dai is all the stronger because he has not kept his promises in the field of internal policy, such as, to put an end to corruption, carry out agrarian reform, put into practice a labour code, &c. The workers' standard of living has fallen 60 per cent. in comparison with 1939. The press censorship is more terrible than ever."

The reports that have been quoted, the number of which could be multiplied many times, show that the internal political situation on the territory of Viet Nam occupied by French troops is catastrophic, since the present Government is not connected with the people and does not express its interests to any extent. The proposal of the Democratic Republic of Viet Nam that free elections should be held is particularly important for a genuine improvement of the political and economic situation in Viet Nam. The recent statement by the United States of America Secretary of State on the immaturity of Viet Nam and his unsympathetic attitude towards the holding of free elections in Indo-China do not provide any evidence of a desire to settle the internal political situation in Viet Nam and in the other States of Indo-China. However, the Geneva Conference ought not to evade giving an answer to the demand of the Viet Namese people that free elections should be held as soon as possible, so as to ensure on the basis of free general elections the formation of a single democratic government for the whole of Viet Nam. The Geneva Conference cannot pass over this question in silence. But this concerns, first and foremost, the Government of France, which must declare its attitude towards free elections in Viet Nam and in the other States of Indo-China.

Of course, the holding of free elections requires that certain conditions be observed. The Viet Namese people should take this matter into their own hands and ensure the freedom of activity of patriotic parties, groups and social organisations in preparing for and conducting free general elections. That would open up a better and really hopeful path towards the restoration of the unity of Viet Nam. It is essential that corresponding measures be carried out also in the other States of Indo-China. The holding of free elections must be preceded by the withdrawal of all foreign troops from the territory of the States of Indo-China, which, of course, requires an appropriate settlement of the military problems under discussion at the Conference.

The Soviet delegation has deemed it necessary to recall the fundamental political problems requiring a solution in respect of all three States of Indo-China. These include, first of all, the question of establishing new mutual relations between France and the three Indo-Chinese States on the basis of genuine recognition of the principles of the national independence and freedom of the peoples of Indo-China. Also included is the question of the holding of free elections in Viet Nam and in the other Indo-Chinese States, which would make it possible to bring about the earliest possible restoration of the unity of the States and the formation of authoritative democratic governments. We cannot leave aside the settlement of these problems, if we wish to ensure the restoration of sure and stable peace in Indo-China.

Direct contact has now been established in Geneva between the parties on questions of a military nature. This contact must also be established on the spot, in Indo-China, as all of us have recently acknowledged. The outcome of these direct negotiations must be examined by us at the Conference.

At the same time, it is necessary to discuss those important political problems, the solution of which will make it possible to establish peace, which is so necessary, in all the States of Indo-China. Naturally, the establishment of direct contact between the parties will also be of great importance for the settlement of the political problems.

The Soviet delegation considers that, besides examining the military problems under discussion at the Conference, it has become necessary to: --

1. Examine without further delay political problems requiring to be settled in connexion with the situation which has arisen in Indo-China. We could for this purpose adopt a procedure whereby military and political questions should be examined simultaneously in such a way that the meetings devoted to military and political questions would be held alternately.

2. Examine in the first place questions connected with the granting of sovereignty and independence to the three Indo-Chinese States, with the holding of free general elections in these States, as well as with the withdrawal of all foreign troops from the territory of Indo-China.

3. Ensure the establishment of direct contact between the representatives of both sides to discuss political questions; this could have a positive significance and would enhance the possibility of reaching an appropriate agreement on these questions.

The Soviet delegation is anxious to help in every way so that both military and political questions may be examined as speedily as possible. We hope that all the participants in the Geneva Conference desire to have these discussions make headway, since the re-establishment of sure and stable peace in Indo-China depends on this.

To-day we have heard the statement by the Head of the French delegation in which he said that the Geneva Conference had already achieved some results on the way to peace. The significance of this statement will depend on how far the subsequent steps of the French delegation will be in keeping with it.

Document No. 22

Speech by Mr. Eden, Secretary of State for Foreign Affairs, June 8, 1954

More than three weeks have gone by since we last discussed Indo-China in plenary session. I think public opinion everywhere will expect to hear what we have achieved during that time. My colleagues will no doubt agree that we have made some progress even if this has been slow. But the differences on the main problems before us are still formidable. Unless we can resolve them we shall have failed in our task.

An important step forward was our agreement, on May 29, that representatives of the two military commands in Viet Nam should discuss the terms of a cessation of hostilities in that country. These talks have now begun in Geneva. It is to be hoped that these military exchanges will soon bear fruit in the shape of agreed recommendations to the Conference. But these talks concern only Viet Nam. The Conference has yet to come to grips with the separate and distinct problems of Laos and Cambodia. I think we can all agree that the cessation of hostilities should be simultaneous throughout Indo-China. It is the arrangements, not the timing, that need to be different in Laos and Cambodia. In Viet Nam the arrangements to be worked out must inevitably be complicated. In Laos and Cambodia we have to deal with the formidable but entirely distinct problem of Vietminh invasion. I cannot regard these aggressive acts, some of which have taken place since this Conference was announced at Berlin, as acts of peace. Nor are they merely symptoms of internal troubles. Therefore no one should be surprised that they cause concern far beyond the confines of the states concerned. If foreign troops are withdrawn from those two countries, the peoples of Laos and Cambodia can be left to work out their own destiny, safeguarded by international supervision from interference from beyond their borders.

In this connexion I note that the representative of Cambodia has told us to-day that Cambodia has no intention of allowing military bases to be established on her territory which might threaten the peace of Indo-China; and that Cambodia is willing, under appropriate conditions, to limit her own forces to those needed for the defence of her territory.

Now I come to another crucial issue—international supervision. We are all agreed that this must form an essential part of the arrangements arrived at for the restoration of peace in Indo-China. This all-important problem, which is common to all the three States of Indo-China, is now the central issue before the Conference. It has, I think, been accepted that in the case of Viet Nam there should be joint committees of the two belligerents, in addition to international supervision. These joint committees could probably render some useful service provided that it was clearly understood that their functions were mainly technical and clearly subordinate to the authority of an International Supervisory Commission.

After eight years of bitter fighting, even with the best will in the world, we must expect that there will be differences between the two sides comprising the joint committees. It is therefore essential to provide for an International Supervisory Commission endowed with power to resolve these differences and to ensure the proper execution of all the provisions of the agreement for the cessation of hostilities.

Here I should like to make a suggestion, which is, I submit, practical. Over a month ago, the Prime Ministers of Burma, Ceylon, India, Indonesia and Pakistan met at Colombo and discussed, among other matters, the problems of Indo-China. The communiqué they issued after their discussions has, I think, been of real value to our deliberations here. I should like to suggest that the Asian Powers represented at that Colombo Conference are admirably qualified to assume the responsibilities of supervising whatever arrangements are reached by this Conference. These five countries meet the essential requirement of impartiality. They have recognised neither the Vietminh nor the Associate States. We are bound to agree that as Asian countries they have a particular concern in the restoration of peace in Indo-China and possess first-hand knowledge of the kind of problems confronting us there. Moreover, they are probably close enough to be able to provide and organise without undue difficulty the large staff of qualified observers that will be needed.

Finally, there could be no danger of a deadlock on an International Supervisory Commission consisting of a panel of these five powers acting by majority vote. This danger would however clearly arise if the Supervisory Commission were to consist of an even number of states—half communist and half non-communist—as has been suggested by M. Molotov. When we have solved the problems of the authority and composition of the proposed International Supervisory Commission, it will be necessary to study in detail its functions and structure. We shall also have to examine more fully the question of a guarantee by the members of this Conference of the arrangements reached. Any such guarantee must be so designed as to ensure that no one power has a veto over action considered necessary to secure observance of the agreements.

To sum up, therefore, the following are the immediate tasks: First, it is necessary for the military representatives of the two commands to submit agreed recommendations to the Conference for its consideration.

Meanwhile, we have two urgent tasks. First, to reach agreement on the composition and powers of the International Supervisory Commission: second, to deal with the special problems of Laos and Cambodia.

Until we have done these things the Conference cannot be held to have made any decisive contribution to the re-establishment of peace in Indo-China.

SIXTH PLENARY SESSION ON INDO-CHINA

Document No. 23

Speech by M. Phoui Sananikone, Head of the Laotian Delegation, June 9, 1954

The delegation of Laos asked to speak yesterday because it thought it desirable to take stock and clarify its position in relation to what has been done so far.

Owing to the course the meeting took, it did not have an opportunity to speak, but does not regard that as a matter for regret since it hopes that what it has to say will enjoy a more propitious atmosphere to-day.

First of all, it must deplore the turn taken at yesterday's meeting. After a month's debate precious time is still being wasted on unjust and immoderate accusations instead of being devoted to discussions expressly dedicated to the search for peace and conciliation.

The delegation of Laos does not consider that such frantic condemnation and biased repetition helps the cause of peace in Indo-China.

M. Molotov is too able and too experienced a statesman not to hearken to what he himself calls the lesson of facts.

Facts are facts.

There is little chance of our agreeing on their origin or their doctrinal explanation. We are not here for that. We are here because, as we understand it, at Berlin the representatives of four Powers wisely agreed that means of ending the war in Indo-China and restoring conditions for a lasting peace there must be sought round a conference table.

To condemn one side by maliciously castigating everything it does or may have done, and praise the other with a reckless disregard for the facts, can only exacerbate differences and in some measure justify the conflict.

We are here, on the contrary, to end the conflict, that is to say, to find common ground for immediate reconciliation and a lasting agreement.

Our view of the world does not recognise unrelieved black and white or unbounded good and evil. Consequently, for the sake of the cease-fire and the peace for which we must jointly and passionately strive, we prefer to remember only one passage from M. Molotov's speech here yesterday, namely, that in which he said: "important prerequisites for an amicable settlement . . . . have been brought about. This settlement has now become possible on honourable terms for both sides."

Those words bring us back, in our view, to the root of the question which concerns us.

All the delegations certainly subscribe to them, while the delegation of Laos interprets them as evidence that peace is on the move and that a continuation of hostilities is condemned.

153

After much apparently inevitable grouping, the Conference gradually reached agreement on an empirical approach which, without shelving the difficult questions, could bring us straight to the immediate objective of our meetings, a cease-fire which would enable the conditions of a lasting peace, based not on illusions but on security and justice, to be considered more calmly at a later date.

Our common aim was thus to begin by fixing the conditions governing a cease-fire throughout Indo-China. The delegation of Laos, like all the delegations here, hopes that this will be rapidly achieved. If such an agreement were concluded for the three States, nothing could be more welcome in Laos than the simultaneous cessation of hostilities throughout Indo-China.

We want to be realistic, however, and it would appear to us to be going too far to decline the advantages of a cease-fire in one of the three countries, on the pretext that agreement had not yet been possible for the whole Indo-Chinese theatre of war.

It is in this spirit, and not out of selfish considerations, that the delegation of Laos supported the proposal that priority should be given to study of the military aspects of the cease-fire in Laos and Cambodia.

To proceed from the simple to the complex seemed to us a procedure acceptable to all. Similarly, it seems to us elementary that separate things should be dealt with separately.

Now the situation in Laos and Cambodia cannot be compared with the situation in Viet Nam; and it is quite simple.

It is different because there is no civil war in Laos and Cambodia; and it is simple because withdrawal of the foreign invading troops would mean *de facto* the cessation of hostilities there.

To support these assertions, I do not intend to go over in detail what I have already said about the situation in Laos.

The statements which we heard yesterday, however, might encourage some confusion about the real state of affairs in our country. We regret that very much, particularly since all the sceptics need to do is to pay a visit to Laos and see just what the situation is and then their prejudices would disappear.

Briefly, there are three fundamental points we can make without fear of contradiction by even the most exacting observers if they would agree to go and seek enlightenment on the spot.

First Point.—Laos is independent.

On October 22, 1953, it signed with France a treaty of independence and association of which M. Molotov and Mr. Dong appear to be ignorant. This treaty, which unequivocally proclaims our national independence, at the same time renews Laos's membership of the French Union on a basis of equality.

We do not think that countries which pride themselves on achieving federal unity amidst a variety of nationalities can fail to recognise that our membership of the French Union merely safeguards and strengthens our independence in a world where absolute autonomy can only lead immediately to the worst forms of enslavement.

Second Point.—We maintain that in Laos national sentiment, centred in His Majesty Sisavang Vong, is unanimous to a degree which many countries might envy us.

The members of the former resistance movement which arose out of the war take a leading part in the country's civic life. Our democratic and parliamentary institutions have been set up without violence to anyone, and all shades of opinion can obtain representation in the National Assembly, which since 1947 has been elected by direct and universal suffrage. Since then two legislatures have seen six governments follow one another in accordance with normal constitutional processes.

There is therefore no room for despotism or coercion. In Laos opinions are not crimes, and political minorities are not persecuted. Any change in the state of opinion resulting from the cessation of hostilities would be reflected in the elections, and the Assembly, to which the government is responsible, would act accordingly, under the Constitution.

Third Point.—We have said, and we repeat, that the military operations in Laos are the work of Vietminh troops, that is to say of troops foreign to the country by race, tradition and ideology.

We maintain that the so-called "free government," which by a gross abuse of language they mis-term "the Laos Resistance Government", has been fabricated lock, stock and barrel by the foreign invaders.

Mr. Pham Van Dong has told us that a "free Laotian administration" was being installed in the occupied zones. For the good of the inhabitants I wish it were so. But alas, that is far from being the case. This so-called Government does not exist apart from the Vietminh, and has no seat other than the Vietminh military command posts. Its widely-advertised plans for reform remain a dead letter. On the other hand, Vietminh imposes relentless social coercion.

In the province of Samneua, which has been occupied since April 1953, children are sent to Viet Nam for communist, indoctrination, the whole population up to the age of 56 (including children and pregnant women) is forced to do haulage and road work, while rice, salt, &c., are requisitioned unmercifully.

To give some idea of the tyranny which the villagers of Laos are suffering at the hands of the Vietminh invaders, all I need to mention is that possession of salt is regarded as "capitalist" hoarding, and that it is forbidden for three people to be seen together if their clothes happen to be red, white and blue, because that would make up the flag of the "French imperialists." In such circumstances it is a paradox to pose as the champions of freedom.

The head of the Vietminh delegation told us a few days ago that the so-called "National Liberation Army of Pathet Lao" entered Laos to carry out land reform and fight against illiteracy.

The redistribution of land certainly figures on the programme of the Popular Movements in many Asian countries. But for anyone who knows Laos and its economic problems, it is almost cruel irony to talk of dividing up the land when there are too few inhabitants to cultivate the immense areas available. As regards the fight against illiteracy, I should be glad if the sole aim of the so-called "Pathet Lao Government" was this praiseworthy campaign. I should then invite its few supporters to waste no time in offering their services to His Majesty's Government, which is short of teachers for the expanding public education programmes, the annual appropriations for which, as voted by the National Assembly, account for one-third of total public expenditure.

That is the situation in Laos, and it must be acknowledged that it is clear enough and cannot be compared with the present situation in Viet Nam. The delegation of Laos therefore felt that it was reasonable that this question should be taken up first. Unfortunately agreement could not be reached on this point, but the Conference, turning its attention to study of the military problems in Viet Nam, has been able to reach a welcome agreement for meetings of military experts to examine the conditions for the regrouping of forces.

We await with confidence the result of their labours and hope that a spirit of mutual conciliation will enable an agreement to be reached which will be a decisive step towards the cessation of hostilities in Viet Nam.

We also hope that the question of the cessation of hostilities in Laos and Cambodia can soon be the subject of thorough examination by the Conference. We shall then give our views in detail as to the conditions which must be met.

Meanwhile, the Conference is continuing its work and is reviewing the various conditions for a cease-fire in Viet Nam.

One of these is of particular importance, that relating to supervision of the agreements. Although we are at present dealing with Viet Nam, the delegation of Laos considers that the general conditions which must be fulfilled by the supervision arrangements will be substantially the same in the three countries. It therefore wishes to make known its point of view.

Delegations have agreed that the supervision must be effective and impartial. They have also recognised the desirability of international supervision. Where differences of view emerge is on how efficacy and impartiality are to be achieved and, especially on the role to be played by international supervision.

By their very nature the duties of the supervisory body cover all fields in which breaches of the agreements are liable to occur. In the case of Viet Nam for example, mention has been made of the regrouping of forces, the release of prisoners of war and civil internees, the ban on the entry of foreign supplies and troops, and on the manufacture of military supplies inside the country. But this list, it seems to me, cannot be exhaustive. As a result of the work of the representatives of the High Commands on the regrouping of forces, attention will doubtless be drawn to certain other points such as troop movements, right of passage, normal supply arrangements, provisional administration in the assembly areas, &c. Would it not also be desirable for a committee to examine in detail all the other aspects of this supervision work in Viet Nam, with a view to submitting recommendations to the Conference?

Moreover, the supervisory body must discharge its duties wherever breaches may occur. Real, impartial supervision will therefore have to extend to the whole of Viet Nam and take a sufficient variety of forms to be able to function even in the most difficult country.

Consequently, the supervisory machinery will need a very large staff and extensive liaison facilities.

Here, in the view of the delegation of Laos, is where the joint commissions in Viet Nam come in. Their duty is not one " of principle." It consists not in exercising supervision but in facilitating it, through knowledge of the country and of local conditions, and also through their opportunities for liaison with the executive authorities of the two parties.

The real responsibility, the actual exercise of supervision, can only fall to a neutral international body.

It must be recognised that, contrary to what was said by the Head of the Viet Nam delegation, it is only outside the two parties concerned that impartial supervision can be established.

It would accordingly seem Utopian to accept Mr. Pham Van Dong's view that the two parties' desire for peace is a guarantee that everything will pass off very well without outside supervision.

We believe, on the contrary, that the selection of the countries to take part in this supervision is a vital question and that it is a test of the good faith of the parties to entrust the task of supervision to an impartial and independent body, whose decisions would be taken by a majority vote.

The delegation of Laos, voicing the thoughts of the Government and of the people of Laos, would have preferred that for this purpose recourse should be had to the machinery of the United Nations. The task to be entrusted to it is appropriate to its fundamental purpose of arbitration,

156

pacification and serene neutrality. On this point we share the view of the delegation of the State of Viet Nam.

If, however, agreement cannot be reached on this point, the delegation of Laos is prepared to examine other possibilities. The absolute essential is neutrality. At the same time, we would like it to be clear-sighted and realistic neutrality. In this respect, Asian countries which are not concerned in the conflict seem to us to be particularly well fitted for this responsibility. If this suggestion were accepted, we would then submit firm proposals. Our preference would be for countries such as Pakistan, Thailand, India, Ceylon and the Philippines.

We are convinced that agreement is possible in this matter. The delegation of Laos, for its part, will display a spirit of broad comprehension.

Document No. 24

Speech by Mr. Chou En-lai, Minister for Foreign Affairs of the People's Republic of China, June 9, 1954

Mr. Chairman and Fellow Delegates:

It is now more than one month since on May 8 the Geneva Conference started to discuss the question of restoring peace in Indo-China. The people of the whole world are earnestly hoping that the Conference will be able to reach agreement speedily, and that it will be possible to stop the war and restore peace in Indo-China at an early date.

During this month we have met in a series of restricted as well as open meetings and taking by common consent the French delegation's proposal of May 8 and the Democratic Republic of Viet Nam delegation's proposal of May 10 as our main basis, have proceeded to discuss the restoration of peace in Indo-China. It cannot be denied that, as a result of the successive discussions, we have made certain progress, and at the meeting on May 29 we adopted the proposal of the United Kingdom delegation. However, if the duration of one month and the actual situation of the Conference are considered, the achievement of the Conference leaves much to be desired, the rate of progress of the Conference has been very slow and our Conference has fallen considerably short of the expectations of the people of the whole world.

The delegation of the People's Republic of China stated at the beginning of this Conference that since the Korean war had been stopped the Indo-China war should be likewise stopped. The early and simultaneous cessation of hostilities throughout Indo-China is the most important and urgent step toward the restoration of peace in Indo-China. It has always been our view that, in order to reach an early agreement on the question of an armistice, our Conference should establish the points in common in the various views, to serve as a basis for further discussion, and should at the same time seek ways to resolve the points of difference. It was for this purpose that the delegation of the People's Republic of China, on the basis of the proposals of the French delegation and of the delegation of the Democratic Republic of Viet Nam and of the supplementary proposal of the delegation of the Soviet Union, put forward on May 27 the following six-point proposal with respect to the question of an armistice:—

" The participants in the Geneva Conference have agreed upon the following basic principles in regard to the cessation of hostilities in Indo-China:—

1. A complete cease-fire by all the armed forces of the two belligerent parties—ground, naval and air forces—to be carried out simultaneously throughout the territory of Indo-China.

2. The two parties to begin negotiations on appropriate readjustments of the areas occupied by them, on the passage of troops of the two parties during the readjustments and on any other related questions that may arise.

3. The entry into Indo-China from outside of all kinds of fresh troops and military personnel as well as of all types of arms and ammunition to cease simultaneously with the cessation of hostilities throughout the territory of Indo-China.

4. Joint Committees composed of representatives of the commands of the two parties to supervise the implementation of the terms of the agreement on the cessation of hostilities.

International supervision by a neutral nations commission of the implementation of the aforesaid agreement also to be carried out.

The question of the composition of the neutral nations commission to be examined separately.

5. The states participating in the Geneva Conference to guarantee the implementation of the agreement.

The question of the nature of the obligations to be undertaken by the states concerned to be examined separately.

6. Prisoners of war and civilian internees to be released by the two parties."

In our view this six-point proposal includes the points in common in the various views, and on these this Conference should reach agreement in principle. We have seen in the course of discussion on this six-point proposal that on certain questions the viewpoints of each of us have been brought closer, but that on other questions there is still a wide gap between the various views, and that some of these views have even been obstructing the progress of this Conference. Now, I would like to make clear the views of the delegation of the People's Republic of China with regard to our six-point proposal.

With regard to the first point of the proposal, this Conference has explicitly defined, in the proposal of the delegation of the United Kingdom which it adopted on May 29, the principle of an early and simultaneous cessation of hostilities in Indo-China. It is the view of the delegation of the People's Republic of China that, since the principle has been laid down, it is necessary to examine, on the basis of that principle, the specific problem of how to effect an early and simultaneous cease-fire in the three states of Indo-China, namely, in Viet Nam, Khmer and Pathet Lao. We consider that an early restoration of peace throughout Indo-China without further delay is the earnest desire of the peoples of the whole world, especially the peoples of Indo-China and of France, and is at the same time the purpose of this Conference. However, even now some people are still arguing that it is not necessary to have a cease-fire simultaneously in Viet Nam, Khmer and Pathet Lao. This is, of course, not true. If hostilities were to cease in one part of Indo-China only, with fighting still going on in other parts, not only would an early restoration of peace in Indo-China be impossible, but there would be a constant danger of the war again spreading over the entire territory of Indo-China. It is true that for convenience of procedure concrete discussions on the question of an armistice in Viet Nam, Khmer and Pathet Lao may take place successively, but the cease-fire must take effect simultaneously.

With regard to the second point of the proposal, in adopting the proposal of the delegation of the United Kingdom on May 29, this Conference decided that the task of the representatives of the commands of the two belligerent sides should be to study the dispositions of forces on the cessation of hostilities, beginning with the question of regrouping areas in Viet Nam. It is the view of the delegation of the People's Republic of China that the principle of studying the question of the dispositions of forces on the cessation of hostilities should undoubtedly be applied to the whole territory of Indo-China. At the same time, we have also noted that the situations in the three states of Indo-China, namely, Viet Nam, Khmer and Pathet Lao, are not entirely similar, so that the measures for settlement will probably not be the same.

It is known to all that there are resistance armies in Khmer as well as in Pathet Lao, and that these resistance armies were organised by the peoples of Khmer and Pathet Lao respectively and are led by the resistance governments of these two countries. Now some people say that the resistance armies of Khmer and Pathet Lao were not organised by the peoples of their respective countries, and demand the evacuation of these armies as a condition for a cease-fire. That is obviously unrealistic, and is consequently also unacceptable. We would like to ask : How could the troops organised by the peoples of Khmer and Pathet Lao respectively be asked to withdraw outside of the territories of Khmer and Pathet Lao?

The representatives of the commands of the two belligerent sides have already started negotiations in Geneva in accordance with the resolution adopted by this Conference on May 29. This has paved the way for direct negotiations between the two belligerent sides. However, it must be pointed out that the representatives of the two commands have not yet entered into contact on the spot. Thus, the overall examination and speedy settlement of the question of the dispositions of troops on the cessation of hostilities has been delayed. We consider that the sides concerned should immediately take measures to carry out at an early date the agreement of this Conference that the representatives of the two commands, besides meeting in Geneva, should at the same time begin to establish contacts on the spot.

With regard to the third point of the proposal, that is the question of cessation of the entry into Indo-China from outside of all kinds of fresh troops and military personnel and all types of arms and ammunition simultaneously with the cessation of hostilities in the whole of Indo-China, this was proposed by Mr. Pham Van Dong, Head of the delegation of the Democratic Republic of Viet Nam. The delegations of the People's Republic of China and of the Soviet Union share the view of Mr. Pham Van Dong on this question. Foreign Minister Molotov has pointed out that the cessation of the entry of troops, arms and ammunition is a most important condition for the cessation of hostilities and the observance of related agreements in Indo-China. M. Bidault, Head of the French Delegation, also considered this an important question, which the international supervisory commission must make every effort to deal with. Since we are all agreed on this principle, the concrete question is then one of the scope and method of implementation and how the supervision should be carried out. With regard to the scope of implementation, we hold that the provisions on the cessation of the entry by land, sea or air into Indo-China from outside of all kinds of fresh troops and military personnel as well as of all types of arms and ammunition should be observed by the two belligerent sides in all the three States of Indo-China and that there should be no exception whatsoever. At the same time, it should be pointed out that the scope of implementation must include cessation of introduction into any area of Indo-China of military personnel, arms and ammunition by the United States of America. As to the question of how the supervision should be carried out, the experience gained from the Korean Armistice Agreement may be used as a guide.

Some people hold that this principle is only applicable to one State in Indo-China but not to another, that for instance it would not be applicable to Cambodia. Such an assertion is obviously untenable. It is known to all that the communiqué of the Berlin Conference of the four Foreign Ministers calls for the restoration of peace throughout Indo-China. If such provisions were carried out only in one State of Indo-China, while the other States were free to introduce fresh military units, or if not fresh military units then military personnel and military materials to reinforce their armed forces, it would then be possible for such states to become military bases for foreign interventionists. This would give rise to a danger of a recurrence of hostilities at any moment, and it would be impossible for the armistice agreement in Indo-China to have a firm basis.

With regard to the fourth point of the proposal, the Delegation of the People's Republic of China considers that, in order to supervise the implementation of the terms of the armistice agreement, two kinds of supervisory organisation should be set up. One is the joint committees as proposed by Mr. Pham Van Dong, *i.e.,* armistice commissions composed of representatives of the two belligerent sides. The other is a neutral nations supervisory commission as proposed by M. Molotov on the basis of the proposal of M. Bidault that an international commission be formed to carry out supervision, this commission to be composed of neutral nations to be invited by agreement of this Conference. The terms of reference of and the mutual relationship between these two kinds of organisation may, I think, be defined in the light of experience of the Korean Armistice Agreement. The Korean Armistice Commission has supervised the implementation by the two belligerent sides in Korea of the provisions of the Armistice Agreement, such as putting the cease-fire into effect, withdrawal of the military forces of both sides from the demilitarised zone, carrying out specific arrangements in the demilitarised zone, withdrawal of the armed forces of each of the two sides from the rear of the other side, &c. The Neutral Nations Supervisory Commission in Korea has carried out the functions of supervision, observation, inspection and investigation as regards the cessation of introduction into Korea from outside of reinforcements in the shape of military personnel, combat aircraft, armoured vehicles, weapons and ammunition, and as regards violations of the Armistice Agreement. Both these commissions have played a positive role in various respects in the implementation of the Korean Armistice. Although supervisory work in Korea has not been free from defects, such defects can be remedied. If, during the discussion on the question of an armistice in Indo-China, some people are even unwilling to accept conditions which are basically the same as those in the Korean Armistice, then it would be very difficult to reach agreement.

With regard to supervision, I would like to refer to the following questions:

(1) The question of the composition of the Neutral Nations Supervisory Commission:

In order to supervise the armistice in Indo-China, the delegation of the Soviet Union has proposed that the Neutral Nations Supervisory Commission shall be composed of representatives of India, Poland, Czechoslovakia and Pakistan. That is entirely reasonable. However, at this Conference, some people persist in objecting to the participation of Poland and Czechoslovakia. Their sole reason for so objecting is that Poland and Czechoslovakia are what they call two communist states and that communist states cannot be neutral nations. This has given rise to the dispute about the definition of neutral nations. What is the correct definition of neutral nations? Paragraph 37 of the Korean Armistice Agreement makes a most explicit provision: " The term ' neutral nations ' as herein used is defined as those nations whose combatant forces have not participated in the hostilities in Korea." This is the definition agreed upon by the governments related to the United Nations Command. This is also the recognised definition in present-day international affairs. If ideology and social system are taken as a criterion in judging neutral nations and if it is insisted that communist states cannot be neutral nations, then capitalist states cannot be neutral nations, either. In that case, where in the world can there be neutral nations? Therefore, if it is insisted that what are called communist states shall be excluded from the Neutral Nations Supervisory Commission, then it will be impossible to reach agreement on the question of composition.

(2) The question of the relationship between the Neutral Nations Supervisory Commission and the joint committees;

The two belligerent sides in Indo-China should be the principals in the armistice. Implementation of the armistice agreement should basically depend on the good faith of the two belligerent sides. Therefore, it is primarily the joint committees composed of the representatives of the commands of the two belligerent sides that should bear the heavy responsibility of supervising the thorough implementation of the armistice agreement. Unless the two belligerent sides primarily bear this heavy reponsibility, how can the Neutral Nations Supervisory Commission impose the armistice on the two belligerent sides? The Korean Armistice Agreement provides that " the general mission of the Military Armistice Commission shall be to supervise the implementation of this Armistice Agreement and to settle through negotiations any violations of this Armistice Agreement." This is not only entirely reasonable but completely necessary. We recognise the fact that, as the result of eight years of fighting, the two belligerent sides in Indo-China may find it difficult to make a *rapprochement* with each other and to have confidence in each other once an armistice is achieved, and that the occurrence of some violations of the armistice agreement may be unavoidable. Therefore, difficulties may arise, if it is left to the two sides alone to pass judgment and take conciliatory action. For this reason, supervision by neutral nations is needed. However, the Neutral Nations Supervisory Commission should not therefore be placed above the joint committees. It is our opinion that in discussing the functions of the joint committees and the Neutral Nations Supervisory Commission, neither of these two kinds of organisation should be given more or less authority than the other. The relationship between the Neutral Nations Supervisory Commission on the one hand and the joint committees on the other should be a parallel one instead of one being subordinate to the other. These two kinds of commissions should have their respective duties defined and arrangements made for their co-operation in accordance with the terms of reference laid down in the armistice agreement, in order to safeguard the effective implementation of the armistice agreement.

(3) The question of the principle of unanimity in the Neutral Nations Supervisory Commission:

There remains one more question from the discussion, namely, whether the Neutral Nations Supervisory Commission should adopt the principle of unanimity. Some people suggest that the method of majority vote in the Neutral Nations Supervisory Commission would be adequate to settle questions. They are against the adoption of the principle of unanimity. The delegation of the People's Republic of China cannot agree to this. We consider that in present-day international affairs the principle of unanimity is a most impartial and most reasonable principle best capable of settling important questions, whereas the method of majority vote has often been used in important international questions as an instrument for attempting to impose the will of the majority of states on the minority of states.

The task of the Neutral Nations Supervisory Commission is to assist the two belligerent sides in supervising the implementation of the armistice agreement. Therefore, the Commission must be able to reflect the views of, and take into consideration the interests of, the two sides, before it is able to make impartial recommendations acceptable to both sides. If the Neutral Nations Supervisory Commission were prejudiced in favour of one side and were unable to reflect the views of, and take into consideration the interests of, both sides, and if it were to rely merely on the majority vote to make recommendations, it would be very difficult for such recommendations to be acceptable to both sides.

Consequently, the Neutral Nations Supervisory Commission can impartially and reasonably settle important questions and accomplish its task of supervision only by a collective effort, by adhering to the powers granted by the armistice agreement and adopting the principle of unanimity. If there are people who attempt to use the method of the majority vote to impose, through the Neutral Nations Supervisory Commission, the views of one of the two belligerent sides on the other, such an attempt would be futile.

Some people say that the Neutral Nations Supervisory Commission in Korea has been paralysed because it has adopted the principle of unanimity. That is erroneous. In actual fact, the Neutral Nations Supervisory Commission in Korea has been effective in carrying out its main functions under the Armistice Agreement. In the ten months following the Korean Armistice, the Neutral Nations Supervisory Commission has supervised and examined the entry into and exit from Korea of over 2,000,000 military personnel of the two sides to the Armistice and of more than 7,000 combat aircraft of the United States side and has thereby enabled the armistice situation in Korea to remain unaffected up to now. How can it be said that the Neutral Nations Supervisory Commission in Korea is not effective? The main argument of Mr. Smith against the Neutral Nations Supervisory Commission in Korea is that the Polish and Czechoslovak members of that Commission disagreed and declined on four occasions to make investigations in compliance with the false charges of the United States side that the Korean and Chinese side were withholding prisoners of war. But it is precisely such disagreement that has safeguarded the Korean Armistice Agreement. There have been cases of the reverse kind. For instance, on January 20 and 21 of 1954, in order to ship the forcibly retained Chinese captured personnel from Inchon to Taiwan, the United States side would not allow the Neutral Nations Inspection Team stationed at Inchon to carry out inspections at the harbour. This was a serious incident and a glaring violation of the Armistice Agreement. The Polish and Czechoslovak members of the Neutral Nations Supervisory Commission proposed that the Commission send a mobile inspection team to Inchon to make a special investigation. However, the Swedish and Swiss members did not agree. In spite of that we did not in consequence write off the role and achievements of the Neutral Nations Supervisory Commission in Korea. Nor did we, like Mr. Smith, make the assertion in consequence that capitalist countries could not be neutral nations. There is still another kind of example. The Neutral Nations Repatriation Commission in Korea adopted the majority vote. But what was the result? I have twice stated that the important decision on the disposal of prisoners of war, agreed upon by the Indian, Polish and Czechoslovak members was not respected by the minority members, and was not carried out by the United Nations Command side. As a result, a deadlock was created in which the United States side forcibly retained more than 21,000 Korean and Chinese captured personnel, a deadlock unresolved up to now.

From this we can see that the experience of the Korean Armistice does not prove in the slightest that the principle of unanimity would inevitably lead to deadlocks nor does it prove that the method of majority vote would definitely not. As to deadlocks, no matter whether the principle of unanimity or of the majority vote prevailed, they have all been caused by the breach of certain terms of the Armistice Agreement in Korea by the United States side.

(4) The question of to whom the Neutral Nations Supervisory Commission should be responsible:

With regard to this question, we consider that the Neutral Nations Supervisory Commission should be responsible to the countries which provide the international guarantee for the restoration of peace in Indo-China. We have not yet heard any objection to this and hope that the Conference will establish this point.

(5) The question of so-called supervision by the United Nations:

In the course of discussion, it has been proposed that the United Nations should supervise the implementation of the armistice in Indo-China. To this the delegation of the People's Republic of China cannot agree. I have repeatedly stated that our Conference has nothing to do with the United Nations. It is self-evident that the United Nations is not suitable to perform the function of supervising the implementation of the armistice in Indo-China. In order to increase their intervention in the war in Indo-China, some people are now trying to place the Indo-China question on the agenda of the United Nations, in an endeavour to create disputes. Under such circumstances, still less should it be suggested that the United Nations assume the responsibility for supervising the armistice in Indo-China.

With regard to the fifth point of the proposal, that is, the question of guarantee by the participating states of this Conference of the implementation of the armistice agreement, this was proposed by M. Bidault, Head of the French delegation. Since no objection has been raised by any of the participating states at this Conference, we consider that this principle should be established and be made an initial agreement of this Conference. In accordance with its original proposal, the delegation of the People's Republic of China hopes at the same time that this Conference will discuss the question of the nature of the obligations to be undertaken by the countries providing the guarantee. As regards this question, the delegation of the People's Republic of China supports the views of the delegation of the Soviet Union, *i.e.*, that the countries which are to provide the guarantee should carry on consultations and adopt collective instead of individual measures with regard to violations of the armistice agreement.

With regard to the sixth point of the proposal, in the light of the experience gained in releasing seriously wounded prisoners of war at Dien Bien Phu, it would not be difficult to reach agreement through direct negotiations between the two belligerent parties on the question of the release by both parties of prisoners of war and civilian internees. Therefore, the delegation of the People's Republic of China is of the opinion that after the cease-fire throughout Indo-China, the question of the release by both parties of prisoners of war and civilian internees may be submitted for discussion in Geneva and on the spot as well, by the representatives of the commands of both parties.

Mr. Chairman, I said in my statement of May 12 that if all the delegates to this Conference are genuinely desirous of restoring peace in Indo-China, there is a possibility of reaching agreement at this Conference. But I also cannot help pointing out that there are still many serious obstacles before us. We must endeavour jointly to surmount these obstacles so as to enable our Conference to reach agreement at an early date.

It should be pointed out that so far there is still no fundamental change in the policy of the United States Government, which aims at extending the war in Indo-China and preventing the Geneva Conference from reaching agreement. At the Geneva Conference, the United States delegation has adopted an unconciliatory attitude and showed distrust of this Conference. At the same time, some delegations often follow this obstructive policy of the United States. Outside the Geneva Conference, persons in power in the United States Government are still clamouring for and instigating an extension of the war in Indo-China, intensifying their activities to organise a South-East Asian aggressive *bloc*, and continuing to create tensions in the Far East so as to threaten the peace and security of Asia and the world. This policy of the United States is seriously blocking the progress of the Geneva Conference.

It should also be pointed out that during the Geneva Conference the war faction in France is still in feverish pursuit of American intervention and enlarged aid in the Indo-China war, and has adopted a dilatory policy in relation to the Geneva Conference. Recently, the French Government and the Government of Bao Dai initialled two treaties in an attempt to counter thereby the movement of the Vietnamese people for real independence, unity and democracy and to prevent France from establishing friendly relations with the whole of Viet Nam on a new basis. Obviously, all this is not conducive to the early restoration of peace in Indo-China and is therefore also not in conformity with the interests of the French people.

We consider that, in order to restore peace in Indo-China at an early date so as to fulfil the earnest expectations of the peace-loving people of the world, such policies of obstructing and delaying the achievement of agreement in the Geneva Conference should continue no longer.

Mr. Chairman, the delegation of the People's Republic of China fully supports the proposals of Mr. Pham Van Dong, Head of the delegation of the Democratic Republic of Viet Nam, and of M. Molotov, Head of the delegation of the Soviet Union, for the discussion of the political questions of Indo-China. As everybody knows, the first six points in the eight-point proposal presented to this Conference on May 10 by Mr. Pham Van Dong have already provided a good basis for the discussion of political problems.

We are of the opinion that in discussing the problem of restoring peace in Indo-China, military issues and political issues are interrelated and cannot be completely separated. It has been suggested that our conference should finish discussing military issues before entering into a discussion of political issues. But the experience we have gained from our discussion of military issues at restricted sessions furnishes ample proof that such an idea is impracticable. For instance, the discussion of an armistice and the re-grouping of forces in the three states of Indo-China inevitably involves the political situation in these three states. Similarly, discussion of questions pertaining to the Neutral Nations Supervisory Commission and international guarantee necessarily involves many political issues. From this it can be seen that political and military issues cannot be completely separated.

It seems that there are still some people who, pointing to the example of the Korean armistice, try to advocate that the Geneva Conference should settle only the problem of a military armistice in Indo-China and leave political issues in Indo-China for future settlement. This suggestion is harmful because it is actually designed to postpone indefinitely the political settlement of the Indo-China question and thus to make the consolidation of peace in Indo-China impossible. As is generally known, paragraph 60 of the Korean Armistice Agreement provides that the two sides hold a political conference to work out a political settlement of the Korean question. But as the result of obstruction and disruptive activity on the part of the United

States Government, it has not been possible to convene the political conference. It is one of the tasks of the Geneva Conference to seek a political settlement of the Korean question. Again, because of the procrastination and obstruction of the United States Government and its followers, the Conference has so far produced no result although we have held thirteen meetings to discuss the Korean question. ˙ At the same time, the Syngman Rhee clique in South Korea is again clamouring outside the Conference about walking out of the Conference and using force or threats of force to unify Korea. This proves that if the political problems of Korea remain unsettled for a long time, it will be impossible to stabilise the Armistice in Korea. One hardly wants the painful experience in Korea to repeat itself in Indo-China.

It has always been our view that it should be the task of the Geneva Conference to settle the political as well as the military questions of Indo-China. That is to say, we should terminate hostilities and restore peace in Indo-China on the basis of recognition of the national rights of the peoples of the three States of Indo-China. Peace in Indo-China can be consolidated and durable only if the political questions are settled. Therefore, the delegation of the People's Republic of China is in favour of the three proposals put forward by the delegation of the Soviet Union on June 8, that both military and political questions of Indo-China be immediately considered by the Conference along parallel lines and in rotation and that the Conference ensure direct contacts between the two sides concerned, so that an agreement on the restoration of peace in Indo-China can be speedily achieved and an early and simultaneous cease-fire brought into effect throughout the territory of Indo-China.

SEVENTH PLENARY SESSION ON INDO-CHINA

Document No. 25

Speech by Mr. Eden, Secretary of State for Foreign Affairs, June 10, 1954

The last two days of public discussion have certainly clarified our differences. I fear that they have also deepened them. I say this with infinite regret, but it is our stern duty to face realities. As a result of the progress we have admittedly made on questions of procedure, our work now seems to me to fall into three main chapters. Let us see where we are in each.

We are agreed that the cessation of hostilities should be simultaneous, and we have also accepted that its examination should begin with Viet Nam. Representatives of the two commands are now meeting. We are all glad of this. We hope that we may soon learn the outcome of their discussions.

Next comes the issue of supervision. We are all agreed that some form of international supervision is necessary. We are not agreed as to how to make it effective and impartial.

Let us first consider the membership of the International Commission. I have stated the proposals of Her Majesty's Government on this. We do not think any the worse of our proposals because they have been ignored by certain delegations. We stand by them. I repeat that I have proposed this group of five Asian Powers because they are truly impartial. I am convinced that a group of four powers, two supporting the views of either side, can only lead to deadlock. My reason for refusing to accept such a proposal is not ideological. It is simply that it wouldn't work.

As to the working of such a commission as we propose, it will clearly be the desire of the impartial powers, if they be chosen, to try to reach agreement among themselves on every issue that comes before them. But if they fail

165

to do so, they must have the right to decide by a majority. There can be no power of veto. May I remind our critics on this point that to insist on unanimity is to declare that you have no confidence in impartiality. The International Commission must therefore be truly impartial, and must have the power to decide by majority. We for our part are firmly convinced that the representatives of India and Pakistan, Ceylon, Burma and Indonesia would form a just and impartial commission.

Now what of the relations of this International Commission with the mixed committees representative of the two commands? There is no dispute that the mixed committees could do useful work in Viet Nam. On the other hand, it has been admitted that even with the best will in the world the two sides cannot be expected after eight years of war to agree on every point. The warning of the representative of the State of Viet Nam about the experience of 1946 should not be forgotten by this Conference.

No one therefore attempts to deny that there will be differences, and they may well be frequent. How are they to be resolved? This is surely where the International Commission will have its part to play. No doubt it will always seek to reconcile these differences. But it will not always succeed. In the event of failure the International Commission must have the authority to decide. There is no other way.

The Conference has a clear choice, and we should face it. Either we can set up a commission which is as impartial as we can make it, and give it the necessary authority and the power to take its decisions by a majority if need be, each of us trusting to its good faith. Or we can at each phase interpose a veto, as some delegations have proposed. According to them, this veto might first be used in the mixed committees themselves. It could next be used in the International Commission. It might even be used once again if in the last resort a question was referred to representatives of this Conference. This issue of effective and impartial supervision seems to me to be crucial. I am sorry to have to record that after the debate of the last two days we are in my judgment further apart than ever upon it.

I come now to the third of the main issues which I wish to discuss—the future of Laos and Cambodia. There is no dispute that it is our duty to examine measures to restore peace in Laos and Cambodia, as in Viet Nam. There is dispute as to what those measures should be. Reference has been made here to the existence of "resistance armies" in Laos and Cambodia, and to the fact that there are "two belligerent sides" in all three States— Viet Nam, Laos and Cambodia. This does not accord with the information which we have from our representatives on the spot. I think it my duty to give this information in all good faith to the Conference.

Laos was first invaded by regular Vietminh forces in April 1953. These forces came from northern Viet Nam. They advanced to within twelve miles of the capital before they were defeated and driven back to the frontier area in North-Eastern Laos, where they have since remained. In December of last year, a further invasion took place. Regular Vietminh troops advanced from the Viet Nam border into central Laos. They were again driven back. But there are still many Vietminh troops in the border areas of Laos. These are regular battalions belonging to Vietminh divisions with their headquarters in Viet Nam. Some of them have heavy weapons, including artillery and anti-aircraft guns. These regular Vietminh units cannot be described as resistance movements.

On April 17 last year the Laotian Government formally notified Her Majesty's Government and other friendly governments of the violation of their frontiers by the Vietminh. On December 25 last year the Laotian Prime Minister appealed to world opinion against renewed aggression by "regular units of the Vietminh corps of battle."

166

Cambodia was invaded in April of this year. This was on the eve of this Conference, and several weeks after we had agreed in Berlin to meet here to discuss the restoration of peace in Indo-China. Once again the invaders were regular Vietminh troops who crossed the border from Viet Nam. They did not come to fight the French. These foreign invaders have in fact merely terrorised and battened on the people of Cambodia. They hold no centre of any importance. On April 23 of this year, a formal protest by the Cambodian Government against Vietminh invasion was delivered to the Secretary-General of the United Nations.

The Laotian and Cambodian delegates have already told us something of the history of the "resistance movements" in their countries. No one denies that there have been such movements in the past. But with unimportant exceptions, the former members of these movements have now rallied to the support of the legitimate Governments of Laos and Cambodia. Armed resistance according to our information now derives overwhelmingly from the Vietminh. It is indeed only since this conference was announced that even communist spokesmen have pretended anything else.

Vietminh aggression is not the only factor that distinguishes the problems of Laos and Cambodia from these of Viet Nam. In race, religion, language and culture, the peoples of these two countries are fundamentally different from those of Viet Nam. The Vietminh invaders not only crossed a political boundary. They crossed the frontier that divides the two great cultures of Asia—the Indian and the Chinese. The Vietminh delegate attempted to excuse this action by saying that there were Viet Namese minorities in Laos and Cambodia. That is true. But it no more justifies Vietminh invasion of Laos and Cambodia than it justified Hitler's invasion of Czechoslovakia. It is also true that in recent years the three different peoples of Indo-China were united under French rule. That is no reason why they should now be united against their wishes under the rule of the Vietminh.

To sum up then, I repeat that there are now three chapters to our work. Military talks between representatives of the two commands are proceeding. As I have said, we await a report upon these. In respect, however, to the arrangements for supervision, and the future of Laos and Cambodia, the divergences are at present wide and deep. Unless we can narrow them now without further delay, we shall have failed in our task. We have exhausted every expedient of procedure which we could devise to assist us in our work. We all know now what the differences are. We have no choice but to resolve them or to admit our failure. For our part, the United Kingdom delegation is still willing to attempt to resolve them, here or in restricted session, or by any other method which our colleagues may prefer. But if the positions remain as they are to-day, then it is our clear duty to say so to the world, and to admit that we have failed.

Document No. 26

Extract from Speech by M. Molotov, Minister for Foreign Affairs of the Union of Soviet Socialist Republics, June 10, 1954

We are now in the process of discussing the setting up of mixed commissions composed of the representatives of the commands on-the-spot and of an international body to supervise the Armistice Agreement. But here, too, artificial obstacles are created hampering the achievement of an agreement. For instance, as far as the Armistice Agreement in Korea is

167

concerned, it was soon agreed that the representatives of Poland and Czechoslovakia should take part in a Neutral Nations Commission to supervise the implementation of the Armistice terms. But at the Geneva Conference, that question was artificially turned into the subject of an endless discussion. One gets a definite impression that some of the participants in the Conference limit themselves to mere words concerning the need to stop hostilities, and that in fact, they think up all sorts of pretexts to prove the impossibility of an agreement, and to make use of that time for talks in Washington and elsewhere regarding the intervention of other countries into the war in Indo-China.

Under the pretext of talking about the cessation of hostilities, all sorts of conditions are advanced, and all sorts of steps taken which have nothing in common with a desire for an early cessation of hostilities in Indo-China. It is perfectly clear wherein the responsibility for that lies.

Document No. 27

Extract from Speech by Mr. Bedell Smith, Head of Delegation of the United States of America, June 10, 1954

The United States delegation has stated repeatedly that, to enable Laos and Cambodia completely to enjoy their sovereignty and independence in peace, it is only necessary for the invading forces of Vietminh to withdraw from their territories. Admittedly, the problem of restoration of peace in the State of Viet Nam presents greater problems but they are not involved in matters of sovereignty or independence which, as I said, we fully recognise.

With regard to our different opinions on matters of history, I leave the judgment to our colleagues.

However, the policy of the United States with regard to the establishment of peace in Indo-China, about which M. Molotov has just asked, is on basic issues identical with that outlined at the beginning of our session by the representative of the United Kingdom, with which statement the United States delegation associates itself completely.

The Chairman : I have no other speakers on my list. I understand that to-morrow we are to have a plenary session on Korea. If it is agreeable to my colleagues, I should suggest that perhaps the two chairmen might discuss together the future course of our work in respect of Indo-China and communicate the suggestions we may have to make to our colleagues. Is that agreeable? (Agreed).

Then the meeting is closed.

Miscellaneous No. 20 (1954)

Further Documents relating to the discussion of Indo-China at the Geneva Conference

June 16—July 21, 1954

*Presented by the Secretary of State for Foreign Affairs to Parliament
by Command of Her Majesty
August 1954*

FURTHER DOCUMENTS RELATING TO THE DISCUSSION OF INDO-CHINA AT THE GENEVA CONFERENCE

June 16–July 21, 1954

CONTENTS

INTRODUCTION

The earlier proceedings of the Geneva Conference on Indo-China were illustrated by the documents published in Miscellaneous No. 16 (1954), Cmd. 9186. These ended with extracts from the record of the 7th Plenary Session on June 10, 1954. After that date only one further Plenary meeting was held, negotiations being conducted either in restricted sessions (at which proceedings are of a confidential character) or by informal contacts between the Delegations. These negotiations resulted in the signature of Agreements on the Cessation of Hostilities by the Belligerents. At its final meeting on July 21, 1954, the Conference took note of these Agreements and of various individual declarations.

This White Paper accordingly consists of extracts from the proceedings of the final meeting of the Conference, together with the texts of the various agreements and declarations considered at that meeting.

Foreign Office,
July 1954.

EXTRACTS FROM VERBATIM RECORD OF EIGHTH
PLENARY SESSION

July 21, 1954

The Chairman (Mr. Eden): As I think my colleagues are aware, agreement has now been reached on certain documents. It is proposed that this Conference should take note of these agreements. I accordingly propose to begin by reading out a list of the subjects covered by the documents, which I understand every delegation has in front of them.

First, agreement on the cessation of hostilities in Viet Nam; second, agreement on the cessation of hostilities in Laos; third, agreement on the cessation of hostilities in Cambodia. I would draw particular attention to the fact that these three agreements now incorporate the texts which were negotiated separately concerning the supervision of the Armistice in the three countries by the International Commission and the joint committees.

I should also like to draw the attention of all delegations to a point of some importance in connexion with the Armistice Agreements and the related maps and documents on supervision. It has been agreed among the parties to each of these Agreements that none of them shall be made public for the present, pending further agreement among the parties. The reason for this, I must explain to my colleagues, is that these Armistice terms come into force at different dates. And it is desired that they should not be made public until they have come into force.

The further documents to which I must draw attention, which are in your possession, are: fourth, declaration by the Government of Laos on elections; fifth, declaration by the Government of Cambodia on elections and integration of all citizens into the national community; sixth, declaration by the Government of Laos on the military status of the country; seventh, declaration by the Government of Cambodia on the military status of the country; eighth, declaration by the Government of the French Republic on the withdrawal of troops from the three countries of Indochina.

Finally, gentlemen, there is the Draft Declaration by the Conference, which takes note of all these documents. I think all my colleagues have copies of this Draft Declaration([1]) before them. I will ask my colleagues in turn to express themselves upon this Declaration.

The Representative of France.

M. Mendès-France (France): Mr. Chairman, the French Delegation approves the terms of this Declaration.

The Chairman : The Representative of Laos.

Mr. Phoui Sananikone (Laos): The Delegation of Laos has no observations to make on this text.

The Chairman : The Representative of the People's Republic of China.

Mr. Chou En-lai (People's Republic of China): We agree.

The Chairman : On behalf of Her Majesty's Government in the United Kingdom, I associate myself with the final Declaration of this Conference.

The Union of Soviet Socialist Republics.

M. Molotov (U.S.S.R.): The Soviet Delegation agrees.

([1]) See page 9 for text.

The Chairman : The Representative of Cambodia.

Mr. Tep Phan (Cambodia): The Delegation of Cambodia wishes to state that, among the documents just listed, one is missing. This is a Cambodian Declaration which we have already circulated to all delegations. Its purport is as follows : Paragraphs 7, 11 and 12 of the final Declaration stipulate respect for the territorial integrity of Viet Nam. The Cambodian Delegation asks the Conference to consider that this provision does not imply the abandonment of such legitimate rights and interests as Cambodia might assert with regard to certain regions of South Viet Nam, about which Cambodia has made express reservations, in particular at the time of the signature of the Franco-Khmer Treaty of November 8, 1949, on relations between Cambodia and France and at the time the French law which linked Cochin-china to Viet Nam was passed. Faithful to the ideal of peace, and to the international principle of non-interference, Cambodia has no intention of interfering in the internal affairs of the State of Viet Nam and associates herself fully with the principle of respect for its integrity, provided certain adjustments and regularisations be arrived at with regard to the borders between this State and Cambodia, borders which so far have been fixed by a mere unilateral act of France.

In support of this Declaration, the Cambodian Delegation communicates to all members of this Conference a note on Cambodian lands in South Viet Nam.

The Chairman: If this Declaration was not inscribed on the agenda on the list of documents I have read out, it is because it has only at this instant reached me. I do not think it is any part of the task of this Conference to deal with any past controversies in respect of the frontiers between Cambodia and Viet Nam.

The Representative of the Democratic Republic of Viet Nam.

Mr. Pham van Dong (Democratic Republic of Viet Nam): Mr. Chairman, I agree completely with the words pronounced by you. In the name of the Government of the Democratic Republic of Viet Nam we make the most express reservations regarding the statement made by the Delegation of Cambodia just now. I do this in the interests of good relations and understanding between our two countries.

The Chairman: I think the Conference can take note of the statements of the Delegation of Cambodia just circulated and of the statement of the Representative of the Democratic Republic of Viet Nam.

I will continue calling upon countries to speak on the subject of the Declaration. I call upon the United States of America.

Mr. Bedell Smith (United States): Mr. Chairman, Fellow Delegates, as I stated to my colleagues during our meeting on July 18, my Government is not prepared to join in a Declaration by the Conference such as is submitted. However, the United States makes this unilateral declaration of its position in these matters : —

DECLARATION

The Government of the United States being resolved to devote its efforts to the strengthening of peace in accordance with the principles and purposes of the United Nations

Takes Note

of the Agreements concluded at Geneva on July 20 and 21, 1954, between (a) the Franco-Laotian Command and the Command of the People's Army of Viet Nam; (b) the Royal Khmer Army Command and the Command of the People's Army of Viet Nam; (c) Franco-Vietnamese Command and the Command of the People's Army of Viet Nam, and of paragraphs 1 to 12 of the Declaration presented to the Geneva Conference on July 21, 1954.

The Government of the United States of America

Declares with regard to the aforesaid Agreements and paragraphs that (i) it will refrain from the threat or the use of force to disturb them, in accordance with Article 2 (Section 4) of the Charter of the United Nations([2]) dealing with the obligation of Members to refrain in their international relations from the threat or use of force; and (ii) it would view any renewal of the aggression in violation of the aforesaid Agreements with grave concern and as seriously threatening international peace and security.

In connexion with the statement in the Declaration concerning free elections in Viet Nam, my Government wishes to make clear its position which it has expressed in a Declaration made in Washington on June 29, 1954, as follows: —

" In the case of nations now divided against their will, we shall continue to seek to achieve unity through free elections, supervised by the United Nations to ensure that they are conducted fairly."

With respect to the statement made by the Representative of the State of Viet Nam, the United States reiterates its traditional position that peoples are entitled to determine their own future and that it will not join in an arrangement which would hinder this. Nothing in its declaration just made is intended to or does indicate any departure from this traditional position.

We share the hope that the agreement will permit Cambodia, Laos and Viet Nam to play their part in full independence and sovereignty, in the peaceful community of nations, and will enable the peoples of that area to determine their own future.

Thank you, Mr. Chairman.

The Chairman: The Conference will, I think, wish to take note of the statement of the Representative of the United States of America.

I call on the Representative of the State of Viet Nam.

Mr. Tran van Do (State of Viet Nam): Mr. Chairman, as regards the final Declaration of the Conference, the Vietnamese Delegation requests the Conference to incorporate in this Declaration after Article 10, the following text: —

" The Conference takes note of the Declaration of the Government of the State of Viet Nam undertaking:
" to make and support every effort to re-establish a real and lasting peace in Viet Nam;
" not to use force to resist the procedures for carrying the cease-fire into effect, in spite of the objections and reservations that the State of Viet Nam has expressed, especially in its final statement."

The Chairman: I shall be glad to hear any views that my colleagues may wish to express. But, as I understand the position, the final Declaration has already been drafted and this additional paragraph has only just now been received; indeed, it has been amended since I received the text a few minutes ago. In all the circumstances, I suggest that the best course we can take is that the Conference should take note of the Declaration of the State of

([2]) " Treaty Series No. 67 (1946)," Cmd. 7015.

7

Viet Nam in this respect. If any of my colleagues has a contrary view, perhaps they would be good enough to say so. (None.) If none of my colleagues wishes to make any other observations, may I pass to certain other points which have to be settled before this Conference can conclude its labours?

The first is that, if it is agreeable to our colleagues, it is suggested that the two Chairmen should at the conclusion of this meeting address telegrams to the Governments of India, Poland and Canada to ask them if they will undertake the duties of supervision which the Conference has invited them to discharge. Is that agreeable? (Agreed.) Thank you.

The last is perhaps the least agreeable chapter of all our work. Certain costs arise from the decisions which the Conference has taken. It is suggested that it should be left here to your Chairmen as their parting gift to try to put before you some proposal in respect of those costs. I only wish to add in that connexion that, as this Conference is peculiar in not having any Secretariat in the usual sense of the term, the two Chairmen with considerable reluctance are prepared to undertake this highly invidious task. The costs to which I refer are not our own but those of the International Commission.

Does any delegate wish to make any further observation? (None.)

Gentlemen, perhaps I may say a final word as your Chairman for this day. We have now come to the end of our work. For a number of reasons it has been prolonged and intricate. The co-operation which all delegates have given to your two Chairmen has enabled us to overcome many procedural difficulties. Without that co-operation, we could not have succeeded in our task. The Agreements concluded to-day could not, in the nature of things, give complete satisfaction to everyone. But they have made it possible to stop a war which has lasted for eight years and brought suffering and hardship to millions of people. They have also, we hope, reduced international tension at a point of instant danger to world peace. These results are surely worth our many weeks of toil. In order to bring about a cease-fire, we have drawn up a series of agreements. They are the best that our hands could devise. All will now depend upon the spirit in which those agreements are observed and carried out.

Gentlemen, before we leave this hospitable town of Geneva I'm sure you would wish your Chairmen to give a message of gratitude to the United Nations and its able staff who have housed and helped us in our work.

And lastly let me express our cordial thanks to the Swiss Government and to the people and authorities of Geneva who have done so much to make our stay here pleasant as well as of service to the cause of peace.

The Representative of the United States of America.

Mr. Bedell Smith (U.S.A.): If I presume to speak for my fellow delegates, it is because I know that they all feel as I do. I hope that they join me in expressing our thanks to the two Chairmen of this Conference. Their patience, their tireless efforts, and their goodwill have done a great deal to make this settlement possible. We owe them our sincere thanks.

The Chairman: The Representative of the Union of Soviet Socialist Republics.

M. Molotov (U.S.S.R.): Mr. Chairman, as one of the Chairmen at the Geneva Conference, I would like to reply to the remarks just made by Mr. Bedell Smith, who spoke highly of the work done by the Chairmen. Naturally I must stress the outstanding services and the outstanding rôle played by our Chairman of to-day, Mr. Eden, whose rôle in the Geneva Conference cannot be exaggerated. And I would also like to reply and thank Mr. Bedell Smith for his warm words of to-day.

The Chairman: Has any other delegate anything else they want to say?

The Representative of Viet Nam.

Mr. Tran van Do (State of Viet Nam): Mr. Chairman, I expressed the view of the Delegation of the State of Viet Nam in my statement and I would have this Conference take note of it in its final act.

The Chairman: As I think I explained, we cannot now amend our final act, which is the statement of the Conference as a whole, but the Declaration of the Representative of the State of Viet Nam will be taken note of.

Any other observations? (None.)

I would like to be allowed to add my thanks for what General Bedell Smith has said and also to thank M. Molotov for his words. Both were undeserved, but even if things are not true, if they are nice things it's pleasant to hear them said.

But I do want to close this Conference with this one sentence: I'm quite sure that each one of us here hopes that the work which we have done will help to strengthen the forces working for peace.

Document No. 2

Final Declaration of the Geneva Conference on the problem of restoring peace in Indo-China, in which the representatives of Cambodia, the Democratic Republic of Viet Nam, France, Laos, the People's Republic of China, the State of Viet Nam, the Union of Soviet Socialist Republics, the United Kingdom and the United States of America took part

July 21, 1954

1. The Conference takes note of the agreements ending hostilities in Cambodia, Laos and Viet Nam and organising international control and the supervision of the execution of the provisions of these agreements.

2. The Conference expresses satisfaction at the ending of hostilities in Cambodia, Laos and Viet Nam; the Conference expresses its conviction that the execution of the provisions set out in the present declaration and in the agreements on the cessation of hostilities will permit Cambodia, Laos and Viet Nam henceforth to play their part, in full independence and sovereignty, in the peaceful community of nations.

3. The Conference takes note of the declarations made by the Governments of Cambodia and of Laos of their intention to adopt measures permitting all citizens to take their place in the national community, in particular by participating in the next general elections, which, in conformity with the constitution of each of these countries, shall take place in the course of the year 1955, by secret ballot and in conditions of respect for fundamental freedoms.

4. The Conference takes note of the clauses in the agreement on the cessation of hostilities in Viet Nam prohibiting the introduction into Viet Nam of foreign troops and military personnel as well as of all kinds of arms and munitions. The Conference also takes note of the declarations made by

the Governments of Cambodia and Laos of their resolution not to request foreign aid, whether in war material, in personnel or in instructors except for the purpose of the effective defence of their territory and, in the case of Laos, to the extent defined by the agreements on the cessation of hostilities in Laos.

5. The Conference takes note of the clauses in the agreement on the cessation of hostilities in Viet Nam to the effect that no military base under the control of a foreign State may be established in the regrouping zones of the two parties, the latter having the obligation to see that the zones allotted to them shall not constitute part of any military alliance and shall not be utilised for the resumption of hostilities or in the service of an aggressive policy. The Conference also takes note of the declarations of the Governments of Cambodia and Laos to the effect that they will not join in any agreement with other States if this agreement includes the obligation to participate in a military alliance not in conformity with the principles of the Charter of the United Nations or, in the case of Laos, with the principles of the agreement on the cessation of hostilities in Laos or, so long as their security is not threatened, the obligation to establish bases on Cambodian or Laotian territory for the military forces of foreign Powers.

6. The Conference recognises that the essential purpose of the agreement relating to Viet Nam is to settle military questions with a view to ending hostilities and that the military demarcation line is provisional and should not in any way be interpreted as constituting a political or territorial boundary. The Conference expresses its conviction that the execution of the provisions set out in the present declaration and in the agreement on the cessation of hostilities creates the necessary basis for the achievement in the near future of a political settlement in Viet Nam.

7. The Conference declares that, so far as Viet Nam is concerned, the settlement of political problems, effected on the basis of respect for the principles of independence, unity and territorial integrity, shall permit the Vietnamese people to enjoy the fundamental freedoms, guaranteed by democratic institutions established as a result of free general elections by secret ballot. In order to ensure that sufficient progress in the restoration of peace has been made, and that all the necessary conditions obtain for free expression of the national will, general elections shall be held in July 1956, under the supervision of an international commission composed of representatives of the Member States of the International Supervisory Commission, referred to in the agreement on the cessation of hostilities. Consultations will be held on this subject between the competent representative authorities of the two zones from July 20, 1955, onwards.

8. The provisions of the agreements on the cessation of hostilities intended to ensure the protection of individuals and of property must be most strictly applied and must, in particular, allow everyone in Viet Nam to decide freely in which zone he wishes to live.

9. The competent representative authorities of the Northern and Southern zones of Viet Nam, as well as the authorities of Laos and Cambodia, must not permit any individual or collective reprisals against persons who have collaborated in any way with one of the parties during the war, or against members of such persons' families.

10. The Conference takes note of the declaration of the Government of the French Republic to the effect that it is ready to withdraw its troops from the territory of Cambodia, Laos and Viet Nam, at the request of the Governments concerned and within periods which shall be fixed by agreement

between the parties except in the cases where, by agreement between the two parties, a certain number of French troops shall remain at specified points and for a specified time.

11. The Conference takes note of the declaration of the French Government to the effect that for the settlement of all the problems connected with the re-establishment and consolidation of peace in Cambodia, Laos and Viet Nam, the French Government will proceed from the principle of respect for the independence and sovereignty, unity and territorial integrity of Cambodia, Laos and Viet Nam.

12. In their relations with Cambodia, Laos and Viet Nam, each member of the Geneva Conference undertakes to respect the sovereignty, the independence, the unity and the territorial integrity of the above-mentioned States, and to refrain from any interference in their internal affairs.

13. The members of the Conference agree to consult one another on any question which may be referred to them by the International Supervisory Commission, in order to study such measures as may prove necessary to ensure that the agreements on the cessation of hostilities in Cambodia, Laos and Viet Nam are respected.

Document No. 3

Agreement on the Cessation of Hostilities in Cambodia
July 20, 1954

CHAPTER I

Principles and Conditions Governing Execution of the Cease-Fire

Article 1

As from twenty-third July, 1954, at 0800 hours (Peking mean time) complete cessation of all hostilities throughout Cambodia shall be ordered and enforced by the Commanders of the Armed Forces of the two parties for all troops and personnel of the land, naval and air forces under their control.

Article 2

In conformity with the principle of a simultaneous cease-fire throughout Indo-China, there shall be a simultaneous cessation of hostilities throughout Cambodia, in all the combat areas and for all the forces of the two parties.

To obviate any mistake or misunderstanding and to ensure that both the ending of hostilities and all other operations arising from cessation of hostilities are in fact simultaneous,

(a) due allowance being made for the time actually required for transmission of the cease-fire order down to the lowest échelons of the combatant forces of both sides, the two parties are agreed that the complete and simultaneous cease-fire throughout the territory of Cambodia shall become effective at 8 hours (local time) on August 7, 1954. It is agreed that Peking mean time shall be taken as local time.

(b) Each side shall comply strictly with the time-table jointly agreed upon between the parties for the execution of all operations connected with the cessation of hostilities.

11

Article 3

All operations and movements connected with the execution of the cessation of hostilities must be carried out in a safe and orderly fashion.

(a) Within a number of days to be determined by the Commanders of both sides, after the cease-fire has been achieved, each party shall be responsible for removing and neutralising mines, booby traps, explosives and any other dangerous devices placed by it. Should it be impossible to complete removal and neutralisation before departure, the party concerned will mark the spot by placing visible signs. Sites thus cleared of mines and any other obstacles to the free movement of the personnel of the International Commission and the Joint Commission shall be notified to the latter by the local military Commanders.

(b) Any incidents that may arise between the forces of the two sides and may result from mistakes or misunderstandings shall be settled on the spot so as to restrict their scope.

(c) During the days immediately preceding the cease-fire each party undertakes not to engage in any large-scale operation between the time when the Agreement on the cessation of hostilities is signed at Geneva and the time when the cease-fire comes into effect.

CHAPTER II

Procedure for the Withdrawal of the Foreign Armed Forces and Foreign Military Personnel from the Territory of Cambodia

Article 4

1. The withdrawal outside the territory of Cambodia shall apply to—

(a) the armed forces and military combatant personnel of the French Union;

(b) the combatant formations of all types which have entered the territory of Cambodia from other countries or regions of the peninsula;

(c) all the foreign elements (or Cambodians not natives of Cambodia) in the military formations of any kind or holding supervisory functions in all political or military, administrative, economic, financial or social bodies, having worked in liaison with the Viet Nam military units.

2. The withdrawals of the forces and elements referred to in the foregoing paragraphs and their military supplies and materials must be completed within 90 days reckoning from the entry into force of the present Agreement.

3. The two parties shall guarantee that the withdrawals of all the forces will be effected in accordance with the purposes of the Agreement, and that they will not permit any hostile action or take any action likely to create difficulties for such withdrawals. They shall assist one another as far as possible.

4. While the withdrawals are proceeding, the two parties shall not permit any destruction or sabotage of public property or any attack on the life or property of the civilian population. They shall not permit any interference with the local civil administration.

5. The Joint Commission and the International Supervisory Commission shall supervise the execution of measures to ensure the safety of the forces during withdrawal.

6. The Joint Commission in Cambodia shall determine the detailed procedures for the withdrawals of the forces on the basis of the above-mentioned principles.

CHAPTER III

Other Questions

A.—THE KHMER ARMED FORCES, NATIVES OF CAMBODIA

Article 5

The two parties shall undertake that within thirty days after the cease-fire order has been proclaimed, the Khmer Resistance Forces shall be demobilised on the spot; simultaneously, the troops of the Royal Khmer Army shall abstain from taking any hostile action against the Khmer Resistance Forces.

Article 6

The situation of these nationals shall be decided in the light of the Declaration made by the Delegation of Cambodia at the Geneva Conference, reading as follows:—

" The Royal Government of Cambodia,
    In the desire to ensure harmony and agreement among the peoples of the Kingdom,
    Declares itself resolved to take the necessary measures to integrate all citizens, without discrimination, into the national community and to guarantee them the enjoyment of the rights and freedoms for which the Constitution of the Kingdom provides;
    Affirms that all Cambodian citizens may freely participate as electors or candidates in general elections by secret ballot."
    No reprisals shall be taken against the said nationals or their families, each national being entitled to the enjoyment, without any discrimination as compared with other nationals, of all constitutional guarantees concerning the protection of person and property and democratic freedoms.
    Applicants therefor may be accepted for service in the Regular Army or local police formations if they satisfy the conditions required for current recruitment of the Army and Police Corps.
    The same procedure shall apply to those persons who have returned to civilian life and who may apply for civilian employment on the same terms as other nationals.

B.—BAN ON THE INTRODUCTION OF FRESH TROOPS, MILITARY PERSONNEL, ARMAMENTS AND MUNITIONS. MILITARY BASES

Article 7

In accordance with the Declaration made by the Delegation of Cambodia at 2400 hours on July 20, 1954 at the Geneva Conference of Foreign Ministers:

" The Royal Government of Cambodia will not join in any agreement with other States if this agreement carries for Cambodia the obligation to enter into a military alliance not in conformity with the principles of the Charter of the United Nations, or, as long as its security is not threatened, the obligation to establish bases on Cambodian territory for the military forces of foreign Powers.

" During the period which will elapse between the date of the cessation of hostilities in Viet Nam and that of the final settlement of political problems in this country, the Royal Government of Cambodia will not solicit foreign aid in war material, personnel or instructors except for the purpose of the effective defence of the territory."

C.—CIVILIAN INTERNEES AND PRISONERS OF WAR.—BURIAL

Article 8

The liberation and repatriation of all civilian internees and prisoners of war detained by each of the two parties at the coming into force of the present Agreement shall be carried out under the following conditions:—

(a) All prisoners of war and civilian internees of whatever nationality, captured since the beginning of hostilities in Cambodia during military operations or in any other circumstances of war and in any part of the territory of Cambodia shall be liberated after the entry into force of the present Armistice Agreement.

(b) The term " civilian internees " is understood to mean all persons who, having in any way contributed to the political and armed struggle between the two parties have been arrested for that reason or kept in detention by either party during the period of hostilities.

(c) All foreign prisoners of war captured by either party shall be surrendered to the appropriate authorities of the other party, who shall give them all possible assistance in proceeding to the destination of their choice.

Article 9

After the entry into force of the present Agreement, if the place of burial is known and the existence of graves has been established, the Cambodian commander shall, within a specified period, authorise the exhumation and removal of the bodies of deceased military personnel of the other party, including the bodies of prisoners of war or personnel deceased and buried on Cambodian territory.

The Joint Commission shall fix the procedures by which this task is to be carried out and the time limit within which it must be completed.

CHAPTER IV

Joint Commission and International Commission for Supervision and Control in Cambodia

Article 10

Responsibility for the execution of the Agreement on the cessation of hostilities shall rest with the parties.

Article 11

An International Commission shall be responsible for control and supervision of the application of the provisions of the Agreement on the cessation of hostilities in Cambodia. It shall be composed of representatives of the following States: Canada, India and Poland. It shall be presided over by the representative of India. Its headquarters shall be at Phnom-Penh.

Article 12

The International Commission shall set up fixed and mobile inspection teams, composed of an equal number of officers appointed by each of the above-mentioned States.

The fixed teams shall be located at the following points: Phnom-Penh, Kompong-Cham, Kratié, Svay-Rieng, Kampot. These points of location may be altered at a later date by agreement between the Government of Cambodia and the International Commission.

The zones of action of the mobile teams shall be the regions bordering on the land and sea frontiers of Cambodia. The mobile teams shall have the right to move freely within the limits of their zones of action, and they shall receive from the local civil and military authorities all facilities they may require for the fulfilment of their tasks (provision of personnel, access to documents needed for supervision, summoning of witnesses needed for enquiries, security and freedom of movement of the inspection teams, &c.). They shall have at their disposal such modern means of transport, observation and communication as they may require.

Outside the zones of action defined above, the mobile teams may, with the agreement of the Cambodian Command, move about as required by the tasks assigned to them under the present Agreement.

Article 13

The International Commission shall be responsible for supervising the execution by the parties of the provisions of the present Agreement. For this purpose it shall fulfil the functions of control, observation, inspection and investigation connected with the implementation of the provisions of the Agreement on the cessation of hostilities, and shall in particular:

(*a*) control the withdrawal of foreign forces in accordance with the provisions of the Agreement on the cessation of hostilities and see that frontiers are respected;

(*b*) control the release of prisoners of war and civilian internees;

(*c*) supervise, at ports and airfields and along all the frontiers of Cambodia, the application of the Cambodian declaration concerning the introduction into Cambodia of military personnel and war materials on grounds of foreign assistance.

Article 14

A Joint Commission shall be set up to facilitate the implementation of the clauses relating to the withdrawal of foreign forces.

The Joint Commission may form joint groups the number of which shall be decided by mutual agreement between the parties.

The Joint Commission shall facilitate the implementation of the clauses of the Agreement on the cessation of hostilities relating to the simultaneous and general cease-fire in Cambodia for all regular and irregular armed forces of the two parties.

It shall assist the parties in the implementation of the said clauses; it shall ensure liaison between them for the purpose of preparing and carrying out plans for the implementation of the said clauses; it shall endeavour to settle any disputes between the parties arising out of the implementation of these clauses. The Joint Commission may send joint groups to follow the forces in their movements; such groups shall be disbanded once the withdrawal plans have been carried out.

15

Article 15

The Joint Commission shall be composed of an equal number of representatives of the Commands of the parties concerned.

Article 16

The International Commission shall, through the medium of the inspection teams mentioned above and as soon as possible, either on its own initiative or at the request of the Joint Commission or of one of the parties, undertake the necessary investigations both documentary and on the ground.

Article 17

The inspection teams shall transmit to the International Commission the results of their supervision, investigations and observations; furthermore, they shall draw up such special reports as they may consider necessary or as may be requested from them by the Commission. In the case of a disagreement within the teams, the findings of each member shall be transmitted to the Commission.

Article 18

If an inspection team is unable to settle an incident or considers that there is a violation or threat of a serious violation, the International Commission shall be informed; the Commission shall examine the reports and findings of the inspection teams and shall inform the parties of the measures to be taken for the settlement of the incident, ending of the violation or removal of the threat of violation.

Article 19

When the Joint Commission is unable to reach agreement on the interpretation of a provision or on the appraisal of a fact, the International Commission shall be informed of the disputed question. Its recommendations shall be sent directly to the parties and shall be notified to the Joint Commission.

Article 20

The recommendations of the International Commission shall be adopted by a majority vote, subject to the provisions of Article 21. If the votes are equally divided, the Chairman's vote shall be decisive.

The International Commission may make recommendations concerning amendments and additions which should be made to the provisions of the Agreement on the cessation of hostilities in Cambodia, in order to ensure more effective execution of the said Agreement. These recommendations shall be adopted unanimously.

Article 21

On questions concerning violations, or threats of violations, which might lead to a resumption of hostilities, and in particular,

(a) refusal by foreign armed forces to effect the movements provided for in the withdrawal plan,

(b) violation or threat of violation of the country's integrity by foreign armed forces,

the decisions of the International Commission must be unanimous.

Article 22

If one of the parties refuses to put a recommendation of the International Commission into effect, the parties concerned or the Commission itself shall inform the members of the Geneva Conference.

If the International Commission does not reach unanimity in the cases provided for in Article 21, it shall transmit a majority report and one or more minority reports to members of the Conference.

The International Commission shall inform the members of the Conference of all cases in which its work is being hindered.

Article 23

The International Commission shall be set up at the time of the cessation of hostilities in Indo-China in order that it may be able to perform the tasks prescribed in Article 13.

Article 24

The International Commission for Supervision and Control in Cambodia shall act in close co-operation with the International Commissions in Viet Nam and Laos.

The Secretaries-General of these three Commissions shall be responsible for co-ordinating their work and for relations between them.

Article 25

The International Commission for Supervision and Control in Cambodia may, after consultation with the International Commissions in Viet Nam and in Laos, and having regard to the development of the situation in Viet Nam and in Laos, progressively reduce its activities. Such a decision must be adopted unanimously.

CHAPTER V

Implementation

Article 26

The Commanders of the forces of the two parties shall ensure that persons under their respective commands who violate any of the provisions of the present Agreement are suitably punished.

Article 27

The present Agreement on the cessation of hostilities shall apply to all the armed forces of either party.

Article 28

The Commanders of the forces of the two parties shall afford full protection and all possible assistance and co-operation to the Joint Commission and to the International Commission and its inspection teams in the performance of their functions.

Article 29

The Joint Commission, composed of an equal number of representatives of the Commands of the two parties, shall assist the parties in the implementation of all the clauses of the Agreement on the cessation of hostilities, ensure liaison between the two parties, draw up plans for the implementation of the Agreement, and endeavour to settle any dispute arising out of the implementation of the said clauses and plans.

17

Article 30

The costs involved in the operation of the Joint Commission shall be shared equally between the two parties.

Article 31

The signatories of the present Agreement on the cessation of hostilities and their successors in their functions shall be responsible for the observance and enforcement of the terms and provisions thereof. The Commanders of the forces of the two parties shall, within their respective commands, take all steps and make all arrangements necessary to ensure full compliance with all the provisions of the present Agreement by all personnel under their command.

Article 32

The procedures laid down in the present Agreement shall, whenever necessary, be examined by the Commands of the two parties and, if necessary, defined more specifically by the Joint Commission.

Article 33

All the provisions of the present Agreement shall enter into force at 00 hours (Geneva time) on July 23, 1954.

Done at Geneva on July 20, 1954.

For the Commander-in-Chief of the Khmer National Armed Forces :

NHIEK TIOULONG,

General.

For the Commander-in-Chief of the Units of the Khmer Resistance Forces and for the Commander-in-Chief of the Vietnamese Military Units :

TA-QUANG-BUU,

Vice-Minister of National Defence
of the Democratic Republic of Viet Nam.

Document No. 4

Agreement on the Cessation of Hostilities in Laos

July 20, 1954

CHAPTER I

Cease-Fire and Evacuation of Foreign Armed Forces and Foreign Military Personnel

Article 1

The Commanders of the armed forces of the parties in Laos shall order and enforce the complete cessation of all hostilities in Laos by all armed forces under their control, including all units and personnel of the ground, naval and air forces.

Article 2

In accordance with the principle of a simultaneous cease-fire throughout Indo-China the cessation of hostilities shall be simultaneous throughout the territory of Laos in all combat areas and for all forces of the two parties.

In order to prevent any mistake or misunderstanding and to ensure that both the cessation of hostilities and the disengagement and movements of the opposing forces are in fact simultaneous,

(a) Taking into account the time effectively required to transmit the cease-fire order down to the lowest échelons of the combatant forces on both sides, the two parties are agreed that the complete and simultaneous cease-fire throughout the territory of Laos shall become effective at 8 hours (local time) on August 6, 1954. It is agreed that Peking mean time shall be taken as local time.

(b) The Joint Commission for Laos shall draw up a schedule for the other operations resulting from the cessation of hostilities.

Article 3

All operations and movements entailed by the cessation of hostilities and re-groupings must proceed in a safe and orderly fashion.

(a) Within a number of days to be determined on the spot by the Joint Commission in Laos each party shall be responsible for removing and neutralising mines, booby traps, explosives and any other dangerous substance placed by it. In the event of its being impossible to complete the work of removal and neutralisation in time, the party concerned shall mark the spot by placing visible signs there.

(b) As regards the security of troops on the move following the lines of communication in accordance with the schedule previously drawn up by the Joint Armistice Commission in Laos, and the safety of the assembly areas, detailed measures shall be adopted in each case by the Joint Armistice Commission in Laos. In particular, while the forces of one party are withdrawing by a line of communication passing through the territory of the other party (roads or waterways) the forces of the latter party shall provisionally withdraw two kilometres on either side of such line of communication, but in such a manner as to avoid interfering with the movements of the civil population.

Article 4

The withdrawals and transfers of military forces, supplies and equipment shall be effected in accordance with the following principles:

(a) The withdrawals and transfers of the military forces, supplies and equipment of the two parties shall be completed within a period of 120 days from the day on which the present Agreement enters into force.

The two parties undertake to communicate their transfer plans to each other, for information, within 25 days of the entry into force of the present Agreement.

(b) The withdrawals of the Vietnamese People's Volunteers from Laos to Viet Nam shall be effected by provinces. The position of those volunteers who were settled in Laos before the hostilities shall form the subject of a special convention.

(c) The routes for the withdrawal of the forces of the French Union and Vietnamese People's Volunteers in Laos from Laotian territory shall be fixed on the spot by the Joint Commission.

19

(*d*) The two parties shall guarantee that the withdrawals and transfers of all forces will be effected in accordance with the purposes of this Agreement, and that they will not permit any hostile action or take action of any kind whatever which might hinder such withdrawals or transfers. The parties shall assist each other as far as possible.

′*e*) While the withdrawals and transfers of the forces are proceeding, the two parties shall not permit any destruction or sabotage of any public property or any attack on the life or property of the local civilian population.

(*f*) The Joint Commission and the International Commission shall supervise the implementation of measures to ensure the safety of the forces during withdrawal and transfer.

(*g*) The Joint Commission in Laos shall determine the detailed procedures for the withdrawals and transfers of the forces in accordance with the above-mentioned principles.

Article 5

During the days immediately preceding the cease-fire each party undertakes not to engage in any large-scale operation between the time when the Agreement on the cessation of hostilities is signed at Geneva and the time when the cease-fire comes into effect.

CHAPTER II

Prohibition of the Introduction of Fresh Troops, Military Personnel, Armaments and Munitions

Article 6

With effect from the proclamation of the cease-fire the introduction into Laos of any reinforcements of troops or military personnel from outside Laotian territory is prohibited.

Nevertheless, the French High Command may leave a specified number of French military personnel required for the training of the Laotian National Army in the territory of Laos; the strength of such personnel shall not exceed one thousand five hundred (1,500) officers and non-commissioned officers.

Article 7

Upon the entry into force of the present Agreement, the establishment of new military bases is prohibited throughout the territory of Laos.

Article 8

The High Command of the French forces shall maintain in the territory of Laos the personnel required for the maintenance of two French military establishments, the first at Seno and the second in the Mekong valley, either in the province of Vientiane or downstream from Vientiane.

The effectives maintained in these military establishments shall not exceed a total of three thousand five hundred (3,500) men.

Article 9

Upon the entry into force of the present Agreement and in accordance with the declaration made at the Geneva Conference by the Royal Government of Laos on July 20, 1954, the introduction into Laos of armaments,

20

munitions and military equipment of all kinds is prohibited, with the exception of a specified quantity of armaments in categories specified as necessary for the defence of Laos.

Article 10

The new armaments and military personnel permitted to enter Laos in accordance with the terms of Article 9 above shall enter Laos at the following points only: Luang-Prabang, Xieng-Khouang, Vientiane, Seno, Paksé, Savannakhet and Tchépone.

CHAPTER III

Disengagement of the Forces—Assembly Areas—Concentration Areas

Article 11

The disengagement of the armed forces of both sides, including concentration of armed forces, movements to rejoin the provisional assembly areas allotted to one party and provisional withdrawal movements by the other party, shall be completed within a period not exceeding fifteen (15) days after the cease-fire.

Article 12

The Joint Commission in Laos shall fix the site and boundaries:—

of the five (5) provisional assembly areas for the reception of the Vietnamese People's Volunteer Forces,

of the five (5) provisional assembly areas for the reception of the French forces in Laos,

of the twelve (12) provisional assembly areas, one to each province, for the reception of the fighting units of "Pathet Lao."

The forces of the Laotian National Army shall remain *in situ* during the entire duration of the operations of disengagement and transfer of foreign forces and fighting units of "Pathet Lao."

Article 13

The foreign forces shall be transferred outside Laotian territory as follows:—

(1) FRENCH FORCES

The French forces shall be moved out of Laos by road (along routes laid down by the Joint Commission in Laos) and also by air and inland waterway;

(2) VIETNAMESE PEOPLE'S VOLUNTEER FORCES

These forces shall be moved out of Laos by land, along routes and in accordance with a schedule to be determined by the Joint Commission in Laos in accordance with the principle of simultaneous withdrawal of foreign forces.

Article 14

Pending a political settlement, the fighting units of "Pathet Lao," concentrated in the provisional assembly areas, shall move into the Provinces of Phongsaly and Sam-Neua, except for any military personnel who wish to

21

be demobilised where they are. They shall be free to move between these two Provinces in a corridor along the frontier between Laos and Viet Nam bounded on the south by the Line Sop Kin, Na Mi, Sop Sang, Muong Son.

Concentration shall be completed within one hundred and twenty (120) days from the date of entry into force of the present Agreement.

Article 15

Each party undertakes to refrain from any reprisals or discrimination against persons or organisations for their activities during the hostilities and also undertakes to guarantee their democratic freedoms.

CHAPTER IV

Prisoners of War and Civilian Internees

Article 16

The liberation and repatriation of all prisoners of war and civilian internees detained by each of the two parties at the coming into force of the present Agreement shall be carried out under the following conditions:—

(a) All prisoners of war and civilian internees of Laotian and other nationalities captured since the beginning of hostilities in Laos, during military operations or in any other circumstances of war and in any part of the territory of Laos, shall be liberated within a period of thirty (30) days after the date when the cease-fire comes into effect.

(b) The term "civilian internees" is understood to mean all persons who, having in any way contributed to the political and armed strife between the two parties, have been arrested for that reason or kept in detention by either party during the period of hostilities.

(c) All foreign prisoners of war captured by either party shall be surrendered to the appropriate authorities of the other party, who shall give them all possible assistance in proceeding to the destination of their choice.

CHAPTER V

Miscellaneous

Article 17

The Commanders of the forces of the two parties shall ensure that persons under their respective commands who violate any of the provisions of the present Agreement are suitably punished.

Article 18

In cases in which the place of burial is known and the existence of graves has been established, the Commander of the forces of each party shall, within a specified period after the entry into force of the present Agreement, permit the graves service of the other party to enter that part of Laotian territory under his military control for the purpose of finding and removing the bodies of deceased military personnel of that party, including the bodies of deceased prisoners of war.

The Joint Commission shall fix the procedures by which this task is carried out and the time limits within which it must be completed. The Commander of the forces of each party shall communicate to the other all information in his possession as to the place of burial of military personnel of the other party.

Article 19

The present Agreement shall apply to all the armed forces of either party. The armed forces of each party shall respect the territory under the military control of the other party, and engage in no hostile act against the other party.

For the purpose of the present article the word "territory" includes territorial waters and air space.

Article 20

The Commanders of the forces of the two parties shall afford full protection and all possible assistance and co-operation to the Joint Commission and its joint groups and to the International Commission and its inspection teams in the performance of the functions and tasks assigned to them by the present Agreement.

Article 21

The costs involved in the operation of the Joint Commission and its joint groups and of the International Commission and its inspection teams shall be shared equally between the two parties.

Article 22

The signatories of the present Agreement and their successors in their functions shall be responsible for the observance and enforcement of the terms and provisions thereof. The Commanders of the forces of the two parties shall, within their respective commands, take all steps and make all arrangements necessary to ensure full compliance with all the provisions of the present Agreement by all military personnel under their command.

Article 23

The procedures laid down in the present Agreement shall, whenever necessary, be examined by the Commanders of the two parties and, if necessary, defined more specifically by the Joint Commission.

CHAPTER VI

Joint Commission and International Commission for Supervision and Control in Laos

Article 24

Responsibility for the execution of the Agreement on the cessation of hostilities shall rest with the parties.

Article 25

An International Commission shall be responsible for control and supervision of the application of the provisions of the Agreement on the cessation of hostilities in Laos. It shall be composed of representatives of the following States: Canada, India and Poland. It shall be presided over by the representative of India. Its headquarters shall be at Vientiane.

Article 26

The International Commission shall set up fixed and mobile inspection teams, composed of an equal number of officers appointed by each of the above-mentioned States.

The fixed teams shall be located at the following points: Paksé, Seno, Tchépone, Vientiane, Xieng-Khouang, Phongsaly, Sophao (province of Sam Neua). These points of location may, at a later date, be altered by agreement between the Government of Laos and the International Commission.

The zones of action of the mobile teams shall be the regions bordering the land frontiers of Laos. Within the limits of their zones of action, they shall have the right to move freely and shall receive from the local civil and military authorities all facilities they may require for the fulfilment of their tasks (provision of personnel, access to documents needed for supervision, summoning of witnesses needed for enquiries, security and freedom of movement of the inspection teams. &c. . . .). They shall have at their disposal such modern means of transport, observation and communication as they may require.

Outside the zones of action defined above, the mobile teams may, with the agreement of the Command of the party concerned, move about as required by the tasks assigned to them by the present Agreement.

Article 27

The International Commission shall be responsible for supervising the execution by the parties of the provisions of the present Agreement. For this purpose it shall fulfil the functions of control, observation, inspection and investigation connected with the implementation of the provisions of the Agreement on the cessation of hostilities, and shall in particular:—

(a) Control the withdrawal of foreign forces in accordance with the provisions of the Agreement on the cessation of hostilities and see that frontiers are respected;

(b) control the release of prisoners of war and civilian internees;

(c) supervise, at ports and airfields and along all the frontiers of Laos, the implementation of the provisions regulating the introduction into Laos of military personnel and war materials;

(d) supervise the implementation of the clauses of the Agreement on the cessation of hostilities relating to rotation of personnel and to supplies for French Union security forces maintained in Laos.

Article 28

A Joint Commission shall be set up to facilitate the implementation of the clauses relating to the withdrawal of foreign forces.

The Joint Commission shall form joint groups, the number of which shall be decided by mutual agreement between the parties.

The Joint Commission shall facilitate the implementation of the clauses of the Agreement on the cessation of hostilities relating to the simultaneous and general cease-fire in Laos for all regular and irregular armed forces of the two parties.

It shall assist the parties in the implementation of the said clauses; it shall ensure liaison between them for the purpose of preparing and carrying out plans for the implementation of the said clauses; it shall endeavour to settle any disputes between the parties arising out of the implementation of these clauses. The joint groups shall follow the forces in their movements and shall be disbanded once the withdrawal plans have been carried out.

24

Article 29

The Joint Commission and the joint groups shall be composed of an equal number of representatives of the Commands of the parties concerned.

Article 30

The International Commission shall, through the medium of the inspection teams mentioned above, and as soon as possible, either on its own initiative, or at the request of the Joint Commission, or of one of the parties, undertake the necessary investigations both documentary and on the ground.

Article 31

The inspection teams shall transmit to the International Commission the results of their supervision, investigations and observations; furthermore, they shall draw up such special reports as they may consider necessary or as may be requested from them by the Commission. In the case of a disagreement within the teams the findings of each member shall be transmitted to the Commission.

Article 32

If an inspection team is unable to settle an incident or considers that there is a violation or threat of a serious violation, the International Commission shall be informed; the latter shall examine the reports and findings of the inspection teams and shall inform the parties of the measures which should be taken for the settlement of the incident, ending of the violation or removal of the threat of violation.

Article 33

When the Joint Commission is unable to reach agreement on the interpretation of a provision or on the appraisal of a fact, the International Commission shall be informed of the disputed question. Its recommendations shall be sent directly to the parties and shall be notified to the Joint Commission.

Article 34

The recommendations of the International Commission shall be adopted by majority vote, subject to the provisions of Article 35. If the votes are equally divided, the chairman's vote shall be decisive.

The International Commission may make recommendations concerning amendments and additions which should be made to the provisions of the Agreement on the cessation of hostilities in Laos, in order to ensure more effective execution of the said Agreement. These recommendations shall be adopted unanimously.

Article 35

On questions concerning violations, or threats of violations, which might lead to a resumption of hostilities and, in particular,

(a) refusal by foreign armed forces to effect the movements provided for in the withdrawal plan,
(b) violation or threat of violation of the country's integrity, by foreign armed forces,

the decisions of the International Commission must be unanimous.

Article 36

If one of the parties refuses to put a recommendation of the International Commission into effect, the parties concerned or the Commission itself shall inform the members of the Geneva Conference.

If the International Commission does not reach unanimity in the cases provided for in Article 35, it shall transmit a majority report and one or more minority reports to the members of the Conference.

The International Commission shall inform the members of the Conference of all cases in which its work is being hindered.

Article 37

The International Commission shall be set up at the time of the cessation of hostilities in Indo-China in order that it may be able to fulfil the tasks prescribed in Article 27.

Article 38

The International Commission for Supervision and Control in Laos shall act in close co-operation with the International Commissions in Viet Nam and Cambodia.

The Secretaries-General of these three Commissions shall be responsible for co-ordinating their work and for relations between them.

Article 39

The International Commission for Supervision and Control in Laos may, after consultation with the International Commissions in Cambodia and Viet Nam, and having regard to the development of the situation in Cambodia and Viet Nam, progressively reduce its activities. Such a decision must be adopted unanimously.

CHAPTER VII

Article 40

All the provisions of the present Agreement, save paragraph (*a*) of Article 2, shall enter into force at 24 hours (Geneva time) on July 22, 1954.

Article 41

Done at Geneva (Switzerland) on July 20, 1954, at 24 hours, in the French language.

For the Commander-in-Chief of the forces of the French Union in Indo-China :

DELTEIL,

Général de Brigade.

For the Commander-in-Chief of the fighting units of " Pathet-Lao " and for the Commander-in-Chief of the People's Army of Viet Nam :

TA-QUANG-BUU,

Vice-Minister of National Defence
of the Democratic Republic of Viet Nam.

Agreement on the Cessation of Hostilities in Viet Nam

July 20, 1954

CHAPTER I

Provisional Military Demarcation Line and Demilitarised Zone

Article 1

A provisional military demarcation line shall be fixed, on either side of which the forces of the two parties shall be regrouped after their withdrawal, the forces of the People's Army of Viet Nam to the north of the line and the forces of the French Union to the south.

The provisional military demarcation line is fixed as shown on the map attached (see Map No. 1).[3]

It is also agreed that a demilitarised zone shall be established on either side of the demarcation line, to a width of not more than 5 kms. from it, to act as a buffer zone and avoid any incidents which might result in the resumption of hostilities.

Article 2

The period within which the movement of all forces of either party into its regrouping zone on either side of the provisional military demarcation line shall be completed shall not exceed three hundred (300) days from the date of the present Agreement's entry into force.

Article 3

When the provisional military demarcation line coincides with a waterway, the waters of such waterway shall be open to civil navigation by both parties wherever one bank is controlled by one party and the other bank by the other party. The Joint Commission shall establish rules of navigation for the stretch of waterway in question. The merchant shipping and other civilian craft of each party shall have unrestricted access to the land under its military control.

Article 4

The provisional military demarcation line between the two final regrouping zones is extended into the territorial waters by a line perpendicular to the general line of the coast.

All coastal islands north of this boundary shall be evacuated by the armed forces of the French Union, and all islands south of it shall be evacuated by the forces of the People's Army of Viet Nam.

Article 5

To avoid any incidents which might result in the resumption of hostilities, all military forces, supplies and equipment shall be withdrawn from the demilitarised zone within twenty-five (25) days of the present Agreement's entry into force.

[3] Map not printed—see Annex for details.

Article 6

No person, military or civilian, shall be permitted to cross the provisional military demarcation line unless specifically authorised to do so by the Joint Commission.

Article 7

No person, military or civilian, shall be permitted to enter the demilitarised zone except persons concerned with the conduct of civil administration and relief and persons specifically authorised to enter by the Joint Commission.

Article 8

Civil administration and relief in the demilitarised zone on either side of the provisional military demarcation line shall be the responsibility of the Commanders-in-Chief of the two parties in their respective zones. The number of persons, military or civilian, from each side who are permitted to enter the demilitarised zone for the conduct of civil administration and relief shall be determined by the respective Commanders, but in no case shall the total number authorised by either side exceed at any one time a figure to be determined by the Trung Gia Military Commission or by the Joint Commission. The number of civil police and the arms to be carried by them shall be determined by the Joint Commission. No one else shall carry arms unless specifically authorised to do so by the Joint Commission.

Article 9

Nothing contained in this chapter shall be construed as limiting the complete freedom of movement, into, out of or within the demilitarised zone, of the Joint Commission, its joint groups, the International Commission to be set up as indicated below, its inspection teams and any other persons, supplies or equipment specifically authorised to enter the demilitarised zone by the Joint Commission. Freedom of movement shall be permitted across the territory under the military control of either side over any road or waterway which has to be taken between points within the demilitarised zone when such points are not connected by roads or waterways lying completely within the demilitarised zone.

CHAPTER II

Principles and procedure governing implementation of the present agreement

Article 10

The Commanders of the Forces on each side, on the one side the Commander-in-Chief of the French Union forces in Indo-China and on the other side the Commander-in-Chief of the People's Army of Viet Nam, shall order and enforce the complete cessation of all hostilities in Viet Nam by all armed forces under their control, including all units and personnel of the ground, naval and air forces.

Article 11

In accordance with the principle of a simultaneous cease-fire throughout Indo-China, the cessation of hostilities shall be simultaneous throughout all parts of Viet Nam, in all areas of hostilities and for all the forces of the two parties.

Taking into account the time effectively required to transmit the cease-fire order down to the lowest échelons of the combatant forces on both sides, the two parties are agreed that the cease-fire shall take effect completely and simultaneously for the different sectors of the country as follows:—

Northern Viet Nam at 8·00 a.m. (local time) on July 27, 1954.
Central Viet Nam at 8·00 a.m. (local time) on August 1, 1954.
Southern Viet Nam at 8·00 a.m. (local time) on August 11, 1954.

It is agreed that Peking mean time shall be taken as local time.

From such time as the cease-fire becomes effective in Northern Viet Nam, both parties undertake not to engage in any large-scale offensive action in any part of the Indo-Chinese theatre of operations and not to commit the air forces based on Northern Viet Nam outside that sector. The two parties also undertake to inform each other of their plans for movement from one regrouping zone to another within twenty-five (25) days of the present Agreement's entry into force.

Article 12

All the operations and movements entailed in the cessation of hostilities and regrouping must proceed in a safe and orderly fashion:—

(a) Within a certain number of days after the cease-fire Agreement shall have become effective, the number to be determined on the spot by the Trung Gia Military Commission, each party shall be responsible for removing and neutralising mines (including river- and sea-mines), booby traps, explosives and any other dangerous substances placed by it. In the event of its being impossible to complete the work of removal and neutralisation in time, the party concerned shall mark the spot by placing visible signs there. All demolitions, mine fields, wire entanglements and other hazards to the free movement of the personnel of the Joint Commission and its joint groups, known to be present after the withdrawal of the military forces, shall be reported to the Joint Commission by the Commanders of the opposing forces;

(b) From the time of the cease-fire until regrouping is completed on either side of the demarcation line:—

(1) The forces of either party shall be provisionally withdrawn from the provisional assembly areas assigned to the other party.

(2) When one party's forces withdraw by a route (road, rail, waterway, sea route) which passes through the territory of the other party (see Article 24), the latter party's forces must provisionally withdraw three kilometres on each side of such route, but in such a manner as to avoid interfering with the movements of the civil population.

Article 13

From the time of the cease-fire until the completion of the movements from one regrouping zone into the other, civil and military transport aircraft shall follow air-corridors between the provisional assembly areas assigned to the French Union forces north of the demarcation line on the one hand and the Laotian frontier and the regrouping zone assigned to the French Union forces on the other hand.

The position of the air-corridors, their width, the safety route for single-engined military aircraft transferred to the south and the search and rescue

29

procedure for aircraft in distress shall be determined on the spot by the Trung Gia Military Commission.

Article 14

Political and administrative measures in the two regrouping zones, on either side of the provisional military demarcation line:—

(a) Pending the general elections which will bring about the unification of Viet Nam, the conduct of civil administration in each regrouping zone shall be in the hands of the party whose forces are to be regrouped there in virtue of the present Agreement.

(b) Any territory controlled by one party which is transferred to the other party by the regrouping plan shall continue to be administered by the former party until such date as all the troops who are to be transferred have completely left that territory so as to free the zone assigned to the party in question. From then on, such territory shall be regarded as transferred to the other party, who shall assume responsibility for it.

Steps shall be taken to ensure that there is no break in the transfer of responsibilities. For this purpose, adequate notice shall be given by the withdrawing party to the other party, which shall make the necessary arrangements, in particular by sending administrative and police detachments to prepare for the assumption of administrative responsibility. The length of such notice shall be determined by the Trung Gia Military Commission. The transfer shall be effected in successive stages for the various territorial sectors.

The transfer of the civil administration of Hanoi and Haiphong to the authorities of the Democratic Republic of Viet Nam shall be completed within the respective time-limits laid down in Article 15 for military movements.

(c) Each party undertakes to refrain from any reprisals or discrimination against persons or organisations on account of their activities during the hostilities and to guarantee their democratic liberties.

(d) From the date of entry into force of the present Agreement until the movement of troops is completed, any civilians residing in a district controlled by one party who wish to go and live in the zone assigned to the other party shall be permitted and helped to do so by the authorities in that district.

Article 15

The disengagement of the combatants, and the withdrawals and transfers of military forces, equipment and supplies shall take place in accordance with the following principles:—

(a) The withdrawals and transfers of the military forces, equipment and supplies of the two parties shall be completed within three hundred (300) days, as laid down in Article 2 of the present Agreement;

(b) Within either territory successive withdrawals shall be made by sectors, portions of sectors or provinces. Transfers from one regrouping zone to another shall be made in successive monthly instalments proportionate to the number of troops to be transferred;

(c) The two parties shall undertake to carry out all troop withdrawals and transfers in accordance with the aims of the present Agreement, shall permit no hostile act and shall take no step whatsoever which might hamper such withdrawals and transfers. They shall assist one another as far as this is possible;

(d) The two parties shall permit no destruction or sabotage of any public property and no injury to the life and property of the civil population. They shall permit no interference in local civil administration;

(e) The Joint Commission and the International Commission shall ensure that steps are taken to safeguard the forces in the course of withdrawal and transfer;

(f) The Trung Gia Military Commission, and later the Joint Commission, shall determine by common agreement the exact procedure for the disengagement of the combatants and for troop withdrawals and transfers, on the basis of the principles mentioned above and within the framework laid down below:—

1. The disengagement of the combatants, including the concentration of the armed forces of all kinds and also each party's movements into the provisional assembly areas assigned to it and the other party's provisional withdrawal from it, shall be completed within a period not exceeding fifteen (15) days after the date when the cease-fire becomes effective.

The general delineation of the provisional assembly areas is set out in the maps([4]) annexed to the present Agreement.

In order to avoid any incidents, no troops shall be stationed less than 1,500 metres from the lines delimiting the provisional assembly areas.

During the period until the transfers are concluded, all the coastal islands west of the following lines shall be included in the Haiphong perimeter:

meridian of the southern point of Kebao Island,
northern coast of Ile Rousse (excluding the island), extended as far as the meridian of Campha-Mines,
meridian of Campha-Mines.

2. The withdrawals and transfers shall be effected in the following order and within the following periods (from the date of the entry into force of the present Agreement):—

Forces of the French Union

Hanoi perimeter	80 days
Haiduong perimeter	100 days
Haiphong perimeter	300 days

Forces of the People's Army of Viet Nam

Ham Tan and Xuyenmoc provisional assembly area	80 days
Central Viet Nam provisional assembly area—first instalment	80 days
Plaine des Joncs provisional assembly area	100 days
Central Viet Nam provisional assembly area—second instalment	100 days
Pointe Camau provisional assembly area	200 days
Central Viet Nam provisional assembly area—last instalment	300 days

([4]) Maps not printed—see Annex for details.

31

Ban on the introduction of fresh troops, military personnel, arms and munitions. Military bases

Article 16

With effect from the date of entry into force of the present Agreement, the introduction into Viet Nam of any troop reinforcements and additional military personnel is prohibited.

It is understood, however, that the rotation of units and groups of personnel, the arrival in Viet Nam of individual personnel on a temporary duty basis and the return to Viet Nam of the individual personnel after short periods of leave or temporary duty outside Viet Nam shall be permitted under the conditions laid down below: —

(a) Rotation of units (defined in paragraph (c) of this Article) and groups of personnel shall not be permitted for French Union troops stationed north of the provisional military demarcation line laid down in Article 1 of the present Agreement during the withdrawal period provided for in Article 2.

However, under the heading of individual personnel not more than fifty (50) men, including officers, shall during any one month be permitted to enter that part of the country north of the provisional military demarcation line on a temporary duty basis or to return there after short periods of leave or temporary duty outside Viet Nam.

(b) " Rotation " is defined as the replacement of units or groups of personnel by other units of the same échelon or by personnel who are arriving in Viet Nam territory to do their overseas service there;

(c) The units rotated shall never be larger than a battalion—or the corresponding échelon for air and naval forces;

(d) Rotation shall be conducted on a man-for-man basis, provided, however, that in any one quarter neither party shall introduce more than fifteen thousand five hundred (15,500) members of its armed forces into Viet Nam under the rotation policy.

(e) Rotation units (defined in paragraph (c) of this Article) and groups of personnel, and the individual personnel mentioned in this Article, shall enter and leave Viet Nam only through the entry points enumerated in Article 20 below;

(f) Each party shall notify the Joint Commission and the International Commission at least two days in advance of any arrivals or departures of units, groups of personnel and individual personnel in or from Viet Nam. Reports on the arrivals or departures of units, groups of personnel and individual personnel in or from Viet Nam shall be submitted daily to the Joint Commission and the International Commission.

All the above-mentioned notifications and reports shall indicate the places and dates of arrival or departure and the number of persons arriving or departing;

(g) The International Commission, through its Inspection Teams, shall supervise and inspect the rotation of units and groups of personnel and the arrival and departure of individual personnel as authorised above, at the points of entry enumerated in Article 20 below.

Article 17

(a) With effect from the date of entry into force of the present Agreement, the introduction into Viet Nam of any reinforcements in the form of all types of arms, munitions and other war material, such as combat aircraft, naval craft, pieces of ordnance, jet engines and jet weapons and armoured vehicles, is prohibited.

(b) It is understood, however, that war material, arms and munitions which have been destroyed, damaged, worn out or used up after the cessation of hostilities may be replaced on the basis of piece-for-piece of the same type and with similar characteristics. Such replacements of war material, arms and ammunitions shall not be permitted for French Union troops stationed north of the provisional military demarcation line laid down in Article 1 of the present Agreement, during the withdrawal period provided for in Article 2.

Naval craft may perform transport operations between the regrouping zones.

(c) The war material, arms and munitions for replacement purposes provided for in paragraph (b) of this Article, shall be introduced into Viet Nam only through the points of entry enumerated in Article 20 below. War material, arms and munitions to be replaced shall be shipped from Viet Nam only through the points of entry enumerated in Article 20 below.

(d) Apart from the replacements permitted within the limits laid down in paragraph (b) of this Article, the introduction of war material, arms and munitions of all types in the form of unassembled parts for subsequent assembly is prohibited.

(e) Each party shall notify the Joint Commission and the International Commission at least two days in advance of any arrivals or departures which may take place of war material, arms and munitions of all types.

In order to justify the requests for the introduction into Viet Nam of arms, munitions and other war material (as defined in paragraph (a) of this Article) for replacement purposes, a report concerning each incoming shipment shall be submitted to the Joint Commission and the International Commission. Such reports shall indicate the use made of the items so replaced.

(f) The International Commission, through its Inspection Teams, shall supervise and inspect the replacements permitted in the circumstances laid down in this Article, at the points of entry enumerated in Article 20 below.

Article 18

With effect from the date of entry into force of the present Agreement, the establishment of new military bases is prohibited throughout Viet Nam territory.

Article 19

With effect from the date of entry into force of the present Agreement, no military base under the control of a foreign State may be established in the re-grouping zone of either party; the two parties shall ensure that the zones assigned to them do not adhere to any military alliance and are not used for the resumption of hostilities or to further an aggressive policy.

Article 20

The points of entry into Viet Nam for rotation personnel and replacements of material are fixed as follows:—

— Zones to the north of the provisional military demarcation line: Laokay, Langson, Tien-Yen, Haiphong, Vinh, Dong-Hoi, Muong-Sen;

— Zone to the south of the provisional military demarcation line: Tourane, Quinhon, Nhatrang, Bangoi, Saigon, Cap St. Jacques, Tanchau.

CHAPTER IV

Prisoners of War and Civilian Internees

Article 21

The liberation and repatriation of all prisoners of war and civilian internees detained by each of the two parties at the coming into force of the present Agreement shall be carried out under the following conditions: —

(a) All prisoners of war and civilian internees of Viet Nam, French and other nationalities captured since the beginning of hostilities in Viet Nam during military operations or in any other circumstances of war and in any part of the territory of Viet Nam shall be liberated within a period of thirty (30) days after the date when the cease-fire becomes effective in each theatre.

(b) The term "civilian internees" is understood to mean all persons who, having in any way contributed to the political and armed struggle between the two parties, have been arrested for that reason and have been kept in detention by either party during the period of hostilities.

(c) All prisoners of war and civilian internees held by either party shall be surrendered to the appropriate authorities of the other party, who shall give them all possible assistance in proceeding to their country of origin, place of habitual residence or the zone of their choice.

CHAPTER V

Miscellaneous

Article 22

The Commanders of the Forces of the two parties shall ensure that persons under their respective commands who violate any of the provisions of the present Agreement are suitably punished.

Article 23

In cases in which the place of burial is known and the existence of graves has been established, the Commander of the Forces of either party shall, within a specific period after the entry into force of the Armistice Agreement, permit the graves service personnel of the other party to enter the part of Viet Nam territory under their military control for the purpose of finding and removing the bodies of deceased military personnel of that party, including the bodies of deceased prisoners of war. The Joint Commission shall determine the procedures and the time limit for the performance of this task. The Commanders of the Forces of the two parties shall communicate to each other all information in their possession as to the place of burial of military personnel of the other party.

Article 24

The present Agreement shall apply to all the armed forces of either party. The armed forces of each party shall respect the demilitarised zone and the territory under the military control of the other party, and shall commit no act and undertake no operation against the other party and shall not engage in blockade of any kind in Viet Nam.

For the purposes of the present Article, the word "territory" includes territorial waters and air space.

Article 25

The Commanders of the Forces of the two parties shall afford full protection and all possible assistance and co-operation to the Joint Commission and its joint groups and to the International Commission and its inspection teams in the performance of the functions and tasks assigned to them by the present Agreement.

Article 26

The costs involved in the operations of the Joint Commission and joint groups and of the International Commission and its Inspection Teams shall be shared equally between the two parties.

Article 27

The signatories of the present Agreement and their successors in their functions shall be responsible for ensuring the observance and enforcement of the terms and provisions thereof. The Commanders of the Forces of the two parties shall, within their respective commands, take all steps and make all arrangements necessary to ensure full compliance with all the provisions of the present Agreement by all elements and military personnel under their command.

The procedures laid down in the present Agreement shall, whenever necessary, be studied by the Commanders of the two parties and, if necessary, defined more specifically by the Joint Commission.

CHAPTER VI

Joint Commission and International Commission for Supervision and Control in Viet Nam

Article 28

Responsibility for the execution of the agreement on the cessation of hostilities shall rest with the parties.

Article 29

An International Commission shall ensure the control and supervision of this execution.

Article 30

In order to facilitate, under the conditions shown below, the execution of provisions concerning joint actions by the two parties, a Joint Commission shall be set up in Viet Nam.

Article 31

The Joint Commission shall be composed of an equal number of representatives of the Commanders of the two parties.

Article 32

The Presidents of the delegations to the Joint Commission shall hold the rank of General.

The Joint Commission shall set up joint groups, the number of which shall be determined by mutual agreement between the parties. The joint groups shall be composed of an equal number of officers from both parties. Their location on the demarcation line between the re-grouping zones shall be determined by the parties whilst taking into account the powers of the Joint Commission.

Article 33

The Joint Commission shall ensure the exicution of the following provisions of the Agreement on the cessation of hostilities: —

(*a*) A simultaneous and general cease-fire in Viet Nam for all regular and irregular armed forces of the two parties.

(*b*) A re-groupment of the armed forces of the two parties.

(*c*) Observance of the demarcation lines between the re-grouping zones and of the demilitarised sectors.

Within the limits of its competence it shall help the parties to execute the said provisions, shall ensure liaison between them for the purpose of preparing and carrying out plans for the application of these provisions, and shall endeavour to solve such disputed questions as may arise between the parties in the course of executing these provisions.

Article 34

An International Commission shall be set up for the control and supervision over the application of the provisions of the agreement on the cessation of hostilities in Viet Nam. It shall be composed of representatives of the following States: Canada, India and Poland.

It shall be presided over by the Representative of India.

Article 35

The International Commission shall set up fixed and mobile inspection teams, composed of an equal number of officers appointed by each of the above-mentioned States. The mixed teams shall be located at the following points: Laokay, Langson, Tien-Yen, Haiphong, Vinh, Dong-Hoi, Muong-Sen, Tourane, Quinhon, Nhatrang, Bangoi, Saigon, Cap St. Jacques, Tranchau. These points of location may, at a later date, be altered at the request of the Joint Commission, or of one of the parties, or of the International Commission itself, by agreement between the International Commission and the command of the party concerned. The zones of action of the mobile teams shall be the regions bordering the land and sea frontiers of Viet Nam, the demarcation lines between the re-grouping zones and the demilitarised zones. Within the limits of these zones they shall have the right to move freely and shall receive from the local civil and military authorities all facilities they may require for the fulfilment of their tasks (provision of personnel, placing at their disposal documents needed for supervision, summoning witnesses necessary for holding enquiries, ensuring the security and freedom of movement of the inspection teams, &c. . . . .). They shall have at their disposal such modern means of transport, observation and communication as they may require. Beyond the zones of action as defined above, the mobile teams may, by agreement with the command of the party concerned, carry out other movements within the limits of the tasks given them by the present agreement.

Article 36

The International Commission shall be responsible for supervising the proper execution by the parties of the provisions of the agreement. For this purpose it shall fulfil the tasks of control, observation, inspection and investigation connected with the application of the provisions of the agreement on the cessation of hostilities, and it shall in particular: —

(a) Control the movement of the armed forces of the two parties, effected within the framework of the regroupment plan.

(b) Supervise the demarcation lines between the regrouping areas, and also the demilitarised zones.

(c) Control the operations of releasing prisoners of war and civilian internees.

(d) Supervise at ports and airfields as well as along all frontiers of Viet Nam the execution of the provisions of the agreement on the cessation of hostilities, regulating the introduction into the country of armed forces, military personnel and of all kinds of arms, munitions and war material.

Article 37

The International Commission shall, through the medium of the inspection teams mentioned above, and as soon as possible either on its own initiative, or at the request of the Joint Commission, or of one of the parties, undertake the necessary investigations both documentary and on the ground.

Article 38

The inspection teams shall submit to the International Commission the results of their supervision, their investigation and their observations, furthermore they shall draw up such special reports as they may consider necessary or as may be requested from them by the Commission. In the case of a disagreement within the teams, the conclusions of each member shall be submitted to the Commission.

Article 39

If any one inspection team is unable to settle an incident or considers that there is a violation or a threat of a serious violation, the International Commission shall be informed; the latter shall study the reports and the conclusions of the inspection teams and shall inform the parties of the measures which should be taken for the settlement of the incident, ending of the violation or removal of the threat of violation.

Article 40

When the Joint Commission is unable to reach an agreement on the interpretation to be given to some provision or on the appraisal of a fact, the International Commission shall be informed of the disputed question. Its recommendations shall be sent directly to the parties and shall be notified to the Joint Commission.

Article 41

The recommendations of the International Commission shall be adopted by majority vote, subject to the provisions contained in Article 42. If the votes are divided, the chairman's vote shall be decisive.

The International Commission may formulate recommendations concerning amendments and additions which should be made to the provisions of the agreement on the cessation of hostilities in Viet Nam, in order to ensure a more effective execution of that agreement. These recommendations shall be adopted unanimously.

Article 42

When dealing with questions concerning violations, or threats of violations, which might lead to a resumption of hostilities, namely:—

(a) Refusal by the armed forces of one party to effect the movements provided for in the regroupment plan;

(b) Violation by the armed forces of one of the parties of the regrouping zones, territorial waters, or air space of the other party;

the decisions of the International Commission must be unanimous.

Article 43

If one of the parties refuses to put into effect a recommendation of the International Commission, the parties concerned or the Commission itself shall inform the members of the Geneva Conference.

If the International Commission does not reach unanimity in the cases provided for in Article 42, it shall submit a majority report and one or more minority reports to the members of the Conference.

The International Commission shall inform the members of the Conference in all cases where its activity is being hindered.

Article 44

The International Commission shall be set up at the time of the cessation of hostilities in Indo-China in order that it should be able to fulfil the tasks provided for in Article 36.

Article 45

The International Commission for Supervision and Control in Viet Nam shall act in close co-operation with the International Commissions for Supervision and Control in Cambodia and Laos.

The Secretaries-General of these three Commissions shall be responsible for co-ordinating their work and for relations between them.

Article 46

The International Commission for Supervision and Control in Viet Nam may, after consultation with the International Commissions for Supervision and Control in Cambodia and Laos, and having regard to the development of the situation in Cambodia and Laos, progressively reduce its activities. Such a decision must be adopted unanimously.

Article 47

All the provisions of the present Agreement, save the second sub-paragraph of Article 11, shall enter into force at 2400 hours (Geneva time) on July 22, 1954.

Done in Geneva at 2400 hours on the 20th of July, 1954, in French and in Vietnamese, both texts being equally authentic.

For the Commander-in-Chief of the French Union Forces in Indo-China :

DELTIEL,

Brigadier-General.

For the Commander-in-Chief of the People's Army of Viet Nam :

TA-QUANG-BUU,

Vice-Minister of National Defence
of the Democratic Republic of Viet Nam.

Annex to the Agreement on the Cessation of Hostilities in Viet Nam

I.—*Delineation of the provisional military demarcation line and the demilitarised zone* (Article 1 of the Agreement; reference map: Indo-China 1/100,000)

(*a*) The provisional military demarcation line is fixed as follows, reading from east to west:—

The mouth of the Song Ben Hat (Cua Tung River) and the course of that river (known as the Rao Thanh in the mountains) to the village of Bo Ho Su, then the parallel of Bo Ho Su to the Laos–Viet Nam frontier.

(*b*) The demilitarised zone shall be delimited by Trung Gia Military Commission in accordance with the provisions of Article 1 of the Agreement on the cessation of hostilities in Viet Nam.

II.—*General delineation of the provisional assembly areas* (Article 15 of the Agreement; reference maps: Indo-China 1/400,000)

(a) North Viet Nam

Delineation of the Boundary of the Provisional Assembly Area of the French Union Forces

1. The perimeter of Hanoi is delimited by the arc of a circle with a radius of 15 kilometres, having as its centre the right bank abutment of Doumer Bridge and running westwards from the Red River to the Rapids Canal in the north-east.

In this particular case no forces of the French Union shall be stationed less than 2 kilometres from this perimeter, on the inside thereof.

2. The perimeter of Haiphong shall be delimited by the Song-Van Uc as far as Kim Thanh and a line running from the Song-Van-Uc three kilometres north-east of Kim Thanh to cut Road No. 18 two kilometres east of Mao-Khé. Thence a line running three kilometres north of Road 18 to Cho-Troi and a straight line from Cho-Troi to the Mong-Duong ferry.

3. *A corridor contained between:*

In the south, the Red River from Thanh-Tri to Bang-Nho, thence a line joining the latter point to Do-My (south-west of Kesat), Gia-Loc and Tien Kieu;

In the north, a line running along the Rapids Canal at a distance of 1,500 metres to the north of the Canal, passing three kilometres north of Pha-Lai and Seven Pagodas and thence parallel to Road No. 18 to its point of intersection with the perimeter of Haiphong.

Note.—Throughout the period of evacuation of the perimeter of Hanoi, the river forces of the French Union shall enjoy complete freedom of movement on the Song-Van-Uc. And the forces of the People's Army of Viet Nam shall withdraw three kilometres south of the south bank of the Song-Van-Uc.

Boundary between the perimeter of Hanoi and the perimeter of Haiduong

A straight line running from the Rapids Canal three kilometres west of Chi-ne and ending at Do-My (eight kilometres south-west of Kesat).

(b) Central Viet Nam

Delineation of the Boundary of the Provisional Assembly Area of the Forces of the Viet Nam People's Army South of the Col des Nuages Parallel

The perimeter of the Central Viet Nam area shall consist of the administrative boundaries of the provinces of Quang-Ngai and Binh-Dinh as they were defined before the hostilities.

(c) South Viet Nam

Three provisional assembly areas shall be provided for the forces of the People's Army of Viet Nam.

The boundaries of these areas are as follows: —

1. *Xuyen-Moc, Ham-Tan Area—*

    Western boundary : The course of the Song-Ray extended northwards as far as Road No. 1 to a point thereon eight kilometres east of the intersection of Road No. 1 and Road No. 3.

    Northern boundary : Road No. 1 from the above-mentioned intersection to the intersection with Route Communale No. 9 situated 27 kilometres west-south-west of Phanthiet and from that intersection a straight line to Kim Thanh on the coast.

2. *Plaine des Joncs Area—*

    Northern boundary : The Viet Nam–Cambodia frontier.

    Western boundary : A straight line from Tong-Binh to Binh-Thanh.

    Southern boundary : Course of the Fleuve Antérieur (Mekong) to ten kilometres south-east of Cao Lanh. From that point, a straight line as far as Ap-My-Dien, and from Ap-My-Dien a line parallel to and three kilometres east and then south of the Tong Doc-Loc Canal, this line reaches My-Hanh-Dong and thence Hung-Thanh-My.

    Eastern boundary : A straight line from Hung-Thanh-My running northwards to the Cambodian frontier south of Doi-Bao-Voi.

3. *Point Camau Area—*

    Northern boundary : The Song-Cai-lon from its mouth to its junction with the Rach-Nuoc-Trong, thence the Rach-Nuoc-Trong to the bend five kilometres north-east of Ap-Xeo-La. Thereafter a line to the Ngan-Dua Canal and following that Canal as far as Vinh-Hung. Finally, from Vinh-Hung a north–south line to the sea.

Document No. 6

Declaration by the Royal Government of Cambodia

July 21, 1954

(Reference : Article 3 of the Final Declaration)

The Royal Government of Cambodia,

In the desire to ensure harmony and agreement among the peoples of the Kingdom,

Declares itself resolved to take the necessary measures to integrate all citizens, without discrimination. into the national community and to guarantee them the enjoyment of the .rights and freedoms for which the Constitution of the Kingdom provides;

Affirms that all Cambodian citizens may freely participate as electors or candidates in general elections by secret ballot.

Document No. 7

Declaration by the Royal Government of Laos

July 21. 1954

(Reference : Article 3 of the Final Declaration)

The Royal Government of Laos,

In the desire to ensure harmony and agreement among the peoples of the Kingdom,

Declares itself resolved to take the necessary measures to integrate all citizens, without discrimination, into the national community and to guarantee them the enjoyment of the rights and freedoms for which the Constitution of the Kingdom provides;

Affirms that all Laotian citizens may freely participate as electors or candidates in general elections by secret ballot;

Announces, furthermore, that it will promulgate measures to provide for special representation in the Royal Administration of the provinces of Phang Saly and Sam Neua during the interval between the cessation of hostilities and the general elections of the interests of Laotian nationals who did not support the Royal forces during hostilties.

Document No. 8

Declaration by the Royal Government of Cambodia

July 21, 1954

(Reference : Articles 4 and 5 of the Final Declaration)

The Royal Government of Cambodia is resolved never to take part in an aggressive policy and never to permit the territory of Cambodia to be utilised in the service of such a policy.

The Royal Government of Cambodia will not join in any agreement with other States, if this agreement carries for Cambodia the obligation to enter into a military alliance not in conformity with the principles of the Charter of the United Nations, or, as long as its security is not threatened, the obligation to establish bases on Cambodian territory for the military forces of foreign Powers.

The Royal Government of Cambodia is resolved to settle its international disputes by peaceful means, in such a manner as not to endanger peace, international security and justice.

During the period which will elapse between the date of the cessation of hostilities in Viet Nam and that of the final settlement of political problems in this country, the Royal Government of Cambodia will not solicit foreign aid in war material, personnel or instructors except for the purpose of the effective defence of the territory.

Document No. 9

Declaration by the Royal Government of Laos

July 21, 1954

(Reference : Articles 4 and 5 of the Final Declaration)

The Royal Government of Laos is resolved never to pursue a policy of aggression and will never permit the territory of Laos to be used in furtherance of such a policy.

The Royal Government of Laos will never join in any agreement with other States if this agreement includes the obligation for the Royal Government of Laos to participate in a military alliance not in conformity with the principles of the Charter of the United Nations or with the principles of the agreement on the cessation of hostilities or, unless its security is threatened, the obligation to establish bases on Laotian territory for military forces of foreign Powers.

The Royal Government of Laos is resolved to settle its international disputes by peaceful means so that international peace and security and justice are not endangered.

During the period between the cessation of hostilities in Viet Nam and the final settlement of that country's political problems, the Royal Government of Laos will not request foreign aid, whether in war material, in personnel or in instructors, except for the purpose of its effective territorial defence and to the extent defined by the agreement on the cessation of hostilities.

Document No. 10

Declaration by the Government of the French Republic

July 21, 1954

(Reference : Article 10 of the Final Declaration)

The Government of the French Republic declares that it is ready to withdraw its troops from the territory of Cambodia, Laos and Viet Nam, at the request of the Governments concerned and within a period which shall be fixed by agreement between the parties, except in the cases where, by agreement between the two parties, a certain number of French troops shall remain at specified points and for a specified time.

Document No. 11

Declaration by the Government of the French Republic

July 21, 1954

(Reference : Article 11 of the Final Declaration)

For the settlement of all the problems connected with the re-establishment and consolidation of peace in Cambodia, Laos and Viet Nam, the French Government will proceed from the principle of respect for the independence and sovereignty, the unity and territorial integrity of Cambodia, Laos and Viet Nam.